FEB 06 2012

Optimism!

Cultivating the Magic Quality That Can Extend Your Lifespan, Boost Your Energy, and Make You Happy Now

edited by

DAWSON CHURCH & STEPHANIE MAROHN

www.optimismbook.com

Elite Books
Author's Publishing Cooperative
Santa Rosa, CA 95404
www.EliteBooks.biz

Library of Congress Cataloging-in-Publication Data

Optimism! : cultivating the magic quality that can extend your lifespan, boost your energy, and make you happy now / edited by Dawson Church & Stephanie Marohn. — 1st ed.
     p. cm.
     ISBN 978-1-60070-069-9
     1. Optimism. 2. Mind and body. 3. Well-being—psychological aspects.
I. Church, Dawson, 1956- II. Marohn, Stephanie.
     BF698.35.O57O69 2011
     155.2'32--dc23

                              2011029553

Interior design by Dawson Church
Typeset in Mona Lisa and Book Antiqua by Karin Kinsey
Cover Design by Vicki Valentine
Printed in USA
First Edition

10 9 8 7 6 5 4 3 2 1

CONTENTS

To All Who Look for the Light

Stephanie Marohn is the author of ten books, including *The Natural Medicine Guide to Bipolar Disorder, The Natural Medicine Guide to Autism, Natural Medicine First Aid Remedies,* and the anthologies *Audacious Aging* and *Goddess Shift: Women Leading for a Change.* She has also published more than fifty magazine and newspaper articles, and had her work included in poetry, prayer, and travel-writing anthologies. Along with her writing, she runs a farm animal sanctuary and Energy Healing for Animals, an energy medicine practice that grew out of years of helping animals on her sanctuary heal from a range of illnesses. www.stephaniemarohn.com

Stephanie Marohn:

Introduction—
The Glass Overflowing

Some people consider optimism to be unrealistic in these times of planetary crisis. But pessimism does not equal realism and research has shown for decades that our thoughts and beliefs have a great effect on what actually happens in our lives. We can go back to the early sociological findings on the effects of negative self-image and the negative projections of teachers and other authority figures on the future prospects of youth; self-fulfilling prophecy has been well demonstrated. We can also turn to research on the reverse relationship of belief and behavior, that is, that attitudes follow behavior, that by behaving "as if," we can instill belief. Combining the evidence of these two lines of research tells us that if we behave as if we humans will be able to solve the serious problems facing us, we will more likely be able to. There is no evidence to support a positive outcome from behaving as if we are unlikely to be able to solve the problems.

It's important to note here that optimism is not merely hope. It is reflected in action as much as in thinking. Optimists don't just sit back and wait for things to get better. Their behavior reflects their positive attitude. In fact, it is more likely that it is the pessimists who will do nothing, believing that there is no point. It is also worth noting that it takes a lot more effort in these dire times to be an optimist, to keep from succumbing to the negativity that is all around us.

Recent research on optimism gives us further motivation to cultivate a positive mind-set:

- In a nine-year study of 999 people aged sixty-five to eighty-five, pessimists were 75 percent more likely to die from cardiovascular disease than optimists. In addition, the more optimistic the individual was, the lower the risk of a cardiac event. These results held regardless of gender, other chronic conditions, older age, smoking, alcohol consumption, and previous heart disease. The optimistic subjects also had lower death rates from all causes over the nine years studied.

- In a study of ninety-six men who had suffered a first heart attack, fifteen of the sixteen most pessimistic men in the group died of heart disease within ten years, while only five of the sixteen most optimistic men died.

- Research has linked a high level of optimism to improved recovery from heart transplant and heart bypass surgery, reduced likelihood of stroke, and decreased risk of the onset of frailty in the elderly.

- A study of 124 first-year law students demonstrated that optimism can affect immune function. The researchers found that the more optimistic the subjects, the better their cell-mediated immunity, which protects the body from bacterial and viral infections and some forms of cancer.

The microcosm is a reflection of the macrocosm. The components of the human body are the same as the components of the rest of the universe. If optimism produces these positive changes in the human body, it is safe to assume that it affects more than just us. This is borne out by the now-famous research of Dr. Masaru Emoto on the effects of positive words such as "love" on the crystalline structure of water in contrast to the effects of negative words such as "hate"; the difference was startling. This has significance for the macrocosm and also further demonstrates the effect of positive energy on people, given that the human body is 55–60 percent water (the brain alone is 70 percent water).

If we consider optimism from an energetic viewpoint, how good can it be for the Earth's energy field (much less ours) to be infused with the negative energy of pessimism? Is it not better for the planet, especially in these dark times, for us to add positive energy to the global field?

We compiled this book, with its powerful messages of optimism from a range of positive thinkers and activists, to add to the much-needed flow of positivism in the world. My own journey of healing taught me how important this is. Though I didn't know where I was heading at the beginning, the trajectory of soul growth took me from the glass-half-empty perspective to the glass-half-full perspective—and beyond. I came to see the glass as overflowing. There is so much to celebrate and be grateful for, even when circumstances are difficult, even dire. Life itself is the glass overflowing. Viewing life from this perspective, I am happier than I've ever been and far more productive and effective in what I choose to do.

In *Optimism!* you will hear from many others who have found their way to the overflowing glass. Optimists exist in all walks of life and here we offer a sampling, from psychologists and other scientists to entertainers and politicians. May their stories and words of wisdom inspire you to gift the world with your own optimistic thoughts and actions.

The Psychology of the Positive

CAROLINE MYSS:

Invisible Facts of Power

CHAPTER 1

Years ago I had a conversation with a man who told me that the most important truth he had learned was to be kind. He learned this, he recounted, during a cab ride in New York City. As he was paying the driver, he said, "Thank you, sir." At this the driver leaped, ran around the back of the cab, and opened the door for his passenger. Startled, the man got out and said to the cab driver, "You didn't have to do that," to which the driver responded, "I wanted to. You are the first person in this country to honor me by calling me sir, and I thank you for that respect." The man had never before considered the power inherent in a respectful gesture, but from then on, kindness became the pillar upon which he built his life and the legacy he hoped to pass on to his children. That exchange, he said, changed his life. He understood at the deepest level that we are all the same—an invisible "fact" of power.

Here are some other invisible facts that you can review when your spirit needs a reminder of the great power you have with which to make a difference in the world.

Fact #1: Life Is a Spiritual Journey

Vest yourself in the belief that your life is a hero's journey of spiritual progress. Mapping your way along the spiritual coordinates of purpose and compassion will help you navigate the storms of change. Life will never be a logical, rational, controllable experience. Some events and relationships will enchant us and others will crack us wide open with pain.

Caroline Myss is a medical intuitive and author. She coauthored her first book, *The Creation of Health*, with C. Norman Shealy, MD. Other of her many books include the *New York Times* best-sellers *Anatomy of the Spirit*, *Why People Don't Heal and How They Can*, and *Sacred Contracts*. She gives lectures and workshops around the world, and has appeared in two highly successful public television programs, *Why People Don't Heal and How They Can* and *Three Levels of Power and How to Use Them*. www.myss.com

Some people might win the lottery and others may end up broke through bizarre twists of fate, but we cannot outrun or outsmart the winds of change. Know that underlying the storm is peace, and under the chaos is order. Use the power of faith as your anchor: faith that there is a reason why things happen as they do; faith that you will make it through a crisis; faith that you are moving forward to a better place.

Whether you are the one in the orbit of change or whether you are helping another person through a cycle of endings and new beginnings, recognizing a crisis — no matter what that crisis may be — as the spiritual experience of "endings and new beginnings" opens up a profound channel of light and grace. One of the most empowering acts of service is to believe in someone when he lacks the faith to believe in himself.

Fact #2: Your Biology and Your Spirit Want to Serve

It's impossible for your body to live separate and apart from the journey of your spirit. Giving makes you feel good; not giving makes you feel bad. Developing compassion and an open heart is good for you and others. His Holiness the Dalai Lama says that as a child, he was as angry as any child and even a bully at times. But after sixty years of meditating and developing compassion, the angry emotions faded away. He doesn't even have to work to suppress any anger; he simply never even feels it.

Following your intuition is vital to your own empowerment and to your physical and spiritual health. All paths of enlightenment direct us to search within ourselves for the right energy to channel to others. Our highest potential cannot be tapped without a commitment to reaching out to others. Service is the most powerful act.

A Personal Act of Power

Increase your attention to your body, especially when you are in need of help or around someone who is reaching out to you. Learn to interpret your physical sensations: they are generated by your intuition. These sensations will direct you to decide whether you should help, how much you should help, and when to say no. At the very least, however, respond with a prayer.

Fact #3: Intuition Influences Every Choice You Make in Life

You are an intuitive being. Intuitive abilities are as natural as breathing; they are not enhanced by diet, incense, or aromatherapy. Your intuition evolves along with your sense of self-esteem, which develops as a by-product of learning how to survive. Your spiritual life enhances your self-esteem and gives you a sense of purpose, which in turn builds your confidence in your ability to survive. That feeling that you can "handle" life—a sensation not based upon the accumulation of wealth or power, but on your spiritual instincts—gives you the mental, emotional, and psychic resources essential for strong intuition.

A Personal Act of Power

Know your intuitive boundaries. Pay attention to both your biological and your intuitive signals. Remember that just because you can sense that someone is in need does not mean that you are the one meant to help him or her. You must ask yourself if you are psychically prepared for the type of assistance required and if not, assist with a prayer and a loving thought. I learned as a matter of my own emotional survival years ago that I cannot possibly do the number of intuitive medical readings that I am asked to do. For the longest time, the guilt was so great that I could no longer even read the letters that poured into my office from all over the world. Finally I began to pray for each one, asking that the divine send someone to them who could help them because I could not. Prayer is powerful medicine.

Fact #4: Your Intuition and Generosity Evolve as Your Personal Power Evolves

Generosity is an expression of our spiritual maturity. I will remind you of the very revealing comment one gentleman made to me, "I would give my friend money to help him get by in life, but not to pass me by." What we have to learn, which this man has not yet, is that empowering someone else empowers all of humanity and ourselves at the same time. When we truly understand that, then we will not hesitate to help someone else.

We go through four stages of learning generosity: tribal (first and second chakras), personal (third), intimate (fourth and fifth), and spiritual (sixth and seventh). This scale of ascension is very, very real. What you are capable of doing for others is as important to understand as what you cannot bring yourself to do. To empower someone's spirit requires that you have empowered yourself, confronted your fears, and realized that your personal power will not be diminished. Otherwise, you are working from the "shadow side" of generosity.

A Personal Act of Power

All forms of service essentially empower a soul. Remind yourself that you can provide this power in many ways: encouragement, hope, kindness, and a nod of approval.

Fact #5: Angels and Grace Are Real

And that's just a fact of life. Period.

A Personal Act of Power

Believe in the presence of angels and in the power of grace. Notice and appreciate synchronicity. Keep an open mind that divine forces are at work in everything that happens to you, whether delightful or difficult.

Fact #6: You Are Never Alone

This is obviously a central lesson for us to learn on Earth School. The divine sends us into that place of aloneness just so that our lives can fill up again and make us realize how precious the people are who share this lifetime with us.

A Personal Act of Power

Whenever you feel that you are alone, release a prayer. Ask for help and let it go. Never underestimate how important you are to someone else. When you feel alone, keep in mind that the aloneness is a temporary place between orbits. You are in motion to another place where there will be love and new friends to meet you. That is a fact of life—and I didn't write the rules. I just know them.

Fact #7: Everything You Do Matters

Everything we do, say, think, and feel matters.

Personal Acts of Power

There is more power in the invisible realm than we can ever imagine. The power of love, kind words, kind thoughts, and a compassionate response, are just a few of the different names we have for the energy of grace. Whenever you are in a bind or frightened, release the prayer, "Fill this moment with grace so that I can find my way," and trust in the presence of grace from that moment onward.

I've gathered a list of the invisible acts of power that meant the most to people and I share them as a to-do list, should an opportunity arise.

1. Hold a door open.
2. Smile.

3. Offer a kind word and encouragement.

4. Give a compliment.

5. Listen without interruption.

6. Make a call when your intuition tells you to.

7. Offer a prayer for a homeless person.

8. Pray — period.

9. Forgive others and yourself.

10. Prepare a meal for a friend.

11. Refrain from judging another person harshly.

12. Remember that life is full of miracles and have faith that every difficult situation can change in the blink of an eye.

13. Remember the truth that there is no such thing as a small or insignificant act of service.

14. Keep your power and attention in present time.

15. Begin and end the day in appreciation of either doing or accepting an invisible act of power.

JOAN BORYSENKO:
Hope Rules

We can all recite the fearful story line of the twenty-first century: The global climate is changing for the worse. A mass die-off of species is under way. Terrorists breed panic and uncertainty. Financial worry creates chronic stress and threatens the survival of business as usual here and abroad. The world population resembles a bacterial culture that has outgrown its petri dish. Pandemics crouch in the wings, ready to pounce. And that's just the beginning of the familiar litany.

But what if there's a more hopeful way to understand this postmodern story—this parenthesis between what used to be and the innovative, sustainable future that can be? Those who will thrive and create that new future are the ones with enough vision and resilience to see the hope through the hype.

The late physicist Ilya Prigogine won a Nobel Prize in 1977 for his theory of dissipative structures. Simply put, all complex systems from subatomic particles to human civilizations reach a point where their current level of organization becomes unstable. Then they melt down. When the old system crashes, it can then reconfigure in a better way, free from the determinism of the past. Prigogine called this daunting event an "escape to a higher order." That's where we are at this moment in history, and although the changes we face are disconcerting in the short run, they're a prelude to great possibility.

Joan Borysenko, PhD, is a world-renowned expert in stress management and mind-body medicine. A biologist, licensed psychologist, and spiritual educator, she is a pioneer in psychoneuroimmunology and the cofounder of one of the first mind-body clinics in the country. A *New York Times* best-selling author, her numerous books include *Your Soul's Compass* and *Fire in the Soul: A New Psychology of Spiritual Optimism*. A former monthly columnist for *Prevention* magazine, her work has been featured in numerous other magazines and newspapers including *O* magazine, *Yoga Journal*, *US News & World Report*, the *Wall Street Journal*, and the *Washington Post*. www.joanborysenko.com

---

My purpose in writing this is to help you overcome fear; stress less; and learn how resilient, creative people think and act. At the risk of sounding prophetic, I believe that in a few years, a new kind of natural selection will have its way with humanity. Hopeful, stress-hardy people will rule the world. And as change and uncertainty escalate, which is likely, those who are stress prone will be less and less able to compete. Read on, and take your place in the new world that's emerging.

Here are ten brief reminders that will help you weather the transition and create a more positive outcome for yourself and for future generations.

1. *Give up trying to change the past* — it's history. Put 100 percent of your energy into creating a more skillful future.

2. *Mobilize resilient thinking.* Incorporate these methods into your life:

   • Look reality in the eyes and accept what is.

   • Find positive meaning in your situation.

   • Use whatever is at your disposal to improvise solutions.

3. *Drop the victim mentality immediately.* Let go of grudges and regain your power.

4. *Exercise regularly.* Stress shrinks your brain, but you can reverse that trend by committing to a moderate fitness program. Be absolutely religious about this!

5. *Don't just sit there — do something.* Optimistic realists take action, but wishful thinking is a dead-end street.

6. *Don't just do something — sit there.* Meditation reduces stress by eliciting the relaxation response, and it stimulates the right-brain thinking necessary to improvise your way to a better future.

7. *Stay engaged with life.* Alienation and isolation breed stress and depression. If you're depressed, get medical help immediately.

8. *Reverse the flow.* Helping others shifts the spotlight off your own troubles and releases feel-good hormones that heal, inspire, and give meaning to life.

9. *Think of one new thing at the end of each day to be grateful for.* Gratitude and other positive feelings enhance resiliency and help you become more expansive and compassionate.

10. *Connect with a friend.* Practice these teachings with a friend so you can support each other as you enact positive, life-affirming changes.

JUDITH ORLOFF:

Four Practical Secrets to Empowering Your Emotional Life

Emotions can come at you hard and fast. You must be prepared. In a flash, negativity can spin you into a tizzy, your center blown to smithereens. Not to worry. You're about to replace that "been there, done that" scenario with more successful ways to cope. I'm going to provide you with strategies for dealing with every angle of emotions—cerebral and intuitive, from earth to heaven. These have repeatedly rescued me, friends, and patients from losing our emotional balance. The four secrets I'll discuss will expose the workings of negativity so that it can't steal your peace of mind or mute your awe for the mind-blowing universe we inhabit.

Secret 1: Reprogram the Biology of Your Emotions

To know thyself, you must know some basics of your biology. Outrageously, most people remain uninformed. Biology lends piercing insights into our emotions, It is the awesome science of life (from the Greek *bios,* meaning "life," and *logos,* meaning "reason") that defines the laws of how living things relate, both physically and emotionally. True, high school or college rarely imparts the subject's magic. And the harrowing sight of that poor limp frog pinned belly up for us to dissect in the ninth grade remains branded in my brain. However, the essence of biology I want to transmit involves dazzling life force; I'll show you how

Judith Orloff, MD, a psychiatrist in private practice and an assistant clinical professor of psychiatry at UCLA, has for more than twenty years been helping patients find emotional freedom. She synthesizes the pearls of traditional medicine with cutting-edge knowledge of intuition, energy, and spirituality to achieve physical and emotional healing. Her book *Second Sight* chronicles her challenges and triumphs embracing her own intuition and integrating it into medicine. She is the author of numerous other books, including the best-sellers *Emotional Freedom, Dr. Judith Orloff's Guide to Intuitive Healing,* and *Positive Energy,* which has been translated into twenty-four languages. www.drjudithorloff.com

to ignite the biochemicals of happiness, turning your mind and body into a finely tuned, mean machine. Taking responsibility for your biology and developing emotional habits to support its highest functioning is a fundamental step toward freedom.

A revelation of twenty-first-century science is that anxiety and loneliness aren't just feelings. Nor are love and hope. All emotions trigger biological reactions that shape your health just as distinctly as what you choose to eat or how you choose to exercise. When you learn to change your emotional reaction to a situation, you change your biological reaction as well. I want to emphasize: *how you react emotionally is a choice in any situation – and those cumulative choices can make or break your chances for well-being.* Appreciating the physical repercussions of emotions makes you more perceptive about how to react, a life-altering realization.

Meditate to Experience Emotional Freedom

Feelings of freedom begin to percolate in us when we calm down. Meditation is the gold standard of calming techniques, For millennia, it's been used by traditions from Zen to Judaism to attain inner stillness. I was overjoyed to see a Time magazine cover story, "The Science of Meditation," a tribute to how Eastern mysticism and Western medicine are finally merging their truths. It's useable in the here and now, not on some rarefied plane. I swear by meditation, practice it daily, and teach it to my patients. It has saved me many times from losing my marbles when life amps up and emotions are swirling. If I stop meditating, even for short spurts, I'll start feeling squirrelly, irritable, and more overwhelmed by the jitter of the world.

Meditation quiets your mind and reprograms your biology (aside from its spiritual and energetic advantages, which you'll discover). The miracle of brain imaging has done wonders to demystify meditation, pinpointing cerebral changes responsible for the calm you feel. Most striking, regular meditation has been shown to literally change the brain by promoting growth in a region responsible for integrating thoughts and emotions; this wires us to deal with stress better. I'm happy to report that it also works fast. In just minutes, meditators have shown increased alpha activity, the brain waves indicating relaxation.

This simple, stress-busting meditation is an initial action step you can take to forge a winning partnership with your biology. Practicing it, you'll become increasingly adept at upping endorphins and short-circuiting your fight-or-flight response, biological gifts of meditation. Once you get the hang of neutralizing stress, it's a merciful reprieve for the body. You'll feel a load lift when uptightness dissipates.

Emotional Action Step
Applying the First Secret:
Reprogram the Biology of Your Emotions

Reduce Stress with This Three-Minute Meditation

1. *Find a comfortable, quiet place.* Wearing loose clothing, settle into a relaxed position in a spot where you won't be interrupted by phones, beepers, or people. It's best to sit upright on a couch, chair, or cushion, so you don't fall asleep. You can be cross-legged or with legs extended, whatever makes you most at ease.

2. *Focus on your breath to quiet your thoughts.* Eyes closed, gently place your awareness on your breath. Be conscious only of breathing in and breathing out. When thoughts come, and they will, visualize them as clouds passing in the sky. Notice your thoughts, but don't attach any judgment to them. Just let them float away and gently return to focusing on your breath. Maintain a centered state of calm by continuing to follow the movement of your breath.

3. *Breathe in calm, breathe out stress.* Let yourself feel the sensuality of inhaling and exhaling as air passes through your nostrils and chest like a cool breeze. Take pleasure in the breath's hypnotic rhythm, what the Buddha described as "breathing in and out sensitive to rapture." With each slow, deep breath, feel yourself inhaling calm, sweet as the scent of summer jasmine, then exhaling stress. Inhale calm, then exhale fear. Inhale calm, then exhale frustration. All negativity is released. Your body unwinds, lulling your biology. You're cocooned by the safety of stillness. Keep refocusing on your breath and the calm. Only the calm.

Secret 2: Uncover the Spiritual Meaning of Your Emotions

As a psychiatrist, I'm in the sacred position of getting to hear what goes on in people's heads, from soccer moms to movie stars. I wish you could be a fly on the wall in my office. Then you'd see why I'm so struck by our basic emotional commonalities, despite how externally different we may seem. To cope with the ongoing saga of life's conundrums, we all have the same set of emotions to choose from (there are only so many) and often keep getting similarly sabotaged. Here's the double bind: everyone wants love, but negativity, our own or another's, often subverts us. So we stay stuck in an unfree limbo of lovelessness for extended periods. Simply put, what is our suffering for? The puzzle can be solved, but it requires a spiritual perspective.

Spirituality, as I'm defining it, is a quest for meaning that goes beyond the linear mind to access a vaster force of compassion to frame everything. Our emotional landscapes are practically unintelligible without this. Why? Because if you don't have an expanded context within which to decipher emotions, the bare bones of many experiences can seem bleak or punishing—a dead-end conclusion that imprisons. Spirituality is freeing because it means opening the heart and doing your darnedest to see every nanosecond of existence through this aperture. Always, you must ask, "How can a situation—any situation—help me grow and develop loving-kindness toward myself or others?" Both with patients and personally, I've seen the authority this question has to recast despair. Adversity of any kind can yield hidden gifts. During boyhood, one of my patients had to walk miles each day to school and thus became great at whistling, a talent that continues to enchant him and his young daughter. Similarly, we can mine goodness in all experiences when we learn to find the spiritual message within emotional turmoil.

Spirituality isn't static. It's an evolving optimism that won't let hardship get the best of you. It apprises you that something good can show up at any time. From my own instincts and from my spiritual teacher, I've also come to define spirituality not just as recognizing that there's more than the material realm, but that we're all points of light bonded together in a vaster continuum. In the context of emotional freedom, a spiritual vantage point is liberating for numerous reasons:

1. By opening yourself to something larger, a compassionate higher power of your own (God, Goddess, nature, love, or something nameless), you'll gain strength beyond your own to conquer adversity. You're not alone. Never have been. You'll feel the safety in that.

2. You'll learn how to be released from what Buddhists call "monkey mind," the circular insecurities that incarcerate you in your smallest self. In Energy Psychiatry I've seen how a problem often can't be solved on a problem's level. To put distance between yourself and negativity, you must view it from higher ground.

3. You'll realize that there's something greater than the emotion of the moment. If you don't know this—and most people don't—you'll think your anger is all there is. You'll get into how justified you are to hold on to it, a lethal stance that fuels war in your kitchen or globally. When you think and act from the framework of spirituality I'm presenting, you'll see anger as an impetus to grow, to resolve differences, to rise above them. You won't stay angry because you believe it's deserved or lose your temper as a pressure-release valve. You won't

want to hurt others, rather, you'll seek to become more expanded in yourself.

Here's my gospel about how to conceptualize emotions in spiritual terms: view each one as a trusted guide whose purpose is to enlarge your heart. I'm presenting emotions as a path to spiritual awakening, a way to break through to the light inside you. Specific emotions play specific roles. For instance; consider how the misery of depression can teach you to develop hope or how bitter jealousy can prompt the cultivation of self-esteem. These key transformations are more than psychological. *They refine your soul, which is your reason to be. There is nothing as important.* Remember this when life gets hard or lonely. I want you to understand that there is meaning and beauty in these difficult experiences too.

Emotional Action Step
Applying the Second Secret: Uncover the Spiritual Meaning of Your Emotions

A Heart-Centering Meditation to Counter Negative Self-Talk

1. *Settle down.* In a tranquil setting, sit comfortably and close your eyes. Take a few long, deep breaths to relieve tension. Even if your negative thoughts are going a mile a minute (you know that broken record: "I'm not good enough, small enough, spiritual enough," yada yada), keep concentrating on your breath as best you can.

2. *Tune in to your heart.* Lightly rest your palm over your heart in the midchest. This energy center is the entryway to compassion and spirit. In a relaxed state, inwardly request to connect with a higher power, a force greater than yourself that links you to love. It can be God, the starlit sky, or a beneficent intelligence, whatever stirs you. Then, in your heart area, notice what you intuitively *feel*, not what you *think*. You may experience a soothing warmth, comfort, clarity, even bliss. I often get shivers, feel a wave of goose bumps, or am moved to tears. It's easiest to first feel spirit inside you. From that home base, you can better sense it everywhere. Stay aware of your heart as it opens more and more, infusing you with compassion. If negative self-talk still arises, keep your compassion flowing. The spiritual meaning of doing this is learning to have mercy on yourself for any perceived lacking, to know that you're enough just as you are. With that meaning in mind, let the freedom of compassion flood your body, a balm for all that ails.

This meditation is a surefire antidote to negative self-talk. I've never seen anyone able to sustain a denigrating diatribe when they're centered in the heart. I'm indefatigable when it comes to equating compassion with freedom. I hope the potency of this pairing really clicks for you. Compassion is the great transformer, of the self and the world. No matter how things seem, your compassion doesn't fall on deaf ears. Remember: Jesus talked about love and the people listened. Whenever you feel lost, return to your heart. It's the doorway to heaven.

Secret 3: Learn the Energetic Power of Your Emotions

In Energy Psychiatry I've learned to see emotions as a stunning expression of energy. Positive ones nurture you. Negative ones deplete you. In terms of wattage, hope, self-acceptance, and compassion make you brighter, freer; shame, envy, and desire for revenge dim your brightness. You feel emotions internally, while their energy extends beyond your body, affecting everyone you contact. Similarly, the emotions of others register in you.

Now, as an Energy psychiatrist, I want to convey to you that emotions are intuitively palpable; you can learn to access their force field to enhance your freedom. I'd like you to begin to think of emotions in terms of subtle energy, a "vibe" emanating from yourself and others, an intimate sensing. Subtle energy is right in front of you but isn't visible. It can be felt inches or feet from the body. I'll describe how to sense it with intuition. Indigenous healing traditions revere subtle energy as our life force. In Chinese medicine it's called *chi*. It's *mana* to Hawaiian kahunas, *prana* to Indian yogic practitioners. Though the molecular structure of subtle energy isn't yet fully defined, scientists have measured increased photon emissions and electromagnetic readings around healing practitioners.

For an unforgettable visual of how the energy of emotions can impact the body, take a look at Dr. Masuro Emoto's book *The Hidden Messages of Water*. His high-speed photographs of frozen water crystals send a valuable message. Listen to what he observed. When sentiments such as "I love you" or "You're wonderful" were directed to water, symmetrical, rainbow-hued snowflake patterns took form, unfolding universes of delight. However, the negative emotions of "I hate you" or "You make me sick" created fractured, ugly shapes with muddled colors — not what you want in your body. (Though some consider this work controversial, Dr. Dean Radin at the Institute of Noetic Sciences has successfully replicated it, and other similar experiments are under way). Take time to assimilate these findings. They have momentous implications for your emotional freedom: since you're composed mostly of water, you must generate maximal positivity to stay healthy and whole. Also, you can't afford to nurse resentments or self-loathing without suffering toxicity.

I realize that it's one thing to know this, yet another to live it. The problem is that negative emotional energy is basically louder and wilder than the positive, and more seductively grabs your attention. Picture a bucking bronco versus a contented cat warming its belly in the sun. If both were in front of you, where would your attention go? Positive emotions, delicious as they are, don't have as dramatic an energetic pull. On an intuitive level, emotions such as grief and terror are easier to sense than the lower-keyed vibes of calmness or confidence. It's important that you channel this knowledge into new behaviors so you're not the doomed moth eternally drawn to the flame.

Emotional Action Step
Applying the Third Secret: Learn the Energetic Power of Your Emotions

Try an Intuitive Experiment: Sense the Difference Between Positive and Negative Emotions

In this experiment, you're going to compare two scenarios. With both observe how your words and tone affect your body and emotional state. Spend at least a few minutes trying these words on.

Scenario 1. Stand in front of a mirror and say to yourself in a loving, appreciative tone, "I look terrific and I'm a fantastic person." Stay focused on your positives. Then feel, don't think. Notice how your body reacts. Are you breathing easier? Do your shoulders relax? Does your gut untighten? Does your energy rise? Do you feel happier? Lighter? Freer? Also, note any other changes.

Scenario 2. Stand in front of the mirror and say in your nastiest, most hateful tone, "I look horrible and I despise myself." Really mean it. Flare those negatives up. How does your body react now? Notice your shoulders, your gut, your chest. Is your energy higher or lower? Are you clenching? Breathing shallowly? Do you feel depressed? Are your aches and pains aggravated? Whatever you sense, note it. Stew in this negativity awhile so you won't forget the feel of toxic energy.

I'm so taken by this exercise because it spells out that positive and negative energy are about as opposite as you can get. No confusing them. Ask yourself which you prefer. It's time to make a choice and go after it. The launching pad for emotional freedom is always yourself. Words, tone, and the positive or negative energy of emotions all figure in. You must

become accountable for the vibes you expose yourself and others to. The next time someone speaks to you, note the physical reaction within your body, not how your brain processes the actual words. Feel the energy beneath those words; notice how your body responds to that. If the content of someone's words is positive, yet the energy beneath it causes you to contract, respect that physical reaction. Energy doesn't lie. Keep sensing it, trusting it, letting it liberate you.

Secret 4: Map the Psychology of Your Emotions

Why do you feel what you feel? Where do fear of commitment, alpha achieving, or looking on the bright side begin? Which emotional coping styles hinder or serve you? These urgent questions are the lifeblood of psychology's study of emotions and behavior. You need to know your psychological self so unhealthy patterning doesn't stifle you. I get a special charge out of picturing all the psychotherapists and their patients around the world valiantly tackling hard issues. Two people sitting across from each other in reverence to growth, a noble undertaking. I've seen it from both sides. Part of my role as psychiatrist is helping patients attain psychological insights, sparkling as always when they pop from the void; my therapist continues to work the same magic for me. Whether I'm the healer or healing recipient, I'm wowed. I lust for those light-bursts of clarity that edge me closer to love and freedom or lift confusion, secrets you'll tap in to yourself. Here's a first look at how psychology can liberate your heart and head. I'll focus on one principle — "You are not your parents" — which is so central to your emotional freedom that it can dictate how you treat yourself and everyone you love.

You Are Not Your Parents:
Learn from Their Assets and Shortcomings

To know your psychology, there's no detour around your parents. Beloved or dreaded, these two people emotionally molded you. Spiritual teacher Ram Dass nails it when he says, "If you think you're enlightened, go spend a week with your parents." There you have it: the good, bad, and the ugly. I say, stir up that pot; examine the relationship with your parents. Why? To achieve emotional freedom, you want to disentangle yourself from their worst traits and embody the best.

Who you are emotionally often reflects who your parents are. While growing up, it's frequently monkey see, monkey do. For better or worse, you emulate your parents' virtues and faults. If your mother was anxious or a worrywart, chances are she transmitted some of that to you. If your father was a bastion of hope, that came through too. In addition, you may contain interesting dualities of both parents. For example, my mother was a people person, my father more a loner. I have both in me, and I've learned to embrace each. You can do likewise with the dualities you've inherited.

Sometimes, in an attempt to be different from your parents, you may develop completely opposite emotional coping styles. For example, if your mother was an inveterate nagger, you may shun all confrontation. If your father was intensely critical, you may be reluctant to be honest with others when you disagree. These styles also deserve examination so that instead of simply doing the opposite of what your parents did, you can find a truly authentic, balanced way to be.

In situations large and small, you have the choice to evolve past your parents' limitations. This choice and the changes that ensue exorcise the unhealthy habits you're unconsciously reenacting. When you refuse to be afraid because your father is fear-ridden, or reject being the victim your mother has become, that's real emancipation. The flip side of freedom is also accepting your parents' positive emotional legacy, the smarts and goodness they've handed down. With parents it's nearly always a mixed bag. Freedom comes from going with the good and striving to shed the rest.

Emotional Action Step
Applying the Fourth Secret: Map the Psychology of Your Emotions

Take an Emotional Inventory of Your Parents

To get a well-rounded picture of your parents, I'd like you to take an inventory of their top five positive and negative traits. Were they caring, good listeners, always there for you? And/or depressed, disappointed in life, blaming? Identifying these traits, do your best to see your parents as human rather than idealizing or demonizing them. Get their pluses and minuses down on paper so they can stare right back at you. When reviewing the inventory, consider ways your parents' asset or liabilities impacted you. Which traits on your list instilled confidence? Humor? A sense of safety? Which ones impaired your well-being? Also, be truthful about the traits you too possess. If they are positive, embrace them. If they are negative, begin to work with one at a time to free yourself. You don't have to worry about turning into your parents if you take action not to parrot their dysfunction. Then decide what you want to retain. Let this inventory begin to help you rewire your psychological programming so it suits the freest you.

CHAPTER THREE

Freedom is about taking charge of who you want to be. Keep referring to this inventory on your journey with emotions. Whenever a feeling comes up, especially a negative one, ask yourself, "Who is reacting—me or my parents?" This is a telling question that reveals if you're a parent clone but don't know it. Like many of us, you may be stuck in the unconscious rut of responding like them, say, being a complainer or a drama queen. However, once you determine who's really running the show, you can decide to behave differently. Doing so lets you locate your true voice and identity.

As everyone with even a little awareness understands, any gutless wonder can walk around oblivious to the effect of his or her emotions. What's it to them to keep acting out and hurting other people with disastrous results? Freedom asks more of you than that. Now that you've been initiated into the four secrets to emotional freedom, you've sampled the collective wisdom of your biology, spirituality, energetic power, and psychology. The more you know about these ingredients of emotions, the more they'll increase consciousness and a connection to your heart. Self-knowledge is a most impressive oracle, crystallizing who you are and can be. As it mounts, expect to feel a coming together inside of you, a beautiful feeling of awakening. I praise consciousness so unflinchingly because it's the path to freedom. The fog will never offer asylum. In all circumstances, make this your mantra: "I will keeping moving toward the light, toward compassion." I promise: it's the right direction. You won't be let down. The bigger your heart grows, the better things will get. Now and always, celebrate the freedom of your life. There's more to come in this adventure.

Carol Look:

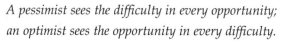

The Choice of Optimism—Welcome Home

CHAPTER 4

A pessimist sees the difficulty in every opportunity;
an optimist sees the opportunity in every difficulty.

—Winston Churchill

The Problem

We are all born optimistic. It's our natural state of being, a biological imprint in our DNA. In my life and work, I have observed that optimism manifests as a joyful appetite for life, a hopefulness about the future, a sense of security that there is a Divine Order to how life unfolds. We also have a need to be optimistic in order to survive. So if our ancestral programming is naturally optimistic, what's the problem? The problem is that over time our environment slowly but surely squeezes the optimistic, positive attitudes out of us.

Let's start with an official definition—what exactly is optimism? The basic definitions from the Internet were what you'd expect: "Hopefulness about the future and about things and situations turning out well." Categorized as a philosophy, the definition is: "The doctrine of the ultimate triumph of good over evil."

From my point of view as a traditionally trained psychotherapist, hypnotist, and energy therapy practitioner with twenty years in the men-

Carol Look, LCSW, DCH, EFT Master, is a success and abundance coach in the energy psychology field. Her specialty is inspiring clients to attract abundance into their lives by combining EFT and the Law of Attraction to clear limiting beliefs and build "prosperity consciousness." A pioneer and leading voice in the EFT community, she is the author of the popular book *Attracting Abundance with EFT* and is a frequent guest speaker at prestigious worldwide conferences and Energy Healing Telesummits. She appears as a primary energy psychology practitioner in the DVD documentaries *The Tapping Solution and Operation: Emotional Freedom.* www.AttractingAbundance.com

tal health field, optimism is also an *energetic pattern*—as is any emotion or behavior we have in our lives—and it carries a signature vibration the same way our voice, posture, colors, books, and foods carry individual vibrations. A vibration is a feeling or mood, a frequency of energy. When you walk into a room, you know whether people are fighting or getting along just by the energy or vibration you feel coming from them. When you are with someone who feels depressed, the vibration is obvious, and in some cases, rather contagious. Optimists operate from emotional and energetic patterns. They have specific perceptions and make the assumption that, in spite of what has just transpired, it will turn out well. Just as an extremely anxious person might operate from fearful perceptions and an assumption that, in spite of what the situation in front of them looks like, it is fraught with danger.

If you don't feel very optimistic now, or don't believe the optimist's philosophy that good will ultimately triumph over evil, it's likely due to the emotional "training" you received from your family, society, teachers, media, and friends. In psychology we often call it *programming.*

I believe optimism is an attitude, a stance, a belief system, and, ultimately, a *choice.* But if the energetic and behavioral patterns we witnessed growing up communicated that we don't have a choice about this life stance, we won't recognize the truth that we do, in fact, have the power to choose to be and feel optimistic in our lives. Most people are under the assumption that we are powerless over our attitudes and feelings, but we're not powerless at all. We may be ignorant, locked in bad habits, accustomed to certain emotional spirals and patterns, but we are not powerless over our emotions.

So how did we get so far away from being naturally optimistic? We ended up miles away from optimism through the same mechanism we learn anything in our lives: through basic conditioning, training, repetition, and programming from our families, friends, and society. From basic modeling principles, we learn how to be optimistic or pessimistic, respectful or disrespectful, cheerful or moody, based on what we see in front of us. Our well-meaning parents, teachers, and societal models of schooling, television, and politics show us how to behave. They program us into believing what they believe. Cell biologist Dr. Bruce Lipton says that we are all being hypnotized until the age of six by other people's beliefs and feelings. No wonder we need new programming!

Simply put, we get trained out of our natural state of optimism. We get taught to be and feel otherwise, then the negativity becomes a habit, then we live in ways that automatically reject optimism. I repeatedly say to my clients who criticize themselves for behaving as their parents did: *"If you grow up in France, you will obviously end up speaking French!"* You don't think you have a choice; so even though you may have been born with the capacity to be and feel optimistic, if you were raised in emotional pessimism, you will start *speaking* pessimism. It's impossible to be immune to that kind of intense programming from your loved ones.

We get taught on a daily basis to have a pessimistic attitude or stance toward life. Our caregivers who teach us are convinced this stance is a good idea. They believe on a deep level that their children's emotional survival depends on it. Think about what "energetic atmosphere" you grew up in: What was the energy regarding hope, or the attitude about your future, or the accepted beliefs about how life unfolds? What were your family's beliefs about the world in general? What were their attitudes about life as it is evolving for humans? Even though you may not be aware that your energetic patterns lean toward negativity, identifying and labeling your beliefs will show you where you are on the continuum between optimism and pessimism.

We often consider our beliefs to represent the truth about life and, as a result, we don't question them (much less categorize them) as optimistic or pessimistic—they just feel like facts to us. Read through these belief statements and identify which ones might be automatic truths for you:

"Nothing ever works in my favor, that's just how it goes."

"I'm not one of the lucky ones this lifetime."

"Other people always get chosen."

"Life has to be a struggle."

"Life is hard and then you die."

So if your parents were trained out of optimism by their parents, they aren't going to know or be able to model a different mode of being. They will teach you what they think is right, based on their attitudes about the world. Consider what your parents thought about the world they brought you into: Were they hopeful? Optimistic about the future of their family? Confident that you as their child would be safe and happy? What attitudes did they impart to you? See if you recognize any of these attitudes and beliefs:

"You need to be more realistic."

"Don't have dreams, they'll never show up."

"It's always better to keep your expectations low."

"Expect the worst and you'll be fine."

"Don't bother feeling happy—it won't last!"

One of the biggest challenges about reclaiming your natural optimism is the extent of the training or programming you received from your family. If your parents didn't think it was safe to be optimistic, they were likely highly motivated to teach you pessimism as a valuable coping mechanism! And they probably taught you this lesson repeatedly. For instance, if they believed from their personal experiences that "It's dangerous to get your hopes up, because you'll never get what you want," they would have valued teaching you to be careful and to avoid being hopeful. Out of their learned "wisdom," they probably tried very hard to convince you that feeling joyful was unsafe. It's possible that their family conditioning wasn't terribly conscious, but they just "knew" that it was dangerous to look forward to anything good. Maybe their hopes were dashed repeatedly, maybe their parents believed being happy was childish and naive, maybe they struggled so much with financial hardship that the notion of looking forward to the future seemed ridiculous to them.

Many times, when we feel joyful or excited, we are criticized or made "wrong" for it. So instead of receiving affirmation or acceptance for being in a good mood, or feeling safe for being who we are, we learn to be afraid of the repercussions of having positive feelings. This translates into a learned code of behavior and making an emotional vow to never show positive feelings again. We would rather be safe at all costs, so we stick to the belief system that shuns a lightness of being or joyful outlook. After all, not only do we want to *fit in* to our family, we don't want to stand out and get into trouble.

For instance, suppose you were feeling joyful about auditioning for the school play when you were in the sixth grade. You were visibly excited, in a playful mood, and eagerly awaiting tryouts. And then your mother, in an effort to "protect" you from the dangers of looking forward to anything, said to you, "Don't get your hopes up; you'll just be disappointed." While her intention was to protect you (a loving, maternal act), she informed you that being in a good mood was foolish and left you with the impression that feeling hopeful would inevitably end in distress. Whether she learned this attitude as a child herself or she became more cynical as she moved through her own life challenges doesn't matter. What matters is that this key emotional figure in your life warned you not to be hopeful, joyful, or carefree. This is a powerful life lesson—one you will likely remember in your conscious as well as unconscious mind until new patterns or programs are created to replace these old ones.

Perhaps your parents were divorced when you were a teenager. And suppose you were feeling excited about a crush you had on someone at school in high school. Your mother, suffering from the trauma and pain of her own divorce, may have said something cynical and negative about relationships, being in a raw place emotionally as a result of a recent separation. So here you are, brimming with adolescent excitement, and you tell your mother you are happy that a boy at school seems to like you. You hear from her, "Boys are nothing but trouble," or "Don't bother, you'll just end up with a broken heart." Those statements would represent her beliefs, her experiences, and may even be an attempt to keep you safe from the same heartbreak she experienced. Again, it doesn't really matter where your parent learned this information. The intention is often protective; the end result is the same. You learn a permanent lesson: "Don't bother being joyful and certainly don't look forward to anything—you'll just end up disappointed anyway."

I worked with a client who was feeling hopeful that her symptoms were not due to an inherited arthritic condition, as she had first thought, but merely fatigue and strain from an intensive exercise program. When she expressed her enthusiasm and hope to her father, he said, "Don't worry, you'll get it sooner or later; we all do!" That is called ancestral pessimism, passed down from one generation to the next. The emotional position he took was: "Knowing you're doomed and preparing for the worst is better than being surprised!"

And do we even need to discuss the negativity in politics and through our media outlets? We watch the negative news and ugly interpersonal political relationships on television over and over again, and wonder why these attitudes stick!

If we were essentially born optimistic, but got trained out of it by our basic interpersonal conditioning, why would we go to such lengths to retrain ourselves and reclaim it? Because optimism is a biological imperative—we need to get back to optimism if we want to be healthy on an energetic, emotional, and spiritual level. Cynicism and negativity are like contagious germs; they undermine our emotional, physical, and spiritual health.

The Solution

In the exciting emerging field of energy therapy, there is so much room for optimism. The protocols and treatments in energy therapy, or Emotional Freedom techniques (EFT), for instance, target the source of a problem at its core: your energy system. Energy psychology experts would define pessimism as a symptom due to "blocks in your energy system"—blockages and congestion that are preventing your natural optimism from coming forward into your life. In the language and theory of energy therapy, having symptoms is the proof that there are energetic blockages in your circuitry of meridians. EFT targets these core issues— blockages—by tapping on the meridian points while focusing on the problem. In this way, these underlying blockages and limiting beliefs get cleared at the deepest level, rather than just symptomatically. This bodes well for permanent clearance.

So if the bad news is that your chronic negativity points to blockages in your energy system, the good news is that you can change these energetic patterns, clean your energy system, and move to a desired emotional stance of hope and joy. Although I have been incredibly resilient most of my life, I have become even more optimistic about life, my clients, and my future since I learned how to treat myself and others with EFT. We no longer have to take an ailment or emotion and cut it out, aim shock treatments at it, or cover it up with medications. Now we have the tools to treat the problem at its core, clear the energy pattern, and choose the emotional direction we'd prefer to take.

So if the problem is clear—that we were trained out of being optimistic by our primary caregivers, (often well-meaning yet dysfunctional caregivers)—how do we get back to being or feeling optimistic?

1. Clear the events or traumas that caused the pessimistic thinking.

2. Practice the attitude and energy of optimism every day.

3. Raise your vibration by using Law of Attraction methods to feel more joyful.

4. Choose your focus, intention, and emotional direction.

5. Ask for and believe in Divine Guidance.

(1) Clear the events/traumas: Remember, you weren't born pessimistic; you have to be trained or programmed to be this way. Clear the events, the statements, and the attitudes that you were taught about the value of being pessimistic, and they no longer have any template to stick to in your energetic system. I highly recommend EFT, or other energy medicine clearing tools. What you might target are typical beliefs that represent the learned pessimism: "Life has to be a struggle" or "You can't rely on anyone for help." These beliefs, if operating, are draining your energy system, and are perfect targets for energy therapy.

(2) Practice, practice, practice. Remember, you were a very good "student" as a child, which is why these childhood lessons stuck so deeply in your energy system. You have practiced something other than joy or good cheer—fear, frustration, depression, cynicism—for at least several decades. Now you need to (as well as deserve to) start practicing being and feeling optimistic again. Define optimism for yourself and start adding it as an ingredient to your daily practices for health and well-being: meditate and practice optimism, exercise and practice optimism, brush your teeth and practice optimism. Put *practice feeling good* on your to-do list every day.

(3) Raise your vibration. This terminology comes from the recently popularized field of Law of Attraction. What it means is *like attracts like.* The theory states that your vibration (your mood and feeling) will attract into your life more similar experiences on an energetic or vibrational basis. When you focus all of your attention on something that is going well or that you appreciate, you tend energetically to invite more positive

interactions and outcomes, even serendipitous events, into your life. If you focus on what has turned out well for you, you tend to notice more of these instances and receive more of them in your life. If you are a complainer and see the dark side to every situation, don't be surprised when more interactions worthy of complaint cross your path. The old saying "Misery loves company" applies to thoughts and experiences, not just people — negative energetic thoughts attract more negative thoughts. So how do we raise our vibration? Write gratitude lists, think of people we appreciate, notice and bask in nature, be still and quiet long enough to get in touch with our creative powers, ask for Divine Guidance, practice feeling good...

(4) Choose your focus. Other people's behavior may be out of our control, but our focus is up to us! This gives us such freedom in our lives. Unfortunately, we are under the illusion that we are not in control of our focus, and we allow our emotions to pull us in all sorts of distressing directions. I'm not saying that we can prevent upsetting events that cross our paths. I'm saying it's up to us to determine the duration and intensity of our pain based on our focus. Do you dwell on what's gone wrong? Is it hard for you to move on? Do you need to tell others repeatedly how you've been victimized? Many of us spend countless hours worrying and fussing about what's not going well. But we have the ability to choose in any moment of any day to turn our attention to appreciation, hope, and how to be of service. Right now, choose to change your focus to gratitude and joy. Believe there is Divine timing, ask for Divine Guidance, and expect it to show up for you. Notice how easy it was to change the channel for your mind...

(5) Ask for and believe in Divine Guidance. Optimists believe there is a Divine plan, even if they reject organized religion of all kinds. When you ask for and believe in Divine (or inner) Guidance, you can relax and know that answers are being sent to you. Guidance about what to do next, how to handle a troubling situation, or how to proceed when presented with an opportunity is available to all of us, regardless of how we view higher wisdom. Knowing there is Divine Guidance available will help you feel calmer, safer, and more hopeful. So make it part of your daily practice to ask for, and believe in, Divine Guidance.

* * *

As an EFT practitioner, the primary focus of the work I do with clients in my workshops is twofold: I help them (1) reduce their emotional resistance, and (2) raise their energetic vibration. Resistance comes from negative thoughts, assumptions, or habits that reduce joy. Resistance often sounds like complaining, taking other people's inventories, fanning the flames of doubt and fear without a plan to be different. Your overall vibration is often described as high or low, and is measured by your emotions and focus. Where is your emotional vibration right now? Hopeful? Joyful? Resentful? I teach my students that we have the power to reduce our resistance and raise our vibration. This gives us back some power, which is hope-giving in itself.

Remember, being hopeful makes you more hopeful and allows you to see the silver lining in all situations — a simplistic example of the Law of Attraction at work. Being negative draws more negativity into your life through energetic resonance. So the challenge is to honor the emotions you experience, validate the feelings you are suffering from, but don't wallow — find a way to move forward. The new age popularity of the Law of Attraction tells us that *like attracts like,* and if you watch your thoughts, feelings, and vibrations for a few days, you'll understand how powerful it is! Right now, sit down and write a gratitude list and then notice your vibration as well as how the rest of your day unfolds.

Make a decision to see the best in others, look for the silver lining, choose optimism now. Simple but not easy, I know. But remember, you actually have the power to make a choice in each moment to continue to be negative or not. You may be a champion at seeing the worst in every situation, you may have practiced it over and over again, but you have the conscious choice to take a different road. Yes, you may have had excellent teachers in your life, but you can change the spiral of this negativity and increase the momentum to move in another direction.

It may be quite challenging in the beginning to practice returning to and reclaiming your optimism. So please ask yourself the following questions to help you along this path:

- What is the *upside* to remaining pessimistic?
  - o Does it help you feel safe?
  - o Do you hide behind the attitude of cynicism?
- What's the *downside* to letting it go?
  - o Are you afraid to change?
  - o Does it feel safer to be pessimistic?
  - o Would you feel disloyal if you broke this family mold?
- How does it serve you to continue being pessimistic?
  - o Does this keep you feeling safe from getting your hopes dashed?
  - o Does it keep your expectations low?
  - o Does it give you permission to keep your performance mediocre?

Keep looking for what's going well in your life because when you do, you often find a long list of successes, happy times, and good opportunities. When you remember or are tempted to wallow in negative memories, events, or unhappy times, clear and release these patterns with a type of energy work.

Is it true that some people find it easier than others to regain an optimistic stance? Yes, of course. Some people are evidently more predisposed to be depressed or down about life, regardless of their family upbringing. They have inherited the chemistry to be a bit more pessimistic, which is then reinforced by their environment. In spite of a chemical predisposition, they, too, have the ability to release energetic patterns of depression, choose appropriate interventions, and use energy therapies to release the old programming.

Conclusion

There's nothing but good news here! You can be trained to speak any language, at any age. You may have been programmed to see the worst, to feel fearful, be mistrustful of other people, but you can change that programming this very moment. We are all entitled to choose our attitude toward life and we have the capacity to look for what's best in each opportunity. We will all experience challenges, troubles, and losses, but resilience is our birthright. We need to clear traumatic events with energy therapy, practice looking for what's going well, raise our vibration, choose our focus, and ask for Divine Guidance.

The ultimate optimistic stance is asking for and believing in Divine Guidance. Good will triumph over evil, more will be revealed, and we have a choice in every moment to feel good. So choose optimism — welcome home!

Susan Russell:

Positive Reflections of the Illness Mirror

I grew up with the Brazilian proverb *"Da um jeitinho"* ("To find a way" or "There is always a way"). In our family, being creative and pitching in were as essential as brushing one's teeth. Our family has tremendous fortitude, forged through the generations and demonstrated by my immigrant grandparents on both sides, as well as by my parents. My mother is of Brazilian and Portuguese extraction, my father of Italian, French, Dutch, and German ancestry. Full of the passions normal in the Brazilian and Italian cultures and the delicious aromas of freshly prepared meals, our household was never dull.

Our dinnertime conversations made multitasking look easy. There were always five to eight conversations going on simultaneously. Requests for food to be passed. May I borrow your book, sweater, pen, money? Or, did you put back my book, sweater, pen, money? Did you see___? How did you like ___? Dinner guests were generally either delighted or baffled by the flurry of conversations that occurred simultaneously and in which we all engaged fully, without missing a beat. At a time when it was awkward not to match the Americana community, we rarely did. The gift from this is an appreciation of different cultures, customs, and approaches as well as an ability to move smoothly into many worlds and hold seemingly different values and possibilities simultaneously without reservation. We children were also raised with noblesse oblige, which included sharing with others who were still making their way in life.

Susan Russell, PhD, ThD, LAc, LMSW, is a licensed psychiatric social worker and psychotherapist, author, educator, shamanic healer, and founder of Turning Point Healing Center, a multimodality healing and education center in Marietta, Georgia. Author of *The Seasonal Meridian Guide: A Guide to Enhancing Your Energy* and *The Body of Qi CD Meditation Series,* she holds a doctorate in Integrative Energy Medicine and the Theology of Holism from Holos University Graduate Seminary and is board chair of Holos. She is also on the program committee for the International Society for the Study of Subtle Energies and Energy Medicine (ISSSEEM) and a member of Acupuncturists Without Borders (AWB). www.turningpointhc.com

I was blessed with three grandmothers; two were more traditional and "aged" appropriately by social standards. My third grandmother was not blood related but, rather, related by spirit. She was my Brazilian grandfather's second wife, Maria. She taught me so much about thinking outside the box. Maria was an avid fisherwoman and played tennis into her nineties because she did not feel she should retire until she was truly old. She drank a Brazilian *choppe* (a traditional Brazilian beer) on the rocks every day after her tennis game and an afternoon *chachaça* (a traditional Brazilian rum drink) into which she liberally poured sugar and squeezed an entire lemon for the vitamin C. Massage, sauna, homeopathy, herbs, and Chinese medicine were norms for her.

Maria loved life and was a joy to be around. Her philosophy was not to linger in sorrow but, rather, *procura a felizidade* (find happiness). She also stood by her convictions, marching in the downtown streets of Rio de Janeiro with many others in protest of a possible military action. This was phenomenal considering my grandfather was an admiral in the Brazilian navy! She also had a full social circle with friends of all ages and walks of life. Her philosophy was that after mourning a friend who had transitioned, she would make another friend ten years younger than the friend who had died. "This way I will not be the last one in my circle of friends as I age and I will always have the same number of friends," she said. "They will become increasingly younger, which will, hopefully, keep my mind and heart active. I will not die lonely." Her death wish was to die in the middle of a winning serve in tennis!

I grew up watching our Brazilian grandfather consult a reference book while listening to a family member relate his or her symptoms; then he created a homeopathic formula for that person. This remained in the recesses of my mind as I moved through my life, to be revived years later in my current profession as a healer.

I lived with my grandparents in Brazil one and a half years, attending school in a bilingual setting and graduating from the Escola Americana do Rio de Janeiro. Brazil offered her rich banquet of different flavors, from visiting with family members who still live in Rio and São Paulo to sports, road trips to the interior, monsoons, going up the Amazon by ship, seeing the magnificent Iguassu Falls, meeting indigenous people. I learned that history is recorded by cultural eyes. The Brazilian aeronautical museum credits Alberto Santos-Dumont, not the Wright brothers, as being the first in flight. I experienced Catholicism Brazilian style and witnessed Macumba and Candomblé ceremonies. I learned that many people who went to Christian church on Sunday participated in the ceremonies of these Afro-Brazilian religions, as well as Carnival. Many Brazilians had no problem holding these very different beliefs and customs and incorporated them into their lives. Samba, one of the many wonderful Brazilian musical rhythms, is also a blend of Brazil's rich Euro-African history and filled the breath of Rio day and night.

My background was replete with both a creative side and a high science side, which fueled my insatiably curious mind. I divided my time between test tubes, experiments, nature, night skies, also designing and creating clothes for my dolls and eventually for myself. By the age of fourteen, I was making many of my own clothes, and soon without patterns, as I was able to see how things fit or could fit together. This has helped me enormously in looking at the psychospiritual patterns that impel us.

The Brazilian proverb that informed my growing up and the family around me has today become a cellular knowing that *there is always a positive way.*

On the Psychiatric Journey

One of the many aspects of my professional background has been as a psychiatric social worker specializing in dual diagnosis, which when I began, translated into working with individuals who experienced "mental" illness along with addictions. I worked in the emergency receiving units of both a state psychiatric hospital and a private psychiatric hospital. I saw people on the edge of sanity. Some howled as though possessed by demons; others tore at padded walls in anguished states of withdrawal. Still others, in their own world, were unable to engage in even marginal conversations, at least upon admission to the psych ward.

I grew extremely dismayed by the psychiatric environment and disillusioned with the Western medicine approach to those who were hospitalized as I saw patients on multiple prescriptions receiving more and more medications to mitigate the side effects of other medications. Then I went to hear neurosurgeon and medical intuitive C. Norman Shealy, MD, speak about a new doctoral program in integrative energy medicine that eventually became Holos University. I was filled with excitement as I listened to his presentation and knew I would be headed in that direction. Eventually, I left the psychiatric hospitals, unable to see myself working there any longer.

What a fabulous gateway opened up for me as I entered the world of energy medicine in the Holos graduate program, spearheaded by Dr. Shealy. These new studies complemented my study of Chinese medicine. Both were invaluable in my private counseling practice. Chinese medicine offers built-in archetypes for every point of energy in the body (which lends insight to Western psychotherapy) and is an excellent template for Western exploration in the field of energy medicine. I studied with and read the works of many masters, including esoteric acupuncture with Dr. Mikio Sankey. Each pearl that resonated with me propelled me further on my journey.

In working with clients and in moving through my own issues, I have come to realize that there are many ways people experience negative impressions and positive expressions. For some people, positive thinking seems easier; for some, negative thinking is their natural way; for others, vacillation between positive and negative thinking is the norm. In looking back at my life, I can see that the times when I remained in a positive outlook resulted in a positive outcome, even when such results seemed improbable or even impossible. The times of holding onto dim views only exacerbated my pain and resulted in a challenging outcome. My passions now are options, information, and awareness.

In Chinese medicine, I learned we live in a binary world; for every yin, there is a yang. A natural example is the hand. The hand is a coming together of the palm with the back of the hand, forming complementary balance. These aspects work together, yet their motion, skin texture, and life journey are very different. In the West, we think in terms of opposition, gas or brake, rather than complementary interrelationship. In acupuncture, we could say that the needles act as antennas to capture and transport vibratory rates or signals. Yin and yang represent static and dynamic flows that are adjusted and sometimes flipped, depending on the placement of the needles. The acupuncturist can place the needles in patterns of sacred geometry or work with the extraordinary meridians for advanced effects.

Acupuncture could be described as a combination of physics, math, music, color, sound, and the power of archetypes such as warrior or philosopher whose absence can be related to stuck qi (the vital life force). It is additionally vibrational, harmonic; it is based on sequencing and synchronizing, which causes shifts in the body's energy fields. The fields then align and flow freely, which moves out debris or old patterns while unlocking stuck patterns and releasing natural, original virtue.

Shifting from Negative to Positive

My private practice became the work of many different healing traditions: psychology, Chinese body-mind medicine, acupuncture and esoteric acupuncture, transpersonal work, and Shamanic and bioenergetic modalities that taught me over and over again that the internal world is a world of symbolic language unique to each person. There is an internal transformation from darkness to light that shifts the external world experience of the individual, in other words from negative thinking to positive thinking. This is possible to cultivate through many means. Healing takes place in remarkable ways.

The concept of the *illness mirror* evolved from my observations in working with clients. A reflecting pattern emerged as I would see family members, close friends, or a couple with one person presenting with a complaint that, once treated, resulted in the other party feeling better. There was a remarkable session with family members being treated in separate rooms. Each presented with different issues. After balancing the first person, I went to work with the second person. The second person noted they no longer felt they had the issue; it just disappeared. This occurred over and over again. It often happens with headaches and stomachaches, especially in children, who often take on the family mental-emotional patterns.

In the psych hospital, we had a name for this phenomenon. If a patient entered grossly disturbed, we would hold a family meeting, which often revealed that the patient was carrying the family dysfunction, as all of the other family members were in denial about any issues. This person was known as the identified patient, or IP. In shamanic traditions, this person would be considered a body surrogate, a person who takes on the issues or illnesses of others. That person comes for help because no one else in the situation can do so. This person can present with issues, phobias, habits, and behavior patterns that clear up upon resolution of the issue in another person. From a bioenergetic perspective, this reflective phenomenon is known as field coupling, bio-resonance, or entrainment. Bioresonance can be emotional, mental, or psychological coherence that occurs when two or more individuals become entrained to each other or a situation.

I began to think of symptoms as reflected by a person but not necessarily stemming directly from that person. Mirrors reflect back information. Our bodies, minds, and emotions do the same. Once resolved, the distortions disappear and positive outcome is the result.

Here are a few outstanding outcomes from the many that regularly occur in my practice.

Case #1. A man who was trained by the military as a remote viewer came in for relief from fragmented flashbacks, headaches, and severe depression. Remote viewing is the practice of seeking impressions about a distant or unseen target using paranormal means, in particular, extrasensory perception (ESP). This person had been trained in a narrow band of reality, taught to locate a target or target area. The deprogramming he received upon leaving military service was insufficient; split-off aspects began surfacing. He was never taught to view all of the possibilities or outcomes. He lived in dread of the worst outcome and was tormented by flashbacks. After I balanced and cleared his nervous system, he eventually became fully integrated into present time. I taught him how to access any event and see a full range of possibilities and then move in the direction of the positive outcome that was the best fit for him while doing no harm to others.

Case #2. A woman requested services for sinus congestion. Upon discussion, a quick snapshot of a young man appeared to me approximately four inches above her heart. I described the man and she said it was her son and that they had not spoken for five years, since an argument during a phone conversation. Deeply regretful, she had attempted to reconnect with her son, but he never returned her calls. The client noted that her sinus congestion had developed at about that time and had increased significantly, despite many attempts to resolve it. I asked her to remember the conversation. As she did so, I focused on her son's face. I tracked the energy patterns of guilt, power struggle, blame, and frustration plus an ancestral pattern of discord between family members. I neutralized these patterns between them by removing the polarities that held them in place. As the energy lifted, the client looked relieved and the sinus congestion was gone; her breathing shifted from laborious to effortless. I asked her to focus on a relaxing imagery, then to imagine her highest outcome, which she reported as a joyful reconciliation. Within two minutes, her cell phone rang. It was her son. We were both speechless. Yes, they reconnected as though no time lapsed!

Case #3. A client injured in the military came in for services. This client's goal was to move through the pain and, once well, complete his tour of duty. As the time drew near to return to duty, the family expressed deep concern about his safety. I held a family session in which each member discussed his or her fears. Through energy work, I brought each person's energy back to the balance of neutral, and then collectively balanced them as a family, including the history of other members who went to war. I invited the entire family to visualize the client returning home unscathed, safe, healthy, and whole. They were encouraged to minimize contact with negative information regarding the military action and to continue to hold the visualization. They agreed on two times a day for the visualization, once in the morning and once in the evening. The client completed his tour of duty and returned home unscathed, safe, healthy, and whole. The client came in for a session and noted that one day while on duty in battle with two other military personnel, the person on each side of him was injured simultaneously, one mortally wounded, the other severely wounded. Yet this person was unharmed, shaken yes, but unharmed. I balanced the client for witnessing the event and experiencing survivor remorse. Would he have returned home unharmed if he and the family were not holding positive outcome? We only know there was a positive outcome on the second tour where others were injured in a situation in which this person remained safe.

Case #4. A mother and her adolescent son came in for services for him. He had been diagnosed as schizophrenic. Upon arrival after extensive travel, both parties were tired. The son was anxious, unable to engage in eye contact, and tending to voices, which is a psychiatric term used to describe a person who is unable to be present to what is occurring and is instead listening to a conversation and possibly engaging in a conversation with unseen and unheard persons. Since the boy was not stable for a session, I asked his mother if she would be willing to have an acupuncture session while her son stayed in the waiting room with staff. She agreed.

I used an acupuncture pattern treatment on her back known as Ghost Gate Points. Ghost syndromes are a group of symptoms generally associated with mania, fright, and schizophrenia. This syndrome includes ghost talk, ghost evil, seeing ghost, and floating ghost talk (Chinese medicine terms for tending to voices and active engagement in conversations with unseen persons, unable to relate to the present). These descriptions depict the symptoms of mental unrest and disruption of the spirit that are recognized in Western psychiatry as tending to voices.

The mother began to relax. I walked back to the waiting area where her son's pacing had begun to slow down. Ten minutes into the treatment of his mother, he demonstrated less pacing; within twenty minutes, he was completely calm and able to have a full cogent, coherent conversation about life aspirations, school, and even future career choices! I returned to the treatment room to speak with his mother, who was now also calm. She disclosed details of her early life traumas and that she had suffered from acute anxiety until the birth of this child.

This opened up a whole new view of the situation. How is it that treating the parent resolved the schizophrenic symptoms of the son? Who was experiencing the anxiety? How is it that one person can mirror the symptoms of the other while the other shows no symptoms? It took eight subsequent treatment sessions for the mother and the son to stabilize permanently within their own energy pattern. The adolescent was able to continue with school and did not experience or exhibit any further symptoms of schizophrenia. The mother resolved her early childhood trauma as well. Such situations reinforce staying open to all possibilities!

Spinning in the Positive

When working with clients, I ask them to project themselves forward or imagine the circumstance with a positive outcome. Some people can do this, while others seem to be oriented to negative outcomes. For those with negative outcome projections, we explore where this is coming from and balance the imprint to a neutral state, and then the client reenvisions. Generally, after this technique the client is then better able to see a positive outcome. All things positive and negative arise simultaneously. Imagine using a hula hoop; at whatever level you spin it, the space between you and the outer ring contains all that pertains to that level. If you hold negative imprints, then you are spinning in the center of negative imprints. If you hold positive outcomes, then you are spinning in the center of positive opportunities. Now imagine there are two people in the center of a single hula hoop, interacting together. If one person is out of sync, the other person either gets derailed or can bring the out-of-balance person back into balancing by compensating for the imbalance or inviting the other person to enter into balance. We often do this in relationships.

Here are some tips for shifting into the positive.

When you feel stuck ask: Is this mine? (Belief, perception, feeling, emotion, outcome, headache, stomachache, etc.) If it becomes more intense, it's yours. If it becomes softer or goes away, it belongs to another person. Those who try this exercise are usually amazed by how often the feeling/belief/physical symptom goes away. This demonstrates how much of our thinking and processing patterns are acquired or inherited. They can and do shift. For a headache, stomachache, or anxiety, you can send it back where it belongs and observe who around you suddenly looks like they do not feel well. If it increases, well, it is yours. You can still get rid of it by placing one hand over the area and another on your forehead then tap on each area with your fingertips. This will shift the energy pattern and generally helps break up or eliminates the headache or stomachache. This is true for nearly any pattern, including depression!

Many exciting possibilities emerge. Who is experiencing what? How do the emotions and beliefs of others impact us? Do you know what thoughts, feelings, emotions, reactions are yours and which ones are not? I have worked with clients who actually release body odors that are part of the emotional memory surrounding an incident or the location of a traumatic memory upon release of that memory.

Several years ago, I climbed up a bookcase to straighten something on the top shelf. I lost my footing and fell, first hitting a desk, then a bench, before landing hard on the floor. I lay on the floor, the wind knocked out of me. I was aghast at what I saw. My right arm was contorted; my wrist and hand were bent and refused to move. Mind chatter arose: "You will never use your hand again; you won't be able to lift your grandchildren, play, drive, or work." My other mind, still calm, said: "You know what to do; apply your knowledge." I scanned the room for the energy patterns and moved through the energy field that contained all of the micro steps that unfolded as I fell. I thanked my arm, hand, and wrist for all of the wonderful things they had allowed me to experience in my life. (This later developed into a gratitude meditation that became part of *The Body of Qi* CD series I produced.) Within fifteen minutes, my hand, wrist, and arm convulsed violently and suddenly my hand straightened out! It was swollen, but it moved! I worked on it a bit longer and was able to begin to use it later that day. Though I would not like to repeat this, it did teach me that staying positive allowed me to act without hesitation.

Our thoughts affect others. While on a trip, I was driving with someone who received a phone call from her dog sitter. The sitter noted the dog was listless and had not eaten since she left. As my companion spoke, the energy concentrated around her. I asked her how she felt about being on the trip and leaving her dog. She was feeling like she should be there instead of being on the trip. I balanced her for these feelings. Within five minutes, the sitter called back to say that the dog was wagging his tail and eating without any issues! We are not separate from our world; we are always communicating with it, and vice versa.

For anyone beginning the journey of positive thinking, I suggest doing like I did and becoming playful with the fearful negative side of yourself. Say to a negative thought, "No such thing, thanks for the commercial interruption, now back to my positive life!" Your positive thoughts will begin to show up quite creatively.

Da um jeitinho!

WAYNE DYER:

Yes, You Can Change Old Habits

Your behaviors are supported by your thinking patterns; that is, your thoughts truly make or break your life. While some of them are operating on a conscious level and are easy to recognize, others are deeply embedded within your subconscious. However, I prefer to call this deeply programmed or almost automatic second-nature part of you, "the habitual mind."

For me, *subconscious* implies being below the level of creative awareness, a sort of mysterious entity that can't be known. Since the central theme here is that anything used to explain thinking and acting in the same self-sabotaging ways is an excuse, it seems to me that calling it "subconscious" is really underscoring this notion: *I can't help it, I can't talk about it, and I certainly can't change it; because it is, after all, below my conscious level, where I do all of my living.*

While excuses are just thoughts or beliefs, you are the decider of what you ultimately store away as your guide to life.

Wayne W. Dyer, PhD, is an internationally renowned author and speaker in the field of self–development. He is the author of more than thirty books, has created numerous audio programs and videos, and has appeared on thousands of television and radio shows. Wayne holds a doctorate in educational counseling from Wayne State University and was an associate professor at St. John's University in New York. www.drwaynedyer.com

The 18 Most Commonly Used Excuses

The affirmations after each excuse will assist you in making a conscious effort to encourage yourself to elevate your beliefs, unquestionably!

1. **It will be difficult:** *I have the ability to accomplish any task I set my mind to with ease and comfort.*

2. **It's going to be risky:** *Being myself involves no risks. It is my ultimate truth, and I live it fearlessly.*

3. **It will take a long time:** *I have infinite patience when it comes to fulfilling my destiny.*

4. **There will be family drama:** *I would rather be loathed for who I am than loved for who I am not.*

5. **I don't deserve it:** *I am a Divine creation, a piece of God, Therefore, I cannot be undeserving.*

6. **It's not my nature:** *My essential nature is perfect and faultless. It is to this nature that I return.*

7. **I can't afford it:** *I am connected to an unlimited source of abundance.*

8. **No one will help me:** *The right circumstances and the right people are already here and will show up on time.*

9. **It has never happened before:** *I am willing to attract all that I desire, beginning here and now.*

10. **I'm not strong enough:** *I have access to unlimited assistance. My strength comes from my connection to my Source of being.*

11. **I'm not smart enough:** *I am a creation of the Divine mind; all is perfect, and I am a genius in my own right.*

12. **I'm too old (or not old enough):** *I am an infinite being. The age of my body has no bearing on what I do or who I am.*

13. **The rules won't let me:** *I live my life according to Divine rules.*

14. **It's too big:** *I think only about what I can do now. By thinking small, I accomplish great things.*

15. **I don't have the energy:** *I feel passionately about my life, and this passion fills me with excitement and energy.*

16. **It's my personal family history:** *I live in the present moment by being grateful for all of my life experiences as a child.*

17. **I'm too busy:** *As I unclutter my life, I free myself to answer the callings of my soul.*

18. **I'm too scared:** *I can accomplish anything I put my mind to, because I know that I am never alone.*

Optimism and Healing

Bernie Siegel:

Faith, Hope, and Joy

CHAPTER 7

I see life as a labor pain of self-birth, and that includes cancer treatment. I have seen many poems describing that view, and one compares the nine months of pregnancy to twelve months of chemotherapy and radiation. The former experience is worthwhile because you give birth to your child, and the latter is worthwhile because you give birth to yourself. Think of yourself as a blank canvas upon which you create a work of art by working and reworking with your brush and palette of colors. Survivors don't just fill their prescriptions; they think about their choices and make their own decisions.

There are many components of the survivor personality; including spiritual faith, and faith in your doctor, in your treatment, and in yourself. Hope is also an important component. I am reminded again of the lines by Emily Dickinson, "Hope is the thing with feathers, that perches in the soul, and sings the tune without the words, and never stops at all." She also wrote, "Surgeons must be very careful, when they take the knife! Underneath their fine incision, stirs the culprit—Life!"

Hope is always real and makes living more joyful. Please understand, there is no false hope. It is not about statistics, it is about possibilities and uncertainties. I know people who have left their troubles to God and had their cancer disappear. I don't recommend it as the only therapy because it isn't easy to do, but I have seen it happen more than once. God can also send a surgeon to help you. However, it shows how powerful faith and hope are; and when they are combined with peace of mind, some remarkable things can happen. When an authority figure tells you what

Bernie Siegel, MD, speaks and runs workshops across the country and is devoted to humanizing medical care and medical education. His books *Love, Medicine, and Miracles; Peace, Love, and Healing;* and *How to Live Between Office Visits* are classics in the field of healing. Since its publication in 1986, *Love, Medicine, and Miracles* has sold millions of copies worldwide. The book sparked controversy when it was first released, but research has since supported Dr. Siegel's exposition of the role the mind plays in disease and healing. www.berniesiegelmd.com

is going to happen, it is hypnotic and can induce the results described. I knew a man who had lung cancer. When he developed cataracts, his health plan refused to pay for the surgery, claiming he would be dead soon and there was no point in wasting money on cataract surgery. The loss of his vision took the joy out of his life, which included playing with his grandchildren, reading the sports page of his newspaper, and betting on horse races. When the doctor denied his request for cataract surgery, he went home, climbed into bed, and died in a week.

That is why doctors need to be trained in communication and consider their patients' requests. I have seen the power of my words with children particularly. I would rub their arm with alcohol and tell them they would not feel the needle because of what I was rubbing on their arm. I deceived people into health at times. One-third of the children had local anesthesia induced by my words and were thrilled by the result. The others would tell me it didn't work but they still had less pain. I've even had children fall asleep being wheeled into the operating room and realized it was because I told them they would go to sleep in the OR. I even had to explain to some of them that I couldn't reach their appendix if they turned over and slept on their stomach.

We cannot survive without hope and meaning. Endless studies show that optimists have better health and longer lives than pessimists, even if they are less accurate about the reality of life. Many studies have come out showing that our feelings have physical consequences. Loneliness affects the genes, which control immune function. Cancer patients who laugh live longer. Treating depression with counseling and group meetings helps survival. How we feel is creating our chemistry.

People who volunteer also have better health, especially when they have a disease and are helping others with the same affliction. In one study of cancer patients, the best survival rates were among those with a fighting spirit. Next came the deniers whose hope, in a sense, came from denying what could happen. The worst survival rates were in the hopeless, helpless group. One man was told he was HIV-positive and went home and developed all the symptoms. He'd had friends who had died of AIDS, so he knew the routine. Some months later, his doctor discovered there was a mistake in the report and he was HIV negative. When he heard about the mistake, he recovered his health in two short weeks.

I think what helped prepare me most for this work were the children I cared for. I'm reminded of a child whose dog was about to be euthanized, who said, "They have shorter lives because they don't need all the time it takes us to learn about love and forgiveness." Children and animals are my teachers because they teach us about living in the moment, having a sense of humor, not worrying about next week, asking for help, and sharing feelings. All of which are survival behavior qualities. It is painful to see a child die, and it has led me on a spiritual journey to try to understand and cope with this experience. I believe we are here on earth to become complete, and anything that helps us to do that is a blessing. The problem is that some blessings do not feel very good when they happen. What you may define as a curse can become a blessing if you let it become your teacher and show you that not all of the side effects of cancer are bad. I mentioned earlier how Lois Becker, a woman who wrote to me about her breast cancer, said, "Cancer made me take a look at myself and I like who I met."

So remember, the issue is: are you willing to be born again and again? As Martin Buber shared in his writings, if a woman goes into labor prematurely doctors treat her to stop her labor, but if she is in the ninth month they help her to deliver the child. Why not think of it this way: when you have a problem but are not ready or capable of change and being reborn, God steps in and answers your prayers. Not so, however, when it is time for you to be born again. Then it is time for you to change and God does not step in to solve the problem. It is now up to you. So again, this is not about God punishing you, instead it is about God giving you the opportunity to change through your efforts and labor pains and give birth to yourself.

I have studied many religions and found that some cause people to feel guilty when they develop an illness. However, for Jewish physician and philosopher Maimonides, disease was a loss of health, and we should all help the person to find their health again. A Muslim, after learning he had a serious illness, said, "All praise be to Allah." Why? Because he could see there would be a blessing associated with it. I know Christians who feel God gives them a disease to bring them closer to Him.

I am talking about self-love and the divinity within each of us. For me it is not about theology but about being a living example of faith, hope, joy, and love. This work has given me the gift of knowing so many inspiring people who have shown me what we are capable of surviving, and I do not mean that in the sense of being cured, but of living with the experience no matter how difficult it may seem. Faith, hope, joy, and love are what sustain us and can be our weapons as we kill with kindness and torment with tenderness. What we are here to do is live and learn, and the people who inspire me are my teachers and role models. William Saroyan, in *The Human Comedy*, wrote, "The best part of a good man stays …for love is immortal and makes all things immortal while hate dies every minute."

I am prepared for my own death and do not fear it or anything else. As one of our children e-mailed me when he was not having a good day, "Life sucks and most people suck and if you wake up one day and the world is beautiful and everyone loves one another, you're dead." So as

I have said, for me death is not the worst outcome. I am not afraid that my life will end. I am more afraid it will never begin, and I try to live my life as if it were the last day of the lives of everyone I love. I hope you all can feel the same way and break out of the cocoon created by the words and actions of others and be transformed. Give your love to the world in the way you want to give it so you do not lose your life in order to please others.

At one point, I had three careers. All day I was the surgeon. Then, when I was done with surgery, I counseled people in the office every evening, and at home, I answered phone calls and letters every night. I realized I needed to focus and consolidate my life. I still meet people who were sustained by the fact that I wrote them a personal letter when they needed help, Today it is easier in some ways because of e-mails, but it also opens me to people from all over the world, So I am a busy man, but the gift is always in helping others, I never mind when people disturb me at home because I know they are survivors who have sought and found me, I have learned not to chase after and try to save them, When I help people find love, hope, joy, and faith, they benefit and so do 1. I may get tired, but I am burning up and not out.

From my experience, I have learned to love myself and others, knowing that I am mortal and here for a limited amount of time, I also accept that I need to be coached by family, patients, and coworkers to become even more loving, I am ready to confess my weaknesses and defects while at the same time being grateful for life and the opportunity it provides.

I conclude with the words of Thornton Wilder in his book *The Bridge of San Luis Rey*: "And we ourselves shall be loved for a while and forgotten but the love will have been enough, All those impulses of love return to the love that made them, Even memory is not necessary for love, There is a land of the living and a land of the dying and the bridge is love, the only survival, the only meaning." So every day in my meditation and prayers, they are still with me and I do not let my tears put out their celestial candles because I know they want me to experience faith, hope, and joy.

Hilary Vreeland:

Learning Optimism Through Depression

Optimism is a wonderful drug. I think it's the best-kept secret. Thinking positively and cultivating a high vibration are dynamic means to creating the life you want to live. I know because that's how I create the life that I most desire. My life is more blissful than I could ever have imagined, and I love that it keeps getting better. I have friends I adore, I live by the ocean, I enjoy my relationships with my family. What makes my heart really sing, though, is my ability to help people by doing what I love. My life these days is a gorgeous symphony of possibilities. When I look back at the pain and suffering I went through before arriving in this flow of deep contentment, I am even more amazed at my present life.

I moved to New York City when I was barely eighteen to study acting at New York University. My transition into adulthood was a tumultuous one. Growing up as a girl in Texas, I was subject to a lot of unwritten, unspoken rules. You should be seen but not heard. You should be beautiful but not sexy. You should be feminine but not have any sexual drives. You should be thin but be able to eat junk food. You should be able to play three sports, be in the choir, be president of student council, get straight A's, have lots of friends, and have a boyfriend. That you only kiss. On the cheek. And above all else, do not get pregnant. In short, you should be "perfect."

Hilary Vreeland is a holistic nutrition coach and energy healer who helps women live from the truest center of themselves: the part from which all the best in life emanates. Hilary helps women balance a satisfying career, personal relationships, family life, and spirituality through nutrition and life coaching. She believes in living from a place of true pleasure and being shameless about it. The basis of her work lies in integrating healthy feminine attitudes into the framework of nourishing ourselves. Hailing from the Institute for Integrative Nutrition in New York City, she is a member of the American Association of Drugless Practitioners. www.hilaryvreeland.com. Photo credit: Christina Morassi

Where these unwritten rules came from, I still don't know. My parents certainly didn't feel this way. In fact, they encouraged me to stop trying to be perfect all of the time. My school, an all-girls school, was feminist in many respects. They were training us to become the leaders of the world. The unwritten rules and mores definitely whirled around young ladies' heads and hearts, however. I suspect that these "rules" lingered in the ether from a time when they were consciously thought of and believed in. By the late 1990s, these rules had become mere whispers. Yet that one haunting little word — "perfect" — caused a lot of problems for me. I was practically perfect in high school. And I was a shell of a human being.

I discovered alcohol during my senior year and quickly became addicted to being drunk. I just loved to be drunk because I didn't feel anything. I felt happy and carefree, free of the stresses of being perfect. I felt beautiful, thin, sexy, and like there were no consequences. As soon as I would sober up after a party, I would long for the next one, need another hit of what I thought was a wonder drug.

I was exercising obsessively, at least once a day and sometimes twice. I was stringently restricting my calories, and the calories I did allow myself didn't contain enough nutrients to sustain me. I didn't let myself eat because I wanted to be thin — to keep my boyfriend interested, to fulfill my dream of being a film actress, to be "perfect." At the time, I thought I was horribly overweight, fat, and ugly. Later my best friend told me that she almost confronted me because she thought I was too thin. I saw food and my body as the enemies. I realize now that I was anorexic.

Spiraling Downward

I carried all of these unconscious ideas and rules with me to New York. Besides the familiar crushing pressure I felt to stay slim, I was in a whole new world. I was living in a tiny shoebox apartment in the middle of Manhattan. I had to think about dressing myself for the first time after thirteen years of wearing a uniform. I had to go grocery shopping and find time to do my laundry. Suddenly, there were boys in all my classes. I had never taken an acting class in my life, but now that's what I was doing full-time. I was desperately trying to get over my breakup with my high school boyfriend without having any friends to lean on.

On top of all this, I was still desperately trying to lose weight. I didn't have access to any truly healthy nutritional choices in the dorm cafeteria. My acting school encouraged us to keep up with our workout routines, but I felt the time crunch, what with being in an acting conservatory and full-time academic college. I was absolutely miserable. I felt like I wasn't able to eat well or exercise, so I swung in the other direction. I started binge eating.

Comforting myself with cookies and brownies and pizza, relaxing with new friends at cafeteria dinners, maybe getting an extra slice of cake—those were the moments I was happiest. I was calm. I felt contained. It felt like I didn't have to worry about anything. For a while, I remember thinking, "How much can I eat before my body starts really packing on the pounds? How much abuse can I inflict on myself?" It was a masochistic yet delicious thought. In those moments of binge eating, I felt momentary relief from the intense stress I was feeling.

I started spiraling downward. I was always in a terrible mood. I didn't want to make friends or meet new people. I wanted to do well in school, do well at acting, get drunk, and not feel any pain. I was still terribly sad about my breakup. I didn't think to consider the effects that the birth control pill I had started taking a few months before might be having on me.

One morning, I thought, "I can't get out of bed. I don't think I can physically bear to do it. What would happen if I never got out of bed again?" And I knew something was wrong. Both of my parents are psychologists, so I asked my mother, "Do you think I should go into therapy?" The next day I was sitting in a therapist's office. I was so upset and depressed that all I wanted was to ask for drugs. I was incredibly relieved when, after five minutes of talking with me, she said, "Let's put you on Lexapro." And I said, "Thank God. Because I feel like my soul is close to death." I started taking this antidepressant, anti-anxiety pharmaceutical and began to feel better.

In therapy, I started untangling what was going on with me. I began to look at why I am the way I am. I slowly became aware of the "Texas rules" by which I had been living without even knowing I was; I realized that I had unconsciously thought that was the way the world worked! I was very judgmental of myself. I was always thinking, "I shouldn't feel this way. I'm bad," because I thought I needed to be perfect to be worthy of love. Even with therapy and antidepressants, I was still in a lot of pain and quite depressed. I was binge eating and binge drinking, and I added drugs to the mix. I started smoking marijuana. At finals time, I got addicted to Adderall (an amphetamine used to treat ADD). I tried the occasional upper or downer if it came my way. I kept searching for something to numb out my sadness, stress, and anxiety.

Choosing Happiness

The summer after my freshman year, my father sat me down at the kitchen table and asked me, "Is this acting program really what you want to be doing?" I got angry at him and snapped back, "Yes, yes! Of course! This is what I've always wanted. This is what I've been doing since I was

in the second grade." As he kept talking to me, I burst into tears. All I could get out between sobs was, "I don't think this is making me happy."

The Dalai Lama once wrote, "Even our physical structure seems more suited to feelings of love and compassion. We can see how a calm, affectionate, wholesome state of mind benefits our health and physical well-being. Conversely, feelings of frustration, fear, agitation, and anger can be destructive to our health. This is why we are impelled to seek happiness."

In that moment, I realized that I needed to follow my happiness. I had always been good at acting; it was my way of getting attention and admiration, but it had never made me truly happy. Being onstage was a way for me to be good at something. At the time, I thought I wasn't good at anything else. The fact was I was good at plenty, but I didn't let myself know it. I was confronted with a fork in the road. I desperately wanted to just stick it out — to finish my undergraduate degree in acting, to suffer through, to maintain the status quo. I thought doing that would be easier in a lot of ways. It was familiar and comfortable. But a soft voice inside me simply would not allow me to do that. Even though it would be more difficult and scarier to walk down the path of the unknown, I knew that it was my only choice if I wanted to be happy and healthy.

So I stopped. I withdrew from my acting school. I was completely lost because I had never thought about what I wanted or what made me happy. I forged on. With a visceral feeling of what misery is, I searched for an as-yet unexperienced emotion: happiness. I was like a newborn calf stumbling through my life. I would try something out, always asking myself the question, "Does this make me happy?" I was met with many noes until I found a course of study that excited and challenged me: Spiritual Healing Journeys.

I had become so enthusiastic and motivated by my own healing journey that I wanted to learn everything I could about spirituality and healing. It just so happens that NYU has a school of individualized study. My life turned a corner when I transferred in. This was the first time I experienced the beautiful alchemy of my hard work and dedication mixed with doing something I love. My passion and the feeling that I was fulfilling my role on Earth fueled me through a grueling course of study. It certainly wasn't easy, but there was a feeling of relief that accompanied finding what I was meant to learn. It was the first time in my life that I got a glimmer of what it would look like to do exactly what I wanted to do — what it would feel like to be happy.

To my surprise, I still had a bunch of problems. I still had depression, and my social anxiety was severe. I was in an unhealthy, codependent relationship with my college boyfriend by this time, I was still binge eating, and I was getting stoned at least once a day. I was overweight. While I was finding fulfillment in some ways, in a lot of ways I was still deeply unhappy. There was an uncomfortable juxtaposition in my life: I had found my path, but I was far from being able to follow it and be happy.

I intuitively knew what I was searching for. I was searching for contentment, for happiness—that nebulous, slippery, indefinable yet unmistakable feeling. I wanted more than fleeting moments of happiness; I wanted a lasting sense of fulfillment. During my last semester at NYU, I took a course called "The Science of Happiness" with a child psychiatrist named Dr. Alan Schlechter. We studied new research being done in the burgeoning field of positive psychology and implemented cutting-edge tools in our lives. As opposed to the classic disease-based model, positive psychology focuses on cultivating wellness. I began to learn about tools I had been using intuitively, the most intriguing of which is optimism. I began to experiment with the tool of positive thinking to create an optimistic mind-set. I gathered data in my own life and was astounded to discover that the more positively I thought, the more optimistic I was, and the happier I seemed to be—in a lasting way.

This is the opposite mind-set from the one I grew up with, which was that cynicism and pessimism are simply a more accurate and honest way to perceive the world. Couple this with teenage angst, raging hormones, and the temperament of a dramatic actress, and I was a living recipe for disaster. I believed that nothing turns out as you wish—that life is tough and then you die. And guess what? My life had mirrored those thoughts back to me! I was playing the victim, and I had cast life as the perpetrator. During all this, I was very privileged and well cared for. It was my mind creating my reality; and my reality was that I was having a very tough time. My perspective during my adolescent and early adult years was extremely narrow. It started to widen when I studied the science of happiness.

Studies have shown that depressed people do, in fact, see the world more accurately, but optimistic people live longer and have less health problems. I knew this through experience. When I was depressed, I always relished the fact that I saw things more clearly than others. The trade-off? I was miserable! I realized during my years at NYU that I would rather be happy than be right. This was my first brush with consciously cultivating positive thinking and an optimistic mind-set.

Quantum Leap

I took a quantum leap with my use of positive thinking and optimism when I met a holistic nutrition coach. With her guidance, I started cleansing my body to clear out environmental toxins as well as the residue of toxins created by all those negative emotions. Clearing these from my system was a major part of healing my depression. From her, I also learned about the Law of Attraction. I had studied vibrational medicine and energy healing at NYU, so I was familiar with the concept that our world is made up of vibrations, that our eyes and brains are merely interpreting those vibrations. But I had never before thought about these principles in terms of myself, my thoughts, my future, and my happiness.

As Otto Hofmann remarks in Richard Linklater's film *Waking Life,* "The quest is to be liberated from the negative, which is really our own will to nothingness. And once having said yes to the instant, the affirmation is contagious. It bursts into a chain of affirmations that knows no limit. To say yes to one instant is to say yes to all of existence."

I continued to experiment with cultivating happy, positive thoughts and feelings for myself, striving to create lasting happiness. Cultivating these thoughts and emotions helped me create a wider optimistic mind-set, and having that mind-set made cultivating those thoughts easier and more natural. It was indeed a contagious affirmation that started to draw my experience of life upward, toward my goal of lasting happiness and fulfillment.

As I cultivated a positive emotional state through thinking positively and raising my vibrational frequency by eating very cleanly and cleansing my body of old toxins, I experienced a spiritual awakening. I was always intuitively drawn toward studying spirituality, but I could never get past my head. I experienced this cut-off feeling in my throat, between my head and my body; I could only understand spirituality intellectually. I could read, write, and think about spirituality, but I never experienced it in my body. During years of spiritual study, I had a deep longing to experience God, Goddess, Spirit, Source, mysticism, something—anything. Hell, I had done my thesis on mysticism and healing—I wanted to experience it! Once I cleansed my body, worked through my eating disorder and substance abuse issues, started nourishing myself healthfully, and cultivating a positive mind-set, the blockage in my throat center that had kept my experience of spirituality in my head vanished.

I remember my first mystical experience. I was sitting outside on a cool summer day listening to music when the wind picked up. I felt the wind pass right through me—through my skin and muscles and bones. It was as if all of my cells had opened up to receive the air into my body. I felt a deep sense of joy and contentment. I felt like just by inhaling I was receiving dense, rich nourishment. I could *feel* happiness and contentment in my cells, their exact vibration in my body. My mind was quiet yet excited, ready, eager, focused. With each breath I felt like I might cry with joy, laugh in ecstasy, or burst into stardust. I felt chills on my skin and fire in my veins. In those moments, I was overwhelmed with a gratitude so deep and rich that it struck grief in my heart: I was terrified to lose this feeling, for this experience to end. The more I watched myself grasp at it, the more it faded. When I relaxed and surrendered to whatever might unfold, the mystical feeling intensified and I felt at ease.

I closed my eyes and meditated in that space. I don't know how long I sat there—it could have been minutes or hours. Waves upon waves of blissful sensation crashed through me. I experienced the world as salivatingly sensuous, and myself as an eager, insatiable soul. The more I surrendered, the richer my experience became. I felt like I was swimming in the waters of my psyche. At first this scared me, but I kept swimming because it felt divine. I realized that when I allowed myself to drift through the dark, stringy, slimy things that once might have startled me—those fields of dark seaweed that would enslave me if I squirmed in fear—if I floated into them, they would actually hold me up and support my weight.

I received this message during my meditation, my mystical experience: "A body likes being paid attention to. It likes to be revered, to be cared for, to be honored, and most important, to be listened to. Its messages to us are vital. It is when we are embodied that we feel ecstasy and when we are disembodied that we feel pain, discomfort, and anxiety. When we feel safe enough in our bodies to open our minds, our mind may relax and enjoy—like that first breath of ocean air after months spent inland." In that moment, I knew that I was put on Earth to help other women remember this truth so that they, too, can live in the flow of the Universe.

I got trained and certified as a holistic health coach, specializing in nutrition, so that I could fulfill my life's purpose, helping other women the way my coach helped me.

Now when I look back at the heartache, turmoil, and depression I endured, I feel differently about those experiences. First of all, I now believe that they were necessary. I have experienced much of what the women who come to me for help are battling. I thank God for the pain I have suffered; it's what allows me to help other women through their suffering. I know that I had to go through these uncomfortable and painful experiences in order to be of service.

I can clearly see now that the difficult events of my young life were made worse by being on the birth control pill and an antidepressant, and using alcohol and drugs to try to numb the pain. These created the perfect storm for a major, ongoing depression. I'm elated to say that since discovering the tools of holistic nutrition coupled with optimism and positive thinking, I'm much more equipped to handle the ups and downs of living with my hereditary predisposition toward depression.

One of my most important and effective tools is optimism, or positive thinking. I can find the positive aspect in just about anything going on in my life. Even if it's tiny, I work to celebrate that positive aspect until it begins to spiral into bigger and better thoughts and feelings. Not to say that negative emotions are bad and positive emotions are good. Our negative emotions are great resources—they give us valuable information. When I look back at my depression, I now see all of those negative emotions as signs. I was viscerally and painfully discovering what I did not want. When I'm happy and thinking positively, I feel like I'm moving toward what I want. So there is great value in negative emotions, for they let us know when we're moving in the opposite direction of our happiness.

Using optimism and positive thinking as tools to create the emotional state I wish to have is empowering. I feel powerful because I feel like I have a choice in the way I feel. When I was depressed, or when I was binge eating, I truly felt like I had no choice. I felt trapped, unsafe, and alone, sentenced to living imprisoned in a body and mind that enslaved my soul. I'm nothing short of ecstatic and deeply grateful that I found a way to move through that suffering. And through that suffering I found my life's work, which is to help others move through their suffering as well.

I recently came across an anonymous quotation: "Our lives are not determined by what happens to us, but by how we react to what happens; not by what life brings to us, but by the attitude we bring to life. A positive attitude causes a chain of reaction of positive thoughts, events, and outcomes. It is a catalyst, a spark that creates extraordinary results." That spark is in each of us, and we all have the ability to nurture it into a roaring flame.

Janine Talty:

Indigo Optimism

I am a multiplicity of awareness projecting through a physical body that is completely enamored with the exploration of the collective perceptions of boundaries and limitations. As such, I manifested some pretty immense challenges in which to explore fully the caverns and crannies of what delicious lessons lie hidden in what appear to be our greatest challenges in life. In this exploration of overcoming, I met my true self and developed the compassion to recognize the same inquisitiveness and similar manifestations in others. My knowing is deeply personal, only reinforced by what I have read in books.

I am not my curriculum vitae. That is only the expression of the curiosity that drove a life in search of its margins, when I had previously been written off as early as the age of six as not expected to amount to much. Hardheaded, you bet. How else does one meet a world that says you can't, you are incapable, mentally deficient, and lazy? I showed them, and in the process realized that the only thing that is important on this journey is one's opinion of oneself. Personal bests. Our own individual "delta" in life, the place from which we start and the place we eventually end up. What is that distance? What possibilities come from exploration purely for the purpose of quenching the churning curiosity within? Knowing you can, you will, and you did. Taking chances when you have nothing to lose, not even your life. Working harder than can possibly be required and taking joy in ignoring others' advice to quit because the task appears too difficult. It is from that resonant knowing that you succeeded in worse

Janine Talty, DO, MPH, is an osteopathic physician, board certified in family medicine. Her private practice in Roanoke, Virginia, specializes in osteopathic manual medicine, with a focus on the diagnosis and treatment of musculoskeletal problems of the spine and extremities, sports medicine, pain management, the diagnosis and treatment of Lyme disease, and natural hormone balance for women and men. She is an assistant clinical professor of manual medicine at Michigan State University, the author of *Indigo Awakening: A Doctor's Memoir of Forging an Authentic Life in a Turbulent World*, and coauthor of *Goddess Shift: Women Leading for a Change.* jmtalty@earthlink.net situations in the past, where the simple expectation of the desired outcome resides. That to me is optimism.

Divine paradox works in creative and wonderful ways. Schooled in the healing arts by tending to myriad sick and injured animals that found their way into my experience all through elementary school left me with a strange knowing that I was being groomed for a life's work in medicine. This while at the same time being considered mentally retarded—severe dyslexia mistaken for retardation until I was twelve. As if that weren't enough of a challenge, at the age of fourteen I broke my back in a severe ski accident, which led to twelve years of chronic back pain.

I have patients now, really sick and injured ones. People who come to me desperate to believe they can one day regain their health, having run out of people who believe they can. Their story is my story. Despite my severe challenges, I ended up qualifying for the Ironman World Triathlon in 1984 and graduated from medical school in 1992. I tell my patients that if I could do it, so can they. Or at least together we will continue to try, never giving up, no matter what the present reality may seem. That to me is optimism.

Having been there, facing a reality that was simply not acceptable and somehow finding the inner strength to climb out of holes that were so deep left me with a resolve that I can accomplish anything as long as I want it enough. Being able to make the necessary sacrifices and tap into an inner strength that allowed me to claw my way to the surface no matter how painful the process let me know I had what it took not only to survive, but also to thrive in the thrill-seeking of it all. In the struggle was where the real nectar of the experience was hidden. Accomplishment became my drug and I its addict. Somewhere lost in this repetitive process of goal setting and attainment came the deeply held inner knowing to trust that the outcome I desired was already held in a vast bank account with my name on it. I knew it was mine. It was just a matter of time until it showed up. That is optimism.

Truth Seeking

Who am I and why have I come here? A dangerous question to ask at five years old when none of the adults I consulted knew the answer either. Some had never thought even to ask the question. Aren't we supposed to start pondering that in our forties? Isn't it usual to live half our lives in a safely protected cocoon of unconsciousness and then be nudged awake when we realize we haven't met all our childhood goals? Isn't that part of the phenomenon known as "the midlife crisis"? Perhaps. Or was it that I came in with my eyes "wide open," unencumbered with the foggy vision of recent wakefulness, as one might experience having had the blessing of forty years to begin even to ponder the deeper questions in life. If that was the case, then the obvious next question was "Why me?" Who was I and why was my ability to see through the mist so effortless? And why couldn't others see what I could?

It all came together for me at the age of forty-two when undeniable synchronistic circumstances and events that occurred in my life in a very short span of time showed me to myself and answered every question and musing I had ever had. I am an adult Indigo whose life's themes and details are not dissimilar to all the other yet-unawakened adult Indigos who are currently repressing their unique traits and characteristics. Why? Because they are "scary."

We possess the natural capability of intuition and psychic awareness, precognition, mental telepathy, telekinesis, invisibility work, cross-species communication, aura reading, and interdimensional viewing. Our inquisitiveness usually gets us into trouble, as we have the ability to see and sense what is true. We detest and resist authority and, because we neurologically process information differently, we were often labeled dyslexic, ADD, ADHD, and autistic when we were in school. Some of us put out yellow sodium vapor streetlights when we walk by and others have electronics misfire, stop working, or ignite in our presence.

As children we share certain physical traits, such as a gaze of angelic knowingness that belies our years, large almond-shaped eyes with dazzling and vivid iris colors, and large hands, feet, and heads. We have never fit into a category because we have never been here in such numbers before: 50 percent of the children born in 1970 are of this persuasion, as are 45 percent of those who are now thirty to forty-five years old and 21 percent of those who are now aged forty-six to sixty.

That laser-beam vision of truth seeking serves me, and thus those who seek my assistance, in remarkable ways. Most patients who come have been told they have reached the end of the known world of medicine. "There is nothing else that can be done for you" seems to be the words the multiple other respected physicians tell people like us. You will never be able to learn to read. Don't expect ever to go to college. You will never be able to return to work, provide for your family, and maintain your dignity. You will never be able to play tennis, jog, ski, or play golf. You will never be able to bear children. You will never amount to much of anything ever again. Done. Finished. Left in the garbage heap, a nothing, a nobody. Your life as you knew it is over.

This is what people are told and this is what they believe. When they walk through my door, they are more than skeptical. They are downright mistrustful. And yet they come. Usually on the tip of a friend, neighbor, a distant relative, or a woman they happened to speak with in the vegetable section at the grocery store. Devastated lives are not uncommon. War stories circulate and so do the tales of success.

It is my job to convince them that what they have been told is not true. What makes it easier is my inner knowing that if I could overcome the challenges that faced me, I will be able to convince them that they are just as capable. The first order of business is to instill hope and gain their trust by unearthing the correct diagnosis. It is my experience that if they are still not better after so much time and treatment, the true reason for their condition has yet to be discovered. It is my job to find it and, in the process, subtly prove to them that there are roads they have not yet traveled that will lead them back to the person they used to be.

I do not dispense false hope, but hope is the key element that has been missing and is absolutely essential in enlisting the assistance of our body and psyche's marvelously complex mechanism of psychoneuroimmunology. Our cells actually listen and respond to our expectations, whether we know it or not. Think negatively and get negative results. Stay truly positive and expect the best. That is what enlists our immune cells and neurotransmitters to affect the vibrational tone of each individual cell wall, which in turn alters and modifies cell membrane transport channels (the gatekeepers for which ions enter or leave the cell). The balance of the ions within the cell eventually affects which parts of the DNA chain get decoded. We actually have the capability to change our cells' genetic expression potential based on our attitudes alone.

Meet Jon and Steve. They both came with devastating stories based on medically devastated lives. They both left as survivors of the system and hopeful of bright and productive lives, once again embarking on a personal journey to explore the perceptions of boundaries and limitations. They are also both adult Indigos.

Twenty Years of Pain

Most conditions that either walk or crawl through my door are eventually fixable. Yet there are certain conditions that, as any physician who deals in chronic degenerative disorders of the spine will tell you, are not. But rather than excuse the patient from the practice, sometimes the best medicine is to instill a dash of optimism. I reframe the situation and get my patients to focus on what they can do, rather than on what they cannot. We also work on accepting what is, rather than the way they wish it could be. We reinforce these concepts, all the while continuing to scour the globe for emerging treatments and technologies.

Jon came in on the recommendation of his acupuncturist who he had been seeing in desperation for months. Unfortunately, many people seeking the assistance of an acupuncturist have already exhausted the usual medical therapies. Jon was suffering from unrelenting severe lower back pain and radiating right leg pain. He had been to physical therapy multiple times, had received and was taking multiple medications for pain and muscle spasm, had been traumatized by cavalier and brutal pain physicians, and had sought the opinion of way too many surgeons, some of whom thought they should do exploratory surgery without a true diagnosis while others said surgery was not indicated. They all eventually told him that there was nothing else they could do for him, save generously supply him with pain medications that barely took the edge off.

Not being a man who accepts defeat lightly, he fought his insurance company for the right to seek "alternative" therapies, because they had worked for him in another dire situation in the past. They eventually agreed, and he began to see an acupuncturist and massage therapist. Both alleviated some of his pain, but the relief didn't last long. Jon had been out of work for two years by then and fear set in. At this point, his acupuncturist recommended me.

Jon was suffering from a cumulative work injury that had occurred over the past twenty years. He had MRI evidence of six areas of the spine that were contributing to his condition and severe pain, none of which could be helped by surgery. He had served in the navy in Viet Nam. His tour included eighteen months on a PT boat cruising upriver behind enemy lines with the simple intent of drawing fire and exposing enemy positions so that U.S. forces could drop Agent Orange and burn them out. The stress of the assignment did not kill him, but the exposure to Agent Orange nearly did. One year after his honorable discharge, he was diagnosed with non-Hodgkin's lymphoma. The military admitted it was likely due to his exposure to the chemical. At the age of twenty-six, Jon went through one round of chemotherapy and radiation, which left him feeling sicker than the actual disease it was intended to treat. He never returned to the oncology ward and elected to treat his cancer with alternative therapies, against medical advice. His lymphoma did not return, but years later we wondered if the extensive degenerative changes in his spine and his unusual lack of response to pain therapies had something to do with the destruction of his connective tissue and nervous system due to his military exposure.

Standing on the edge of the abyss facing the vast nothingness of the river of possibilities was a familiar and comfortable place for me. Standing in solidarity with another Indigo seeker, firm in the resolve that answers do in fact exist and together we can set out to find them was my apparent lot in life. And so we did.

Jon was willing to try everything that sounded reasonable. We worked him up from head to toe, which confirmed what we already knew. There were no easy anatomical fixes for the years of repetitive, degenerative destruction and the possible long-term effects of Agent Orange. We then embarked on a journey into a different pain-treatment world than he had been before: vertebral axial spinal decompression therapy, Prolotherapy, lumbar epidural blocks, selective nerve root blocks, medial branch blocks, intradiscal blocks, spinal cord stimulation, and a trial for an indwelling medication pump. He seemed to have either no benefit from or adverse reactions to every one. I sometimes wondered why he kept showing up and trying.

The only thing that worked to reduce his pain most times and for almost two weeks at a time was Osteopathic Manual Medicine, a hands-on healing technique in which I specialize. It restores normal joint and tissue motion to areas and spinal segments that are restricted, and also helps balance and recalibrate the central and peripheral nervous systems. Jon and I saw each other every other week for ten years, more frequently than I had ever had to see any other patient. We knew each other's stories. He would often tell me how grateful he was that I kept on trying and never gave up on him.

Over the years we managed to manage his pain. Meanwhile, the legal battles over just how disabled he was raged on. He had long ago moved an adjustable hospital bed into his living room and slept half of the night in a Swedish zero gravity recliner. Sleeping no more than three hours at a time and never reaching restorative REM sleep only aggravated his growing mood instability and adrenal exhaustion. Jon's world had shrunk to his kitchen, bedroom, living room, and bathroom and short walks in his suburban backyard with his two cocker spaniels. He left the house for his bimonthly appointments with me and his pain psychologist, after each of which he would have to go to bed for three days because it all took so much out of him. The massage therapist and physical therapist made house calls.

Jon kept trying and so did I.

Several months after the legal issues were resolved, it was as if he could finally relax and not feel as if he were being persecuted because he was injured. At that point, a huge shift occurred. He wanted to see what life was like without the medications and, with my help, started to wean himself from his daily regime. It was a revelation to him that he could do with so little, based on the massive doses previously required just to take the edge off his terrible pain.

Once out of the fog of the medications—the inevitable consequence of conventional chronic pain management—Jon rediscovered the man he used to be. He now felt confident that he could venture farther than his medical appointments, taking two- and three-hour car trips to visit family and friends, go shopping, and attend weddings, funerals, and birthday parties. He and his wife even contemplated a Hawaiian vacation.

I Am Not My Curriculum Vitae

Steve and I were friends before he became my patient. I met him at a medical conference just six months after he was diagnosed with multiple sclerosis. Born to a mom on disability who subsequently became single after divorcing his father when he was just two, he was fueled at a young age by a passion to be one day able to perform lifesaving reconstructive surgery on baby's malformed hearts. Fascinated by the heart for what it symbolized both physically and emotionally, he also felt empathy for children whose lives could be "fixed" forever with the proper reconstructive corrective surgery, a situation unlike the condition he was born with.

As an infant, it soon became clear that Steve had the same rare genetic disorder that had disabled his mother. Familial angioedema manifests as regional uncontrolled swelling of a body part or organ. It goes unchecked and expands until the immune system runs out of substrate (fuel). This process takes approximately thirty-six hours to complete and, in the meantime, the area that is affected continues to swell to monstrous deforming dimensions. It causes indescribable ischemic pain as the tissue stretches beyond its normal capacity and cuts off its own blood supply. There is no treatment and, when he was a child, no good way to prevent these episodes. Through no fault of his own, he would be ravaged by these bouts every time he fell and bumped his knee, forehead, hand, foot, leg, arm, or face, causing him to look like a monster. It also occurred every time he got a viral infection, or for what seemed like no reason at all. It also commonly attacked his intestines, causing them to swell inside him, cutting off their blood supply, which then caused horrendous, cramping colic-like pain and bowel obstructions resulting in uncontrollable vomiting.

Steve fought his way out of poverty, all the while dealing with his unique genetic gift. He bagged groceries at the local Kroger grocery store while he was in high school. Then he became an EMT over the summer between his sophomore and junior years in college to pay his tuition at UC Davis while working nights and weekends on the rig. He then went on to physicians assistant school at Duke, was summa cum laude in his class, completed a one-year residency in cardiothoracic surgery at Yale, attended medical school at Wake Forrest, followed by six years of general surgical training at Vanderbilt, and was in his second of three required years of thoracic surgical training at UC San Francisco when his hands and feet suddenly went numb, he lost the hearing in his right ear, and his sight became temporarily blurry.

Following our introduction, over the next three years I watched him lose his health, his career, and his family.

He was worked up and treated by the finest physicians on the West Coast and tried to stay in his program. Interferon injections every other day left him with severe flu-like symptoms as he watched his life and his dream slip away. He became so fatigued and weak he could not keep up his daunting surgical resident schedule. He spent the next year on disability. A former marathon runner, his legs were so numb and weak he could barely stand. After making out his will at the age of thirty-seven and considering his six-year-old son who would never know him if Steve's haunting suicidal fantasies came true, he resolved to devise his own rehabilitation program.

Steve began with vacuuming a small part of the living room, then the entire room, and eventually the whole house. He then purchased a mountain bike and started equally slowly. As the weeks and months passed, he was eventually spending six to eight hours ridding in the coastal hills where he lived.

Recently divorced by his wife and kicked out of their home, he was homeless. He eventually returned to cardiothoracic surgery as a first assistant surgeon at an HMO, watching the head surgeons fumble with "shots" (fine suture knots used to sew heart tissue) that he knew he could throw with ease. Over the next fourteen years, he would have recurrent "flares" of his MS symptoms but was never left with any permanent numbness or weakness or disability. These episodes always cleared completely. This was highly uncharacteristic of typical MS.

After a three-year trek through various plastic surgery fellowships all over the country, he landed back in the San Francisco Bay Area to attempt to reconstruct his career in a field where he could do reconstructive hand surgery sitting down if he became permanently unable to stand. At this point, I had the opportunity to spend more time with him. Listening to his story again in more detail and observing other signs and symptoms that were not typical of MS, I encouraged him to undergo a workup for chronic Lyme disease. I shared with him all the stories of the patients I had helped over the years who were still in search of answers for their chronic pain, severe fatigue, and symptoms in multiple other organ systems, some with severe intermittent neuropathy that caused the same symptoms he was demonstrating. The test showed that he was CDC criteria positive for Lyme disease and likely had two other coinfections that live inside the Lyme-bearing tick and are thus transferred to the unsuspecting host.

This changed everything.

He was no longer going to die or end up in a wheelchair alone, on the streets panhandling, unable to take care of himself. He had a future. He had a treatable disease that with the proper therapy had a high likelihood of a cure. With one simple lab test, he got his life back.

I had already recognized him as a fellow Indigo and seeker of the perceptions of boundaries and limitations. What drives a life such as this?

What fire burns so bright that nothing can extinguish it? Steve knew all along he was capable, driven, and guided to pursue a dream that put his life in perspective. He didn't set out to be a just doctor or a surgeon. He set out to save infant human beings whose lives were threatened through no fault of their own. He was burgeoning with compassion for the less fortunate, recognizing something of him in their situations and stories. Fixing miniature broken hearts with his own that had been so badly broken.

Steve persevered and in the process met his true self. He realized once his health, his profession, and his personal life were all taken away that he did not come to Earth to do a job. That was not who he was. He too was not his curriculum vitae. He came for the purpose of exploring what we think holds us back.

Choosing an Optimistic Reality

Perceptions of reality, that's all our chosen experience is. We have the ability to pick good and healthy ones that bring to us magnitudes of magnificent knowledge and ideas. We also have the ability to view the world as a dark and dangerous place filled with impossibilities, distrust, and limitations. Our experiences and what we do with them are up to each of us individually.

I prefer to seek the joy and always expect the best. Optimism is infectious. Don't cover your mouth. Spread it around!

Susan Kolb:

Energy Management— A Blueprint for Optimism

CHAPTER 10

In this world, learning to focus on positive emotions such as love, gratitude, and passion is an imperative part of creating the life you desire. Of course, focusing on negative emotions also affects your creative process, though not always in the ways you want. In the spiritual boot camp that is the third dimension, your soul learns to refine its creative potential through the lessons of your life experience, and sometimes you have to learn the hard way. Until you learn to create consistently in positive, healthy, and productive ways, it is perhaps a blessing that your creations take some time to manifest.

Spiritual teachings throughout time emphasize a common universal principle: "as above, so below." The ancient mysteries teach that what transpires in the higher realms of existence will naturally be reflected in the physical world. The physical, emotional, mental, and spiritual realms are intricately related, bound in a universal web and, in essence, cannot be separated. All things are independent, yet interrelated: mind and body, atom and galaxy, the individual and the collective, the microcosm and the macrocosm. All exists together in a universe in which everything is connected, and in which each of the parts mirrors the sum of the whole. According to this principle, your thoughts, beliefs, and attitudes are reflected back to you from the higher realms into the lower physical dimension. What you create in your thoughts manifests itself in your physical world.

Susan Kolb, MD, FACS, ABHM, is a medical doctor with a specialty in plastic and reconstructive surgery. A founding diplomat of the American Board of Holistic Medicine, she is the director and founder of Millennium Healthcare, a holistic integrative medical center; Avatar Cancer Center, an alternative cancer treatment institute; and Plastikos, a holistic plastic surgery center. Her practice is an international healing center for women with breast implant disease and other immune disorders. A pioneering authority on the health hazards of implants, she is the author of *The Naked Truth about Breast Implants: From Harm to Healing* and coauthor of *Goddess Shift: Women Leading for a Change*. www.templeofhealth.ws

To paraphrase a proverb, it is important for you to watch your thoughts, for thoughts turn into words, words turn into actions, actions turn into habits, habits turn into character, and character determines destiny. The truth of this saying is nowhere more apparent than in the effects of thoughts and feelings on your physical body. Unresolved conflict in the mental and emotional realms can result in infection in the physical realm; unresolved aggression in the mental and emotional realms can result in autoimmune disease (including allergies) in the physical realm; and unresolved issues of love (separation of self and non-self) in the mental and emotional realms can result in cancer in the physical realm. This is not to say, of course, that there are not also physical causes of disease. Stepping on a rusty nail can certainly cause an infection, and exposure to radiation is related to cancer. As a physician who specializes in the treatment of breast implant disease, I certainly understand the devastating effects of silicone toxicity, for instance, on the endocrine, immunologic, and neurologic systems of the human body. A tendency exists, however, for negative emotional states to contribute to disease, because such emotions can drain energy from certain parts and organs of the body, creating an environment in which infection, autoimmune disease, cancer, or other illnesses may be more likely to occur. Thus, learning to manage the energetic environment that constitutes your thoughts and feelings is one of the most important contributions you can make to your own health and well-being.

Energy Management

Have you ever been around someone who is the energetic equivalent of a black hole? They seem to suck the life force energy out of everyone they encounter and never offer a hint of gratitude or optimism. Their entire world is fear-based. Every thought and action is designed to avoid a scenario that they have blown up in their minds to larger-than-life disaster proportions. These people provide excellent examples of energy mismanagement and can serve as role models for what to avoid in your own thoughts and emotions.

Energy management involves developing the capacity to recognize those thoughts and emotions that increase your energy, as well as those that deplete it. When you become mindful of the positive effects of particular thoughts, feelings, and ideas on your energy level, you can begin to foster the presence of those attitudes in your consciousness. Likewise, your awareness of negative patterns will allow you to take the steps necessary to eliminate attitudes that rob you of vital energy.

One good method for cultivating this kind of energetic awareness is through the practice of meditation. Meditation involves observing your thoughts and feelings, rather than being unconsciously immersed in the chatter of the mind. Research shows that meditation shifts brain waves to the left frontal cortex. Activity in that part of the brain seems to have a calming effect and is associated with enhanced concentration, metacognition, and positive emotions. Meditation is effective in treating insomnia, posttraumatic stress disorder, attention deficit disorder, depression, anxiety, high blood pressure, headaches, and a host of other medical and psychological conditions. Recent studies indicate that meditation strengthens the immune system, increasing the activity of natural killer cells, which fight infection and kill cancer cells.

Meditation begins with focused attention on the flow of thoughts going through your mind, and with practice, you learn to still the random thoughts. Resting in this stillness, you become aware of the "observer" or the "witness" within. Through continued cultivation, you develop the capacity to step back from your life drama and observe your thoughts, feelings, reactions, and attitudes with objective awareness. Your choices of how to respond to the drama increase exponentially. From the observer's viewpoint, you can see more clearly how to solve problems and resolve conflicts. You become more focused and less reactive emotionally. As you discipline your thoughts, you train yourself to think in constructive, productive, and healthy ways.

Everyone has an internal critic. Sometimes this critic is the voice of a parent or other authority figure that acts as an inner judge or saboteur, limiting your interactions and stifling your potential. When you create a quiet inner landscape through meditating, however, you not only silence these negative voices, but you also actually gain information and insight from a higher level that can be quite useful in your life. The "still, small voice" that emerges out of the silence is the expression of your inner guidance. The inner work that you do through meditation and other spiritual practices helps prepare the fertile inner landscape so that you can steer away from fear-based thoughts and move toward the guidance you can receive from higher levels. This guidance has a transcendent, multidimensional viewpoint, and only when your mind is elevated to this level do you really have enough information to know what is truly important in the road ahead.

In addition to increased awareness of your emotions, energy management includes developing healthy outlets for the expression of feelings. Rather than suppress internal conflict, which can depress your immune system and result in disease, it is important to determine how to release negative feelings such as anger and sadness. Just as physical toxins must be released from the body, emotional and mental toxins must be eliminated as well. Through therapeutic forms of expression, you can process and transform negative feelings into positive, productive energy. Whether you talk to a professional therapist (or supportive friend), or use creative methods such as writing, art or movement, communicating your feelings in a safe way results in a cathartic release of energy that elevates your consciousness and enhances your creativity. Again, cultivating this important practice increases your level of health and well-being.

Another important energy management skill can be gained through monitoring the effects of your relationships. Your energy is either enhanced or depleted by the relationships in which you engage. Recognizing and responding to the effects of your relationships on your energy level is a major step toward self-empowerment. Otherwise, your relationships can control your world, and your reactions to others can dictate your experience. Some relationships are amazing sources of dynamic exchange, increasing the energy of both parties involved. Other relationships contain exchanges that diminish your energy and leave you feeling angry, confused, or frustrated. These relationships can throw your energy system into chaos. In most cases, you have a choice as to whom you allow to be in a relationship with you, that is, you can choose whether or not you want to continue interacting with someone. If the person happens to be in your immediate family or is in another close, unavoidable relationship, it is important to find ways to manage your difficult feelings and emotions in order to neutralize the toxic effects the relationship may be having on your energy. Although you cannot control another person, you can learn to control your responses to him or her. In fact, learning to manage your responses to negative relationships presents an excellent opportunity for spiritual growth.

Perhaps nothing in life has the power to transform your spirit as much as a truly difficult relationship. In Carlos Castaneda's Don Juan legends, the knowing master teaches his student how to deal with the "petty tyrant" character type. Don Juan defines the petty tyrant as a tormentor, "someone who either holds the power of life and death over warriors or simply annoys them to distraction." You have undoubtedly faced a petty tyrant at some time in your life, be it a parent, sibling, teacher, boss, mate, or the schoolyard bully. The petty tyrant has the capacity to bring out the worst in you. Some enlightened teachers say that encountering the petty tyrant is an initiation on the path, because it pushes you to develop the discipline necessary for the next level of spiritual advancement.

The petty tyrant for me was my boss in the air force. He was a surgeon who took an immediate dislike to me, and, in his opinion, I could do nothing right. Once he threatened me with disciplinary action for taking "too much leave," even though he had signed off on all my leave, and the computerized system would not allow anyone to take more leave than they had earned. My fellow officers took me aside and gave me advice on how to handle this critic whose accusations defied logic. The Air Force Academy had trained them to respond to such petty tyrants without becoming consumed by negative emotions and losing energy. I took their advice and learned to respond differently to my boss. For instance,

I decided to stop whatever I was doing (even to the point of pulling off the highway when driving) any time I became upset about his treatment of me. I would then go into meditation and send him the energy of love. I continued this practice until I no longer had any negative thoughts or feelings about him.

Then, to my surprise and to the surprise of my fellow officers, his behavior toward me took a dramatic turn. He started praising me in conferences, telling others what a great job I was doing, and remarking that he had gotten letters of thanks from my patients. The change in his behavior was remarkable. This experience allowed me to realize that, without him in my life, I might not have developed the spiritual skill of sending love to those who would try to harm me. The concept that all the players that appear in one's life are there for a reason suddenly became clear to me.

Spiritual teachers say the petty tyrant teaches you the practice of forgiveness, patience, responsibility, and unconditional love. He or she cultivates in you the ability to follow your inner guidance and not be thrown off course by your own negative emotions. So, though you cannot change others or learn their lessons for them, you can change your response to their words and actions. This takes practice, yet such practice renders you more conscious of how your thoughts determine your experience. The practice of transmuting negative emotions into feelings of love reverses the trajectory of karma (the causal effect of past actions) and creates a more positive future.

Martin Luther King Jr., whose life exemplified the power of loving your enemies, delivered in one of his most famous sermons an outline of how to accomplish this arduous spiritual discipline. Dr. King taught that the initial step in developing the capacity to love your enemy is to look first within yourself. Are there spiritual qualities you need to cultivate such as gratitude or patience? If there are, ask for assistance from the higher realms. Is there something you may have done to offend? Is there something for which you need to ask forgiveness? If you find that there is, you can take steps to correct your own behavior and make amends. Of course, it may be that your enemy dislikes you for reasons that have nothing to do with you. It may be due to feelings of jealousy or insecurity, or the harboring of irrational prejudices. If your internal search reveals this to be the case, then you will begin to see your enemy as weak rather than powerful. Dr. King reminds us that there is "something of a civil war going on in all of us," that we are all in need of grace. Once you see your enemy within the matrix of a struggling humanity, you realize you can afford to be compassionate. You can then channel your compassion into prayer for the heart and soul of your adversary, which is what I did when I sent the energy of love to my boss.

The second step Dr. King advised is that you try to find the good in the other person. He said that even in the worst of us, there is good, and in the best of us, there still lurks some evil. If you can focus on the good in others, it helps to neutralize and reverse the trajectory of your own negative energy. He further emphasized that you must relinquish any opportunity to extract vengeance and, instead, act only out of love. He said that hate "destroys the very center of your creative response to life and the universe; so love everybody." We learn from Dr. King that love is the universal law of creation and hate is the distortion of that law.

According to Dr. Michael Ryce, a naturopath and world-renowned teacher of health and healing, there are two qualities of energy: integrative and dis-integrative. Integrative energies like joy, enthusiasm, and love create health; dis-integrative energies, such as fear and revenge, lead to disease. Pain is the body's signal that you are holding onto dis-integrative energy that needs to be released in order for healing to occur. Ryce likens hating your enemies to taking a poison pill and expecting it to poison your enemy. The only true cure for the dis-ease caused by dis-integrative energies is release and forgiveness. When the negative energies are released, the body actually uses them in the recuperative healing process. Thus, you need to forgive, not primarily for the benefit of your "enemies," but for your own healing. Both King and Ryce emphasize that forgiveness is an "inside" job.

If through mindfulness and meditation, you can get to the root of your self-limiting thoughts and release their corresponding emotional tension, you can neutralize the negative charge that is draining your energy. After such release, your perspective naturally rises to a higher spiritual plane. When you can further channel this energy in positive directions, such as loving your enemies, your creative potential is greatly enhanced.

Transcending Fear

People who believe in their fears simply haven't developed the faith to transcend them. The apostle Paul said, "We see through a glass darkly. " This means that until you develop spiritual vision, you do not have the capacity to see things as they actually are. For instance, a fear that plagues many is the fear of abandonment. Feelings of abandonment can be triggered when a parent leaves a child, a partner decides to move on, or a loved one dies. In the final analysis, if you have the good fortune to live long enough, you may outlive all of your significant relationships. You can take a pessimistic view that you are alone and therefore lonely or an optimistic view that you have been blessed with a long life and will reunite with others in the hereafter. If your true love leaves you for another, you can take the pessimistic view that you will never have another true love or the more rational view that the opportunity for a happier and more satisfying relationship with another has arrived. In the end, the best course is always to work on your own spiritual development, for after you connect with the higher aspects of yourself, loneliness is gone for good and you have access to an inner world that allows you to be content without unhealthy dependency on others. Once you make this spiritual shift, you may be surprised to find that others begin to seek you out for help and advice, as well as for the pleasure of your company.

Perhaps the most common fear is the fear of death. Some people lack the faith that anything exists once you drop the physical aspect of your body. Others, especially those with religious backgrounds, fear that their sins will determine their destiny in the afterlife. Current research indicates that human consciousness continues after death. Russell Targ, a laser physicist and cofounder of the Stanford Research Institute, discussed this research with me on my weekly *Temple of Health* radio show. He cited the April 2006 issue of the *Journal of the Society of Psychical Research,* in which Drs. Wolfgang Eisenbeiss and Dieter Hassler reported their experiment investigating the survival of consciousness after death. They asked a medium to find a former chess grandmaster in the afterlife. The medium reportedly contacted a Hungarian man named Maróczy who had been a chess grandmaster when living. Then, through the medium (who did not play chess), Maróczy played a current living grandmaster, Korchnoi. They played forty-seven moves before Maróczy resigned, saying he was disappointed in his performance due to lack of practice (indicating he had not played chess in the afterlife). Maróczy explained his motive for engaging in the chess game as follows: "I want to do something to aid mankind living on earth to become convinced that death does not end everything, but instead the mind is separated from the physical body and comes up in a new world, where individual life continues to manifest itself in a new unknown dimension." Bobby Fisher, who was Targ's brother-in-law, looked at the series of chess moves in the game and said that only a grandmaster could have played them. This experiment, along with others showing similar results, is consistent with the idea that consciousness survives death. If this is the case, fear of death may be an unnecessary waste of energy.

Another common fear is the fear of loss: loss of material things or money, loss of security, loss of health, or loss of whatever we perceive is important for our happiness. Those who fear loss lack faith that the universe will provide them with what they need in life. I often ask people experiencing this fear to think back on situations in which they really needed something to manifest and to remember how the universe did, indeed, come through for them. The universe sometimes delivered in ways they could not imagine, and sometimes they did not even realize that they got what they needed until after the fact (as they may not have known exactly what they needed at the time of the request).

A blessing in disguise occurred in my own life when I fell and broke my left upper arm several years ago. At the time, this seemed like a terrible accident to me. I am a surgeon and because of the nature of the injury, I could not operate for several months. Only later did I realize it was one of the best things that could have happened to me. I believe now that I was on a collision course with lung cancer, having smoked for twenty years and spent the majority of my time taking care of others rather than myself. Over-focus on the care of others to the exclusion of one's self is a behavior that is sometimes associated with the development of cancer, and I was so busy taking care of my patients that I had neglected my own care. I was forced to take four months off work and thereby given the opportunity to learn how important it was to take care of myself, to rest, to eat well, and to nurture my spirit. I realized that self-care is a prerequisite in caring for others. This "accident" likely resulted in my dodging an encounter with lung cancer (which several medical intuitives confirmed both before and after the event).

Other cancer survivors have shared with me their belief that cancer allowed them the freedom to take care of themselves and pursue what was important for them, rather than continuing only to care for others. My breast implant patients, many of whom have overcome seemingly insurmountable odds to find healing, have taught me that any illness can be a gift. Indeed, recognizing the gift an illness brings seems to be an important part of the healing process. When everything that happens in your life is welcomed for the grace it brings, your life opens up to reveal the magic and mystery of being alive.

Only from the higher vantage point of spiritual vision can you see that it is possible to live your life without the burden of fear. When fear and negativity are released, your energy is literally uplifted and you move into a state of higher awareness. Consequently, you have more time to enjoy yourself, as well as more energy available to create the life you want. As your relationship with Spirit is strengthened, your mind opens to inner guidance and your path seems to unfold effortlessly. At this point, optimism becomes a natural state and gratitude becomes a spontaneous response. If your energy is mired in fear and negativity, you cannot access spiritual guidance with any real clarity. It is as if the radio signal is jammed by outside interference and the channel has to be cleared.

In the end, with spiritual insight, you come to understand that you are not your belongings; you are not your achievements; you are not defined by your relationships; and you are not your emotions or your thoughts. That which is at the core of your being has been with you since before your birth and will survive after your physical death. This aspect of yourself is connected to a multidimensional source of energy that is life itself and is connected to every other living thing that has ever existed. Once you are able to access the awareness of who you are and use it to interact with the resources you have at your disposal, you find yourself in a dynamic, creative relationship with your own life. When you identify with the immense power and beauty of celestial being, your life unfolds according to your heart's desire and your soul's purpose.

Pamela Wible:

Dream Unrestrained

My dream was to be a doctor like my mom and dad. I wasn't sure they loved each other, but they loved work. So I tagged along. Raised in the morgue, I spent my childhood playing in the hospital halls. My father made it fun. He even talked to the dead people in the coolers. So I did too. From the morgue, we made our rounds to the city jail, methadone clinic, and the psychiatric hospital. Introduced as a doctor-in-training, I was set loose on inmates, heroin addicts, and schizophrenics while most girls my age were playing with Barbies.

I was going to be one of those doctors who could do everything. I'd deliver babies and help people die, plus treat criminals and people on drugs and people nobody else could help. I'd be a superhero and save a whole town. So I went to medical school and then graduated from residency in family and community medicine.

My first job was at a small clinic in Oregon. I didn't feel heroic. I felt like a factory worker. I tried other clinics, but they were the same: assembly-line medicine. People were often excluded if they had no insurance, or neglected if they took too long to express themselves or were shy, or different, or addicted to heroin, or in jail, or were not easy, simple, healthy, English-speaking patients with good insurance.

But I quit those jobs to pursue a dream.

This is the story of my dream come true and seven lessons to help your dream come true even when it seems impossible.

Lesson 1: Never, never give up on your dream.

Pamela Wible, MD, is a family physician born into a family of physicians. Her parents warned her not to pursue medicine. She followed her heart only to discover that to heal her patients she had first to heal her profession. So she invited citizens to design the clinic of their dreams. Celebrated since 2005, Dr. Wible's pioneering model has sparked a populist movement that has inspired Americans to create ideal clinics and hospitals nationwide. Dr. Wible is coauthor of *Goddess Shift: Women Leading for a Change*. www.idealmedicalcare.org. Photo credit: Digital Latte 2010

CHAPTER ELEVEN

Dreaming an Ideal Clinic

What if Americans were free to dream their wildest dreams? And what if ordinary people across America joined together to dream an ideal health-care system—a system not designed by experts, lobbyists, or politicians? And what if I promise to bring that dream to life?

Lesson 2: All revolutionary new ideas start as a dream.

From a stack of handmade flyers sprinkled with glitter, a series of e-mail blasts, and a blurb in the newspaper is born a movement: Health care of, by, and for the people. It begins in Eugene, Oregon—in my bedroom. Early December 2004, I jump out of bed with a vision of thousands of people gathering in churches and community centers: doctors, preachers, grandmothers holding grandchildren, masses of hands, every size and color, palm-to-palm, fingers interlaced—the universal symbol of solidarity.

With no time to wait for politician-saviors, I host a town hall meeting and challenge citizens to do something extraordinary: create the clinic of their dreams.

Housewives and hippies, bus drivers and businessmen, artisans, farmers, and folks of all ages convene to design a new model, a template for the nation. I welcome their wildest fantasies. Every off-the-wall idea is now on the table.

Pages overflow with floor plans, diagrams and doodles, poetry and prose as townspeople share their dreams unrestrained.

Mimi, a free-spirited mother of two reads, "An ideal clinic is a sanctuary, a safe place, a place of wisdom where we learn to live harmlessly, listen with empathy, observe without judgment. It's a place where a revolution starts, where we rediscover our priorities."

Then Lynette, a Chinese woman with an Australian accent, interjects, "No front counters separating people from people, complimentary massage while waiting, fun surgical gowns!"

Jacob, a soft-spoken young man with dreadlocks, imagines "intriguing magazines" and a "pet cat that greets people at the door" plus "a big garden and a running stream where you come over for lunch and play with the pet goats who inadvertently heal your broken leg."

I drift away on a montage of images: fairies and fountains, fizzy peppermint foot baths, physicians on house calls...when Anjali, a shy East-Indian college student, summarizes, "Most importantly, the doctor would be someone with a big heart and a great love for people and service, someone whose presence itself is enough to cheer a patient..."

In their words I rediscover myself, but I'm wondering how one doctor might manifest a community's dream when Nancy, an elder, clarifies that an ideal doctor is "a relatively relaxed physician in a calm space, someone who has plenty of time off." Ahh...I begin to imagine what's possible...

From living rooms and Main Street cafes to yoga studios and neighborhood centers—nine town hall meetings in six weeks—I collect one hundred pages of written testimony. Finally, my job description is written by patients, not administrators. I organize the papers scattered across my bed, bind them into a book, and carry it with me everywhere.

During the day, I purchase equipment, negotiate contracts, but at night under my comforter I enter a sanctuary with joyful, peaceful music ...I see the steam rising from the hot tub...and the clinic cat rubs his face against my leg as I open the door to a Caribbean-themed exam room filled with balloons...and each night I return to this place where nobody is turned away for lack of money, where the doctor answers the phone, says come right over, and is waiting when you arrive...

One month later we're open. Minus the pet goats.

Lesson 3: A dream is a prerequisite for a dream come true.

Doctors Who Dare to Dream

Some doctors accuse me of practicing "Alice-in-Wonderland" medicine. Others believe I live in "La-La Land" or on "Planet Oregon." When our community clinic is ridiculed, I often wonder why. After all, who could be against ideal health care?

Even the *Journal of Family Practice* praises our innovative community-focused model. And now our clinic is featured in Harvard School of Public Health's *Renegotiating Health Care,* a text that examines major trends with the potential to change the dynamics of health care. Yet some journals reject ideal care. Why? One editor responds: It's "too utopian." But Americans are ready for utopian health care, so why the resistance?

Robert F. Kennedy acknowledged: "One-fifth of people are against everything all of the time." I want to know why.

In 2007, I'm crisscrossing the country to recruit naysayers after *Physicians Practice,* America's top practice management journal, invites me on a seven-city speaking tour. My medical keynotes are declared "gospel revivals" by docs who envelop the stage and line the hall where I answer questions for hours...

But not all docs are so inspired. Center stage at the Houston Convention Center, I proclaim: "Doctors deserve to be happy" and three old white men run out of the room.

Why resist happiness? What are physicians thinking? To discover, I review hundreds of comment cards: "She's a nut; Too ideal; Excellent & informative; Complete waste of time; Thoroughly enjoyed her talk and will start a similar practice; Charming, sweet, encouraging, and completely impractical; Oh my! Love and peace! No help at all with reality!"

Most feedback is appreciative; some is skeptical. I'm drawn to the comments that sting, the ones that ridicule me, the docs who don't believe in happily-ever-after endings. The most common response goes something like this: "Okay in Eugene, Oregon, but would never work in fill-in-the-blank city — Beverly Hills, Chicago, Manhattan..."

The reality: community-designed clinics are thriving in small towns and large cities all across America.

Take Dr. Amy Solomon, a blond-haired, blue-eyed mother of two who spends a weekend in front of Johnnie's Supermarket in Boulder Creek, California, surveying citizens about how she can serve them. Six months later, Amy leaves corporate medicine and enters her town's beautiful new integrative medical center, complete with massage therapist, life coach, and yoga teacher. Amy believes in her community's dream. Now she lives it every day.

Dr. Soma Mandal's small high-tech, high-touch office is a dream come true in a large metropolis like Manhattan. With no answering service, she's available directly to patients who enjoy online scheduling and same-day appointments. Average office wait time: one minute. When busy patients can't come by, Dr. Soma checks in on them at their workplace. A Web review by *sickandlovingit*: "If you want the mind of a scientist, the efficiency of the Tokyo metro and the caring of Doc Baker from *Little House on the Prairie*, this is your woman."

Meet Dr. Bob Forester who leaves a lucrative practice in Modesto, California, to serve migrant farmworkers. He hosts three community meetings and develops a "Benefactor Model." Half the clients are benefactors who pay a modest yearly fee to cover all their office visits, house calls, and 24/7-physician access, but their fee also fully subsidizes primary care for recipients who receive unlimited care at no charge. Townspeople volunteer to jump-start the clinic. Anonymous donors drop off unsolicited checks. Since opening in 2004, the clinic has provided more than one million dollars in free care to the community. Dr. Bob says, "We pretty much have the local market cornered on giving away services to the uninsured for free!"

I love Dr. Megan Lewis of Durango, Colorado. Like her patients, she's tough and resourceful. When Dr. Lewis needs help, she hosts a town hall meeting. Turnout exceeds capacity so people cram into the cafe next door where Dr. Lewis recounts recent hassles, asks for solutions, and closes the meeting with a call to action: "Speak to your neighbors, elected officials, anyone who will listen, and return with ideas, implementation strategies." Citizens arrange meetings for Dr. Lewis with State of Colorado representatives who are most intrigued that physicians and patients are collaborating to design ideal health care.

And here's Dr. Myria Emeny's "Cinderella Story:" Burdened with $273,000 of student loans while single parenting a daughter with cerebral palsy, Myria wants off the hamster wheel. She dreams of life as a country doc. After two town hall meetings with the citizens of Westerlo, New York, Myria's dream comes true. Townspeople raise $2,500 with bake sales, spaghetti dinners, ice cream socials; they sew gowns and blankets; donate a washer and dryer, snow tires for her car, remodel an apartment for her family, and post "Doc Myria's Health Care Center" on the building she pays one dollar per year to lease. Patients volunteer to do billing and office work; one is teaching her horseback riding. Despite oppressive insurance regulations and layers of bureaucracy, Doc Myria keeps smiling as strangers snowplow her driveway and patients arrive with her favorite triple-chocolate cake on her birthday.

What's important, Myria says, is "believing it is possible. Most people give up on dreams like this."

Lesson 4: Believe all is possible.

Dream Your Hospital

It's July 2010. This guy Bob is driving to his farm in Wisconsin when he hears my interview on public radio. Turns out Bob is the chairman of the board of a local hospital. Suddenly, the CEO of a Wisconsin hospital system is calling to tell me: "You are the answer to all of our dreams." I welcome him to the movement; he invites me to Wisconsin.

Citizens in Wisconsin will now lead the nation in health-care reform by designing their own hospitals!

A late-night voicemail confirms the CEO's enthusiasm for our project: "Dr. Wible, I wanted to thank you…You've just opened up my mind and my heart toward so many things, and I'm very excited that you will come to our community and help us become a better place and help our doctors become happier practitioners. I really think this is divinely inspired…and we are all really grateful that you are coming and excited that you will help us. God bless you."

Lesson 5: To bring big dreams to life, keep company with dreamers, people who believe nothing is impossible.

Lesson 6: It's always good to meet a CEO who's more excited about your dream than you are.

CHAPTER ELEVEN

Three months later I'm welcomed to Wisconsin: First a dinner with the hospital team. Then, Peter, a Native American flute player, whisks me away to an impromptu bonfire and powwow where I'm embraced by townspeople. Over the next forty-eight hours, I speak with nearly eight hundred citizens as I lead nine small sessions and two community-wide visioning luncheons packed with three hundred attendees each.

The lights dim in the ballroom...Peter accompanies me on bamboo flute as I invite the audience to close their eyes...to walk into the dream that is called a hospital...Notice how it feels...See the colors...textures... How does your hospital serve the community...and heal the wounds of a nation?

And the voices of the people are heard:

A hospital is energetically sound, every nail pounded with love... It's a place that feels like home...where families can be close...where there is hands-on healing...waterfalls, warm floors, essential oils...with prayer and God's loving light...It's a place where a sick person does not feel alone...where fears are addressed...and life and death are embraced with grace...

At Longfellow Elementary in Eau Claire, kindergartners want dinosaur and princess books in their rooms. A fourth grade girl requests a "mural," a big picture on the side of the hospital building of people who are having fun. Kids see zoo animals and aquariums everywhere and a glass floor under their beds with fish swimming by...

And at Chippewa Falls Middle School, eighth grade boys beg for massage and more kids to share rooms so it won't be so lonely. How about a walk-through garden on the roof so patients can have fresh food?

Down the street, the women at Wissota Springs Assisted Living in Chippewa Falls say an ideal hospital is small and personal, not built like a five-star hotel. Remove the fancy stuff and put the money back into staff salaries. Arrange rooms with glass doors around the nurses' station so patients can see caregivers. Tell greeters to stop the scripted "How can I help you?" and come out from around the welcome desk, embrace guests, and say, "We're so glad you're here!"

Then the CEO and I head southeast to the tiny town of Augusta. Upstairs on the third floor of Unity Bank, we enter an empty conference room and flip on the lights to discover twelve bearded Amish men in matching black work boots, navy-blue pants, shirts, and zip-up jackets. They're seated evenly spaced from eldest to youngest in a slight semi-circle. I smile, introduce myself, and ask them to share their dreams, their visions of ideal health care. Like most Americans, they're stunned by the question itself. No response. I lean forward and ask, "Well, what can we do to make you more comfortable in the hospital?" Silence...

I wait…

They sit quietly. Eventually, an elder states, "We're comfortable now."

I continue with questions about their culture, their views on health, disease, death. Stone-faced silence. No reaction. Nothing. So I get a little frisky, "Well, let me tell you about me…I'm a family doc from Oregon. I got tired of just pushing people through, so I quit and held a town hall meeting to ask people what they want. You know what people want? They want to go back to the 1950s when you could walk to the doctor's office right in the neighborhood…"

And all at once all the men smile the same little smile. So I keep rambling and a moment later they all burst into laughter, some jump up from the sheer force of emotion. Now they're all smiles, big, beautiful smiles… and they share their lives…their hopes and dreams with me…

I learn the Amish are proud. They pay their bills by collecting money door-to-door in their community, but hospitals often write off their debt. That offends them. With the new health-care laws, of course, they'll be covered by insurance, but they inform us: "To have health insurance means one doesn't trust in God." What they request is a "fair bill." Yes, that's what all Americans want: a fair bill. The CEO promises to work on it. I say give 50 percent off at the door for anyone religiously opposed to lawsuits.

Standing up, I approach the twelve men. One by one, I lean over to shake their hands and thank them. The first gentleman looks up and asks, "So you're moving to Wisconsin to be our doctor?" I reply, "No, I'm going home to Oregon," just as the next pleads, "You're not moving here to be our doctor?" I respond, "No." And I pause, hold his hand, and add, "But I'm helping doctors all over the country be the kind of doctors people want."

As we drive away, I wonder what would actually happen if we adopted a few common-sense strategies from the Amish or followed the advice of the wise women of Wissota Springs or brought the dreams of kindergartners at Longfellow Elementary to life…

I won't have to wonder for long; it's happening now in Wisconsin…

Lesson 7: Our greatest healing takes place when we are willing to transcend artificial boundaries, love freely, and embrace each others' dreams as our own.

Andrew Weil:
Medicine of the Future

The medicine of the future has already arrived and is available to those who seek it. Throughout America doctors of integrative medicine are practicing in the prevention-oriented, more natural, and cost-effective style that must become standard. Although disease management and high-tech interventions still dominate mainstream practice, integrative medicine has been a growing theme in health care for the past decade.

In 1994 I founded the Program in Integrative Medicine at the University of Arizona Health Sciences Center in Tucson. In 2008 the program became the Arizona Center for Integrative Medicine, a center of excellence at the university with an annual budget of $4.5 million, an endowment, a large faculty and staff, and worldwide recognition as the leader in training physicians and allied health professionals to practice medicine more effectively. The Center has graduated more than five hundred physicians, from residents to senior academicians, family doctors and internists, cardiac surgeons and oncologists.

Back in 1994 the term "integrative medicine" was not in common use; few people understood it. As I used it more frequently, my medical colleagues gradually adopted it. I thought the term best described the transformative style of medicine that I knew to be central to health care of the future, and it was free of the negative associations many doctors had to such words as "holistic," "alternative," and "complementary."

"Holistic medicine," popular in the 1970s, suggests treating patients as more than physical bodies—an important concept. But the term has a

Andrew Weil, MD, author of *Spontaneous Healing, 8 Weeks to Optimum Health,* and *Healthy Aging,* among numerous other books, is known for bringing the field of integrative medicine to public awareness. A graduate of Harvard Medical School, he is a professor of public health and a clinical professor of medicine at the University of Arizona, as well as the director of the Arizona Center for Integrative Medicine. www.drwei1.com, www.weilfoundation.org

distinctly New Age ring; moreover, practitioners of holistic medicine often reject conventional treatments and are antagonistic toward those who use them. I consider "whole-person medicine" to be a central principle of integrative medicine (IM), but I avoid the word "holistic." "Alternative medicine" has had a much longer life. Although integrative medicine frequently makes use of alternative therapies in place of pharmaceutical drugs, it never hesitates to rely on conventional methods when those are indicated. We are not trying to replace conventional medicine with something else; rather, we are trying to make it more effective and more cost-effective by broadening its perspective and options for treatment. "Complementary medicine" is another inaccurate description of our practice, because it suggests that we mostly use adjuncts to conventional treatments, add-ons that are secondary and less important. Today, "complementary and alternative" medicine (CAM) is in vogue. We have a National Center for CAM (NCCAM) at NIH. I hope it will soon be renamed the National Center for Integrative Medicine. Whenever I speak to audiences throughout this country and abroad, I must patiently explain that integrative medicine is not synonymous with CAM. IM will use all appropriate therapies in treating disease, whether conventional or unconventional, as long as they do no harm and are supported by reasonable evidence for efficacy, but it has much broader goals than simply bringing complementary and alternative therapies into mainstream practice. In particular, it aims to do the following:

1. Restore the focus of medical teaching, research, and practice on health and healing

2. Develop "whole person" medicine, in which the mental, emotional, and spiritual dimensions of human beings are included in diagnosis and treatment, along with the physical body

3. Take all aspects of lifestyle into account in assessing health and disease

4. Protect and emphasize the practitioner-patient relationship as central to the healing process

5. Emphasize disease prevention and health promotion

These five goals must characterize American health care in the future, as it rises above the inadequacy of technology-based disease management. As I have said, the ascendancy of technology in the last century inadvertently distorted medical philosophy and practice. Integrative medicine seeks to correct this distortion and reconnect medicine with its roots.

Accepting the Unfamiliar

Long before I started the original program in integrative medicine, I had investigated other forms of healing around the world: in North

America, South America, Africa, India, and East Asia. In these explorations I came across many noteworthy practitioners and treatments that were far afield from the ones I learned at Harvard. Some of the ideas and practices I encountered struck me as nonsensical. Some were clearly in conflict with my scientific understanding. Others seemed strange but worth considering. A few were so sensible and so useful that. I wanted to learn more about them and include them in my own practice.

Soon after I returned from my travels and settled in the desert outside of Tucson, Arizona, in the mid-1970s, I began to see patients at my home. I first described what I did as "natural and preventive medicine." Later I came to call it integrative medicine, because I wanted people to know that I combined the conventional medicine I had learned at Harvard with ideas and practices from other systems and traditions. I explained that IM neither rejects conventional medicine nor embraces alternative therapies uncritically. In fact, I have always taught that the worst mistake an IM practitioner can make is to miss the diagnosis of a condition that should go straight to standard care. In other words: Send a patient with possible acute appendicitis to an emergency room, not to a hypnotherapist.

Even in those early days it was obvious to me that there was great demand for the service I offered. Those who came to me were frustrated with their health care. They had not been helped or had been harmed by conventional medicine and wanted to take greater responsibility for their own well-being. They were overjoyed to be able to sit with a medical doctor who was open-minded about treatments other than drugs and surgery; who took the time to listen to their stories; who gave advice about diet and products in health food stores and alternative therapies; and who could help them figure out their best options for treatment. I was delighted that some of the people who sought me out were in good health and simply wanted to know more about how to maintain it.

Most of the patients I saw had been through the medical mill many times. They brought extensive medical records and results of diagnostic workups, so I rarely had to worry about missing problems that required standard treatment. If I thought some possibility had been overlooked, I would send the patient to an internist or specialist whom I knew and trusted. Most of my consultations lasted an hour. At the end of that time I would give my impressions along with a treatment plan that addressed not only the presenting problem but other issues that caught my attention. My treatment plans included dietary recommendations (about both foods and supplements), other lifestyle advice (about exercise, for example, and use of alcohol and caffeine), information about botanical remedies, instructions for breath work and other relaxation methods, and suggested reading. I also made referrals to other practitioners, most frequently mind-body therapists (for hypnotherapy or guided imagery), osteopathic physicians (for manipulation), practitioners of traditional Chinese medicine, psycho-therapists, and teachers of yoga and meditation.

Patients came to see me from far and wide, many for a one-time con-sultation to get direction on the path to better health. I asked all of them to report on their progress two months after the visit, or sooner if they had more questions or new problems. The follow-up communications I received reinforced my conviction that the integrative approach worked well for many people and many health conditions. It was especially gratify-ing to learn of recoveries from chronic illnesses that had not responded to standard treatment.

I am quick to admit that much of my clinical success had to do with the kinds of patients I saw. I do not mean that they had trivial problems. Quite the opposite: Many presented with very difficult multisystem diseases that would be challenging for any practitioner and any system of medicine. Some came to see me as a last resort, with advanced life-threatening condi-tions. But they were all self-selected patients who were highly motivated to make changes in their lives. They sought good information, answers to questions, and sound advice. Compliance was not an issue; they were eager to take greater control of their lives and more than willing to implement the suggestions I gave them.

One of the greatest rewards of practicing IM is that you attract such motivated patients. Motivated patients are a pleasure to work with. It is easy to mobilize their innate healing potential, which increases the prob-ability that simple treatments and targeted lifestyle changes will produce the desired results. The frustration of many doctors today is that they have to work in impersonal settings with patients who think of their bodies as appliances brought into the shop for repair. That attitude, especially with insufficient time to form a productive therapeutic relationship, reduces the likelihood of clinical success and true healing.

Integrative medicine has been the focus of my professional life for the past three decades. As you can see, I am passionate about its potential to improve our health and heal our ailing health-care system. There are other encouraging trends in American medicine. Terms like "patient-centered medicine" and "spirituality and medicine" are now in common use on campuses of academic health centers. Many thoughtful physicians are working to increase awareness of cultural factors affecting health and outcomes of medical encounters. (For example, Hmong patients coming to a clinic in Minneapolis may have very different perceptions of symp-toms and procedures from those of the American doctors seeing them.) And many providers are trying to bring better health care to impov-erished communities.

All of this helps, but I believe integrative medicine, with its compre-hensive philosophy and rational practices, is the specific corrective needed to get American medicine back on track. IM doctors are ideally qualified to practice the kinds of preventive and lifestyle medicine I have described. Along with like-minded nurses, pharmacists, and others, they are best positioned to improve our dismal health outcomes and create a functional, cost-effective health-care system that serves all of our citizens.

Forerunners in Optimism

Helen Keller: Optimism Within

CHAPTER
13

Could we choose our environment, and were desire in human undertakings synonymous with endowment, all men would, I suppose, be optimists. Certainly most of us regard happiness as the proper end of all earthly enterprise. The will to be happy animates alike the philosopher, the prince and the chimney-sweep. No matter how dull, or how mean, or how wise a man is, he feels that happiness is his indisputable right.

It is curious to observe what different ideals of happiness people cherish, and in what singular places they look for this well-spring of their life. Many look for it in the hoarding of riches, some in the pride of power, and others in the achievements of art and literature; a few seek it in the exploration of their own minds, or in the search for knowledge.

Most people measure their happiness in terms of physical pleasure and material possession. Could they win some visible goal which they have set on the horizon, how happy they would be! Lacking this gift or that circumstance, they would be miserable. If happiness is to be so measured, I who cannot hear or see have every reason to sit in a corner with folded hands and weep. If I am happy in spite of my deprivations, if my happiness is so deep that it is a faith, so thoughtful that it becomes a philosophy of life—if, in short, I am an optimist, my testimony to the creed of optimism is worth hearing. As sinners stand up in meeting and testify to the goodness of God, so one who is called afflicted may rise up in gladness of conviction and testify to the goodness of life.

Helen Keller (1880–1968), author, lecturer, pacifist, suffragist, and advocate for people with disabilities, among other activism, was the first deaf and blind person to earn a bachelor of arts degree, graduating cum laude from Radcliffe in 1904. She helped found the American Civil Liberties Union (ACLU). In 1955, in recognition of her significant achievements and contribution to social causes, Harvard awarded her its first honorary degree ever granted to a woman. This chapter is part 1 of *Optimism, An Essay*, which Helen wrote while in college. It was originally published in 1903 in New York by T. Y. Crowell and Company.

Once I knew the depth where no hope was, and darkness lay on the face of all things. Then love came and set my soul free. Once I knew only darkness and stillness. Now I know hope and joy. Once I fretted and beat myself against the wall that shut me in. Now I rejoice in the consciousness that I can think, act, and attain heaven. My life was without past or future; death, the pessimist would say, "a consummation devoutly to be wished." But a little word from the fingers of another fell into my hand that clutched at emptiness, and my heart leaped to the rapture of living. Night fled before the day of thought, and love and joy and hope came up in a passion of obedience to knowledge. Can anyone who has escaped such captivity, who has felt the thrill and glory of freedom, be a pessimist?

My early experience was thus a leap from bad to good. If I tried, I could not check the momentum of my first leap out of the dark; to move breast forward is a habit learned suddenly at that first moment of release and rush into the light. With the first word I used intelligently, I learned to live, to think, to hope. Darkness cannot shut me in again. I have had a glimpse of the shore, and can now live by the hope of reaching it.

So my optimism is no mild and unreasoning satisfaction. A poet once said I must be happy because I did not see the bare, cold present, but lived in a beautiful dream. I do live in a beautiful dream; but that dream is the actual, the present—not cold, but warm; not bare, but furnished with a thousand blessings. The very evil which the poet supposed would be a cruel disillusionment is necessary to the fullest knowledge of joy. Only by contact with evil could I have learned to feel by contrast the beauty of truth and love and goodness.

It is a mistake always to contemplate the good and ignore the evil, because by making people neglectful it lets in disaster. There is a dangerous optimism of ignorance and indifference. It is not enough to say that the twentieth century is the best age in the history of mankind, and to take refuge from the evils of the world in skyey dreams of good. How many good men, prosperous and contented, looked around and saw naught but good, while millions of their fellowmen were bartered and sold like cattle! No doubt, there were comfortable optimists who thought Wilberforce a meddlesome fanatic when he was working with might and main to free the slaves. I distrust the rash optimism in this country that cries, "Hurrah, we're all right! This is the greatest nation on earth," when there are grievances that call loudly for redress. That is false optimism. Optimism that does not count the cost is like a house builded on sand. A man must understand evil and be acquainted with sorrow before he can write himself an optimist and expect others to believe that he has reason for the faith that is in him.

I know what evil is. Once or twice I have wrestled with it, and for a time felt its chilling touch on my life; so I speak with knowledge when I say that evil is of no consequence, except as a sort of mental gymnastic. For the very reason that I have come in contact with it, I am more truly an optimist. I can say with conviction that the struggle which evil necessitates is one of the greatest blessings. It makes us strong, patient, helpful men and women. It lets us into the soul of things and teaches us that although the world is full of suffering, it is full also of the overcoming of it. My optimism, then, does not rest on the absence of evil, but on a glad belief in the preponderance of good and a willing effort always to cooperate with the good, that it may prevail. I try to increase the power God has given me to see the best in everything and every one, and make that Best a part of my life. The world is sown with good; but unless I turn my glad thoughts into practical living and till my own field, I cannot reap a kernel of the good.

Thus my optimism is grounded in two worlds, myself and what is about me. I demand that the world be good, and lo, it obeys. I proclaim the world good, and facts range themselves to prove my proclamation overwhelmingly true. To what is good I open the doors of my being, and jealously shut them against what is bad. Such is the force of this beautiful and wilful conviction, it carries itself in the face of all opposition. I am never discouraged by absence of good. I never can be argued into hopelessness. Doubt and mistrust are the mere panic of timid imagination, which the steadfast heart will conquer, and the large mind transcend.

As my college days draw to a close, I find myself looking forward with beating heart and bright anticipations to what the future holds of activity for me. My share in the work of the world may be limited; but the fact that it is work makes it precious. Nay, the desire and will to work is optimism itself.

Two generations ago Carlyle flung forth his gospel of work. To the dreamers of the Revolution, who built cloud-castles of happiness, and, when the inevitable winds rent the castles asunder, turned pessimists — to those ineffectual Endymions, Alastors and Werthers, this Scots peasant, man of dreams in the hard, practical world, cried aloud his creed of labor. "Be no longer a Chaos, but a World. Produce! produce! Were it but the pitifullest infinitesimal fraction of a product, produce it, in God's name! 'T is the utmost thou hast in thee; out with it, then. Up, up! whatsoever thy hand findeth to do, do it with thy whole might. Work while it is called To-day; for the Night cometh wherein no man may work."

Some have said Carlyle was taking refuge from a hard world by bidding men grind and toil, eyes to the earth, and so forget their misery. This is not Carlyle's thought. "Fool!" he cries, "the Ideal is in thyself; the Impediment is also in thyself. Work out the Ideal in the poor, miserable

Actual; live, think, believe, and be free!" It is plain what he says, that work, production, brings life out of chaos, makes the individual a world, an order; and order is optimism.

I, too, can work, and because I love to labor with my head and my hands, I am an optimist in spite of all. I used to think I should be thwarted in my desire to do something useful. But I have found out that though the ways in which I can make myself useful are few, yet the work open to me is endless. The gladdest laborer in the vineyard may be a cripple. Even should the others outstrip him, yet the vineyard ripens in the sun each year, and the full clusters weigh into his hand. Darwin could work only half an hour at a time; yet in many diligent half-hours he laid anew the foundations of philosophy. I long to accomplish a great and noble task; but it is my chief duty and joy to accomplish humble tasks as though they were great and noble. It is my service to think how I can best fulfil the demands that each day makes upon me, and to rejoice that others can do what I cannot. Green, the historian,* tells us that the world is moved along, not only by the mighty shoves of its heroes, but also by the aggregate of the tiny pushes of each honest worker; and that thought alone suffices to guide me in this dark world and wide. I love the good that others do; for their activity is an assurance that whether I can help or not, the true and the good will stand sure.

I trust, and nothing that happens disturbs my trust. I recognize the beneficence of the power which we all worship as supreme — Order, Fate, the Great Spirit, Nature, God. I recognize this power in the sun that makes all things grow and keeps life afoot. I make a friend of this indefinable force, and straightway I feel glad, brave and ready for any lot Heaven may decree for me. This is my religion of optimism.

---

* *Life and Letters of John Richard Green,* edited by Leslie Stephen.

ELEANOR ROOSEVELT:

What I Hope to Leave Behind

CHAPTER 14

Ipersonally have never formulated exactly what I would like to leave behind me. I am afraid I have been too busy living, accepting such opportunities as come my way and using them to the best of my ability, and the thought of what would come after has lain rather lightly in the back of my mind.

However, I suppose we all would like to feel that when we leave we have left the world a little better and brighter as a place to live in. A man said to me recently, "I would like before I die to live in a community where no individual has an income that could not provide his family with the ordinary comforts and pleasures of life, and where no individual has an income so large that he did not have to think about his expenditures, and where the spread between is not so great but that the essentials of life may lie within the possession of all concerned. There could be no give and take in many ways for pleasure, but there need be no acceptance of charity."

Men have dreamed of Utopia since the world began, and perfect communities and even states have been founded over and over again. One could hardly call the community that this man likes to visualize Utopia, but it would have the germs of a really new deal for the race.

As I see it we can have no new deal until great groups of people, particularly the women, are willing to have a revolution in thought; are willing to look ahead, completely unconscious of losing the house

Eleanor Roosevelt (1884–1962), one of the most important women in American history, was First Lady of the United States from 1933 to 1945, instrumental in the formation of the United Nations, and was the first U.S. Delegate to the United Nations General Assembly, the first chair of the UN Commission on Human Rights, and the first chair of the Presidential Commission on the Status of Women. Her work on behalf of human rights led President Truman to call her the "First Lady of the World." Through her books, speeches, articles, and essays, she gave the world a clear vision of human rights and democratic responsibilities. The essay reprinted here was originally published in the *Pictorial Review* in April 1933.

on Fifth Avenue as long as somewhere they have a place to live which they themselves may gradually make into a home; are willing to give up constant competition for a little more material welfare and cooperate in everything which will make all those around them acquire a little more freedom and graciousness in life.

If a sufficient number of women can honestly say that they will willingly accept a reduction in the things which are not really essentials to happiness but which actually consume a good deal of the money spent by the rich, in order that more people may have those things which are essential to happy living, then we may look, I believe, for the dawn of a new day.

When enough women feel that way there may grow up a generation of children with entirely different ambitions, and before we know it, a new deal and a new civilization may be upon us. Perhaps this result is that which technocracy is preaching; but though I have read a little on the subject, I am not yet quite clear just what is the ultimate result that technocrats desire; but I gather that they do expect a revolution of some kind unless we make right use of the information which they have gathered.

If these methods of theirs bring about the type of community which I have in mind, the type of education and the ability to appreciate and enjoy, then technocracy has served a good purpose, But if that result does not come to us through technocracy, I still believe it may come to us through the efforts of the men and women of this generation in using their common sense and their dreams.

If I had Aladdin's lamp and could wish for whatever I desired, and see my desires materialize before me, I think the world would be a perfect place to live in, but I doubt if it really would be any more interesting than it is today, for in a way we all of us have wishing rings or something of the kind at hand all of the time. These age-old fairy tales were told simply to remind a generation of people, who happened to learn things more readily by stories, of the realities of life.

We learn things today just as readily by tales, only our tales are a little different. Aladdin's lamp, interpreted, means an individual's will to accomplish, and the wishes are the purposes, the dreams, if you will, the point on which we shape our lives. Of course, we may not be able to make all our dreams come true, but it is an astonishing thing how often, in the words of *Peter Ibbetson*, we can "dream true."

Unconsciously our characters shape themselves to meet the requirements which our dreams put upon our life. A great doctor dreamed in his youth that he would save people, that he would help a suffering humanity. He completed his long training; he steeled himself to see suffering in order that he might alleviate it. Instead of sliding out from under responsibility, he accepted it because he knew that he had to develop all those qualities of mind and heart if he were going to be a great doctor or a great surgeon.

Most women dream first of a happy family. The instinct for reproduction is inborn in most of us. If we have known happy homes, we want to reproduce the same type of thing we have had; and even though we may always be critical of some things in our past, time nearly always puts a halo around even a few of the disagreeable things, and most women dream, as they rock their babies or busy themselves in household tasks, that their daughters will do the same things someday.

In some intangible way it satisfies our hunger for eternity. We may not actually figure it out, but the long line that we see streaming down uncounted years, going back of us and going on beyond us, comes to mean for us immortality.

For a number of years it took so much vitality to keep the home going, and that home represented so many different kinds of activities, that none of us had any urge to go outside of this sphere.

Gradually in every civilization there comes a time when work of the household is done by servants, either human or mechanical.

When the care of the children ceases to be entirely in one person's hands, then in the past, as in the present, women have turned to other things. Some have changed the map of the world, some of them have influenced literature, some have inspired music. Today we are dreaming dreams of individual careers.

I find I have a sense of satisfaction whenever I learn that there is a new field being opened up where women may enter. A woman will rejoice in her freedom to enter on a new career. She will know that she has to make some sacrifice as far as her own life is concerned, and for that reason you will find more and more women analyzing what are the really valuable things in human life, deciding whether a job of some kind will be worthwhile for them from several points of view, whether it will give them sufficient financial return to provide for the doing of certain household things better than they could do themselves, and whether the job they do will give them more satisfaction and make them better-rounded people and, therefore, more companionable and worthwhile in their associations with the human beings that make up their home life.

What is the real value of a home? To me the answer is that the value lies in human contacts and associations—the help which I can be to my children, which my husband and I can be to each other, and what the children can be to us. These are the real values of home life. A sense of physical comfort and security can be produced quite as well by well-trained servants.

I feel that if holding a job will make a woman more of a person, so that her charm, her intelligence, and her experience will be of greater value to the other lives around her, then holding a job is obviously the thing for her to do. Sometimes a woman works not only to make money and to develop her personality, and be more of a person in herself, but also because she is conscious that she wishes to make some kind of contribution in a larger field than that of her home surroundings.

In all the ages there have been people whose hearts have been somehow so touched by the misery of human beings that they wanted to give their lives in some way to alleviate it. We have some examples of women like this today: Lillian Wald and Mary Simkhovitch in New York, Jane Addams in Chicago. They were none of them actuated, when they started out on their careers, by any small personal ambitions. They have achieved great personal success, but that is simply as a by-product; for what they set out to do and have done was to alleviate some of the trials of humanity in the places where they were able to work.

The conditions which are governing the world today are obliging many women to set up a new set of values, and in this country they will, on the whole, be rather a good thing.

We have come to a place where success cannot be measured by the old standard. Just to make money is no gauge anymore of success. A man may not be able to make as much as his wife, may not be able to make enough to support his family, and yet he may be a success. He may have learned to be happy and to give happiness, too, in striving for things which are not material.

A painter may do his best work and yet not be able to sell it, but he is nonetheless a success. You may make your home a success and spend one-tenth of what you spent last year. Bread and cheese cheerfully eaten and shared with other congenial souls may bring a larger return on the investment than do the four- or five-course dinners of a year ago.

There is no doubt that we women must lead the way in setting new standards of what is really valuable in life.

It is a far cry from our pioneer ancestors to a lady who owns a house on Fifth Avenue, and yet if you have to give up your house on Fifth Avenue and you have to change to some other conditions in life, it is not so very difficult to go back and reproduce certain conditions which have faded out of our minds and which, after all, were the essentials of life in, let us say, Governor Winthrop's time.

One of my favorite quotations is:

To be honest, to be kind—to earn a little and to spend a little less, to make upon the whole a family happier for his presence, to renounce when that shall be necessary and not be embittered, to keep a few friends but these without capitulation—above all, on the same grim condition to keep friends with himself—here is a task for all that a man has of fortitude and delicacy.

I often wish that more people would read Stevenson's "Christmas Sermon." He expresses a philosophy which, if it were carried out and accepted without bitterness, might make of us again a happy nation in spite of the loss of many material things.

As I grow older I realize that the only pleasure I have in anything is to share it with someone else. That is true of memories, and it is true of all you do after you reach a certain age. The real joy in things, or in the doing of things, just for the sake of doing or possessing, is gone; but to me the joy in sharing something that you like with someone else is doubly enhanced.

I could not today start out with any zest to see the most marvelous sight in the world unless I were taking with me someone to whom I knew the journey would be a joy. It may be a drawback which comes with age—you do not crave any new sensations and experiences as much as you did in youth—but it is one of its compensations that you are so much better able to enjoy through other people. You can even sit at home and be happy visualizing others that you love enjoying things which you have prepared them to see and to understand.

One of the things which I hope are coming home to us with a lessening of the abstract desire for money is an appreciation of the fact that some people have an ability to enjoy where others have not, and that one of the things that we must do is to give that ability to enjoy to more and more people.

It is almost entirely a question of education. There is such a thing as going through the world blindfolded. I have known people who were quite unconscious of the play of the sun and shadow on the hills. There was no joy to them in the view from a high hill. A landscape was simply a landscape—nothing else.

As one political dignitary once said to me, "Don't ask me to admire the scenery. I cannot see anything in it." His eyes had never been opened. The waves on the shore and the sweep of the ocean meant little to him. The sound of the wind in the trees, the breath of a crisp October day, all went unnoticed and uncatalogued as a beauty or a pleasure. I doubt if his ear had ever heard music; and the pitiful thing is that so many people can go through the world with the same handicaps either because they will not learn or because they haven't had the opportunity to see things through the eyes and hear things through the ears of a really educated person.

With advancing years I feel I must give this question of what I want to leave behind me greater thought, for before long I shall be moving on to fields unknown, and perhaps it may make a difference if I actually know what I would like to bequeath to a new generation. Perhaps the best I can do is to pray that the youth of today will have the ability to live simply and to get joy out of living, the desire to give of themselves and to make themselves worthy of giving, and the strength to do without anything which does not serve the interests of the brotherhood of man. If I can bequeath these desires to my own children, it seems to me I will not have lived in vain.

NORMAN VINCENT PEALE:

Inflow of New Thoughts Can Remake You

A t the time I wrote [*The Power of Positive Thinking*] it never occurred to me that more than two million copies would be sold in various hardcover editions and that it would one day attract a vast new readership through a paperback edition. Frankly, however, my gratitude for this event is not from the viewpoint of books sold, but in terms of the many persons to whom I have been privileged to suggest a simple, workable philosophy of living.

The dynamic laws which the book teaches were learned the hard way by trial and error in my personal search for a way of life. But I found in them an answer to my own problems and, believe me, I am the most difficult person with whom I have worked. The book is my effort to share my spiritual experience, for if it helped me, I felt it might also be of help to others.

The book is written with deep concern for the pain, difficulty, and struggle of human existence. It teaches the cultivation of peace of mind, not as an escape from life into protected quiescence, but as a power center out of which comes driving energy for constructive personal and social living. It teaches positive thinking, not as a means to fame, riches, or power, but as the practical application of faith to overcome defeat and accomplish worthwhile creative values in life. It teaches a hard, disciplinary way of life, but one which offers great joy to the person who achieves victory over himself and the difficult circumstances of the world.

Norman Vincent Peale (1898–1993) was a minister and author whose landmark book *The Power of Positive Thinking*, first published in 1952, brought optimism as a life-changing possibility into public awareness on a large scale. The book has sold five million copies to date. Though Dr. Peale's model of positive thinking invoked much criticism, including that it is a form of self-hypnosis, and Martin Seligman (see chapter 16), for one, emphasized that it is not the same as positive psychology, it nevertheless paved the way for acceptance of the concept that one's thinking can affect one's reality, which science has since amply demonstrated.

One of the most important and powerful facts about you is expressed in the following statement by William James, who was one of the wisest men America has produced. William James said, "The greatest discovery of my generation is that human beings can alter their lives by altering their attitudes of mind." As you think, so shall you be. So flush out all old, tired, worn-out thoughts. Fill your mind with fresh, new creative thoughts of faith, love, and goodness. By this process you can actually remake your life.

You can think your way to failure and unhappiness, but you can also think your way to success and happiness. The world in which you live is not primarily determined by outward conditions and circumstances but by thoughts that habitually occupy your mind. Remember the wise words of Marcus Aurelius, one of the great thinkers of antiquity, who said, "A man's life is what his thoughts make of it."

It has been said that the wisest man who ever lived in America was Ralph Waldo Emerson, the Sage of Concord. Emerson declared, "A man is what he thinks about all day long."

A famous psychologist says, "There is a deep tendency in human nature to become precisely like that which you habitually imagine yourself to be."

It has been said that thoughts are things, that they actually possess dynamic power. Judged by the power they exercise one can readily accept such an appraisal. You can actually think yourself into or out of situations. You can make yourself ill with your thoughts and by the same token you can make yourself well by the use of a different and healing type of thought. Think one way and you attract the conditions which that type of thinking indicates. Think another way and you can create an entirely different set of conditions. Conditions are created by thoughts far more powerfully than conditions create thoughts.

Think positively, for example, and you set in motion positive forces which bring positive results to pass. Positive thoughts create around yourself an atmosphere propitious to the development of positive outcomes. On the contrary, think negative thoughts and you create around yourself an atmosphere propitious to the development of negative results.

To change your circumstances, first start thinking differently. Do not passively accept unsatisfactory circumstances, but form a picture in your mind of circumstances as they should be. Hold that picture, develop it firmly in all details, believe in it, pray about it, work at it, and you can actualize it according to that mental image emphasized in your positive thinking.

This is one of the greatest laws in the universe. Fervently do I wish I had discovered it as a very young man. It dawned upon me much later in life and I have found it to be one of the greatest if not my greatest discovery, outside of my relationship to God. And in a deep sense this law is a factor in one's relationship with God because it channels God's power into personality.

This great law briefly and simply stated is that if you think in negative terms you will get negative results. If you think in positive terms you will achieve positive results. That is the simple fact which is at the basis of an astonishing law of prosperity and success. In three words: Believe and succeed.

Following are seven practical steps for changing your mental attitudes from negative to positive, for releasing creative new thoughts, and for shifting from error patterns to truth patterns. Try them—keep on trying them. They will work.

1. For the next twenty-four hours, deliberately speak hopefully about everything, about your job, about your health, about your future. Go out of your way to talk optimistically about everything. This will be difficult, for possibly it is your habit to talk pessimistically. From this negative habit you must restrain yourself even if it requires an act of will.

2. After speaking hopefully for twenty-four hours, continue the practice for one week, then you can be permitted to be "realistic" for a day or two. You will discover that what you meant by "realistic" a week ago was actually pessimistic, but what you now mean by "realistic" is something entirely different; it is the dawning of the positive outlook. When most people say they are being "realistic" they delude themselves: they are simply being negative.

3. You must feed your mind even as you feed your body, and to make your mind healthy you must feed it nourishing, wholesome thoughts. Therefore, today start to shift your mind from negative to positive thinking. Start at the beginning of the New Testament and underscore every sentence about Faith. Continue doing this until you have marked every such passage in the four books, Matthew, Mark, Luke, and John. Particularly note Mark 11, verses 22, 23, 24. They will serve as samples of the verses you are to underscore and fix deeply in your consciousness. [Instead of the Bible, you can use whatever writing is most inspirational to you, whether poems, prayers, or uplifting quotes.]

4. Then commit the underscored passages to memory. Commit one each day until you can recite the entire list from memory. This will take time, but remember you have consumed much more time becoming a negative thinker than this will require. Effort and time will be needed to unlearn your negative pattern.

5. Make a list of your friends to determine who is the most positive thinker among them and deliberately cultivate his society. Do not abandon your negative friends, but get closer to those with a positive point of view for a while, until you have absorbed their spirit, then you can go back among your negative friends and give them your newly acquired thought pattern without taking on their negativism.

6. Avoid argument, but whenever a negative attitude is expressed, counter with a positive and optimistic opinion.

7. Pray a great deal and always let your prayer take the form of thanksgiving on the assumption that God is giving you great and wonderful things; for if you think He is, He surely is. God will not give you any greater blessing than you can believe in. He wants to give you great things, but even He cannot make you take anything greater than you are equipped by faith to receive.

The secret of a better and more successful life is to cast out those old, dead, unhealthy thoughts. Substitute for them new, vital, dynamic faith thoughts. You can depend upon it—an inflow of new thought will remake you and your life.

Martin Seligman:

Two Ways of Looking at Life

CHAPTER

16

When I first began to work on learned optimism, I thought I was working on pessimism. Like almost all researchers with a background in clinical psychology, I was accustomed to focusing on what was wrong with individuals and then on how to fix it. Looking closely at what was right and how to make it even better did not enter my mind.

The turning point was a meeting in 1988 with Richard Pine, the person who was destined to become my literary agent, intellectual advisor, and friend. I described my work on pessimism and Richard said, "Your work is not about pessimism; it's about optimism." No one had said this to me before. As I left his office, somewhat shaken, he called out, "I pray you'll write a book about this. They make religions out of this stuff!"

I did. No religions sprouted up, but the book [*Learned Optimism: How to Change Your Mind and Your Life*] has sold steadily for fifteen years. And something did happen: Positive Psychology. In 1996, I was elected president of the American Psychological Association by what they tell me was the largest vote in history, thanks in part to the popularity of this book and the field of research that it spawned.

The president of the American Psychological Association is supposed to have an initiative, a theme of office, and as I looked over the modern history of psychology, I saw that Richard had given me my theme.

Martin Seligman, PhD, founder of the field of positive psychology, is professor of psychology and director of the Positive Psychology Center at the University of Pennsylvania and a past president of the American Psychological Association. A leading motivational expert and an authority on learned helplessness, he has published two hundred articles and twenty books, including *Learned Optimism, Authentic Happiness,* and *The Optimistic Child.* His research has been supported by the National Institute on Mental Health, the National Institute on Aging, the National Science Foundation, the Department of Education, the MacArthur Foundation, the Templeton Foundation, and the Guggenheim Foundation. www.authentichappiness. sas.upenn.edu

Psychology now seemed half-baked to me. The half that was fully baked was devoted to suffering, victims, mental illness, and trauma. Psychology had worked steadily and with considerable success for fifty years on the pathologies that disable the good life, which make life not worth living. By my count fourteen of the major mental illnesses are now treatable by psychotherapy or by medications, with two of them (panic disorder and blood and injury phobia) virtually curable. But clinical psychologists also began to find something disconcerting emerging from therapy: even on that rare occasion when therapy goes superbly and unusually well, and you help the client rid herself of depression, anxiety, and anger, happiness is not guaranteed. Emptiness is not an uncommon result. How can this be?

Curing the negatives does not produce the positives. In jargon, the correlation between sadness and happiness is not anything close to –1.00; it is more like –0.40. Strangely one can both be happy and sad (although not in the same instant). Women, in fact, being more emotionally labile, are both happier and sadder than men. The skills of becoming happy turn out to be almost entirely different from the skills of not being sad, not being anxious, or not being angry. Psychology had told us a great deal about pathology, about suffering, about victims, and how to acquire the skills to combat sadness and anxiety. But discovering the skills of becoming happier had been relegated to amusement parks, Hollywood, and beer commercials. Science had played no role.

When you lie in bed at night and contemplate your life and the lives of the people you love, you are usually thinking about how to go from +2 to +6, not how to go from –5 to –2. But at its best, psychology had only told us how to relieve misery, not how to find what is best in life and live it accordingly. This was the unbaked half that would become Positive Psychology.

What if the great majority of depressions are much simpler than the psychoanalysts believe?

- What if depression is not something you are motivated to bring upon yourself but something that just descends upon you?
- What if depression is not an illness but a severe low mood?
- What if you are not a prisoner of past conflicts in the way you react? What if depression is in fact set off by present troubles?
- What if you are not a prisoner of your genes or your brain chemistry, either?
- What if depression arises from mistaken inferences we make from the tragedies and setbacks we all experience over the course of a life?
- What if depression occurs merely when we harbor pessimistic beliefs about the causes of our setbacks?

- What if we can unlearn pessimism and acquire the skills of looking at setbacks optimistically?

  What if the traditional view of the components of success is wrong?

- What if there is a third factor — optimism or pessimism — that matters as much as talent or desire?

- What if you can have all the talent and desire necessary — yet, if you are a pessimist, still fail?

- What if optimists do better at school, at work, and on the playing field?

- What if optimism is a learned skill, one that can be *permanently* acquired?

- What if we can instill this skill in our children?

The traditional view of health turns out to be as flawed as the traditional view of talent. Optimism and pessimism affect health itself, almost as clearly as do physical factors. Our physical health is something over which we can have far greater personal control than we probably suspect. For example:

- The way we think, especially about health, changes our health.
- Optimists catch fewer infectious diseases than pessimists do.
- Optimists have better health habits than pessimists do.
- Our immune system may work better when we are optimistic.
- Evidence suggests that optimists live longer than pessimists.

Learned optimism is not a rediscovery of the "power of positive thinking." The skills of optimism do not emerge from the pink Sunday-school world of happy events. They do not consist in learning to say positive things to yourself. We have found over the years that positive statements you make to yourself have little if any effect. What is crucial is what you think when you fail, using the power of "non-negative thinking." Changing the destructive things you say to yourself when you experience the setbacks life deals all of us is the central skill of optimism.

Most psychologists spend their lives working within traditional categories of problems: depression, achievement, health, political upsets, parenting, business organizations, and the like. I have spent my life trying a new category, which cuts across many of the traditional ones. I see events as successes or failures of personal control.

Viewing things this way makes the world look quite different. Take an apparently unrelated collection of events: depression and suicide becoming commonplace; a society elevating personal fulfillment to a right; the race going not to the swift but to the self-confident; people suffering chronic illness frighteningly early in life and dying before their time; intelligent, devoted parents producing fragile, spoiled children; a therapy curing depression just by changing conscious thinking. Where others would see this mélange of success and failure, suffering and triumph, as absurd and puzzling, I see it as all of a piece.

We begin with the theory of personal control. I will introduce to you two principal concepts: learned helplessness and explanatory style. They are intimately related.

Learned helplessness is the giving-up reaction, the quitting response that follows from the belief that whatever you do doesn't matter. *Explanatory style* is the manner in which you habitually explain to yourself why events happen. It is the great modulator of learned helplessness. An optimistic explanatory style stops helplessness, whereas a pessimistic explanatory style spreads helplessness. Your way of explaining events to yourself determines how helpless you can become, or how energized, when you encounter the everyday setbacks as well as momentous defeats. I think of your explanatory style as reflecting "the word in your heart."

Each of us carries a word in his heart, a "no" or a "yes." You probably don't know intuitively which word lives there, but you can learn, with a fair degree of accuracy, which it is.

Unlike many personal qualities, basic pessimism is not fixed and unchangeable. You can learn a set of skills that free you from the tyranny of pessimism and allow you to use optimism when you choose. These skills are not mindlessly simple to acquire, but they can be mastered. The first step is to discover the word in your heart. Not coincidentally, that is also the initial step toward a new understanding of the human mind, one that has unfolded over the past quarter-century—an understanding of how an individual's sense of personal control determines his fate.

The Science of Optimism

Bruce Lipton:

The Biology of Inspiration

While I hold a vision of a wholesome future, we are currently confronted with a crisis of global proportions. Scientists have determined that Earth's biosphere is in the throes of experiencing its sixth mass extinction. Five previous mass extinctions, each of which almost wiped out life on the planet, are attributed to extraterrestrial forces such as comets or asteroids hitting the Earth. The current extinction is driven by forces much closer to home, for it is recognized that human civilization is the primary cause behind the current crisis.

This is not the first time, nor will it be the last, that civilization will come face to face with its own mortality. Historian Arnold Toynbee described society as a living "organism" that grows with momentum, reaches equilibrium—and then goes into "overbalance," which produces new environmental *challenges*. Social cycles are driven by patterns of *challenge-and-response*. *Challenges* from the environment provoke a *response* in society.

According to Toynbee, the cultural mainstream inevitably clings to fixed ideas and rigid patterns in the face of imposing challenges. From among their ranks arise *creative minorities* that resolve the threatening *challenges* with more viable *responses*. Creative minorities are active agents that transform old, outdated philosophical elements into new, life-sustaining cultural beliefs.

For over four hundred years, Western civilization has chosen Science as its source of truths and wisdom about the mysteries of life. Allegorically, we may picture the wisdom of the universe as resembling a large

Bruce H. Lipton, PhD, author of *The Biology of Belief* and *Spontaneous Evolution,* is an internationally recognized authority in bridging science and spirit. A cell biologist by training, he taught cell biology at the University of Wisconsin School of Medicine and later conducted pioneering research at Stanford University. His breakthrough studies on the cell membrane presaged the new science of epigenetics and have made him a leading voice of the new biology.

mountain. We scale the mountain as we acquire knowledge. Our drive to reach the top of that mountain is fueled by the notion that with knowledge, we may become "masters" of our universe. Conjure the image of the all-knowing guru seated atop the mountain.

Scientists are professional seekers, forging the path up the Mountain of Knowledge. Their search takes them into the uncharted unknowns of the universe. Through each scientific discovery, humanity gains a better foothold in scaling the mountain. Ascension is paved one scientific discovery at a time. Along its path, Science occasionally encounters a fork in the road. Do we take the left turn or the right? When confronted with this dilemma, the direction chosen by Science is determined by the consensus of scientists interpreting the acquired facts, as they are understood at the time.

Occasionally, scientists have embarked in a direction that ultimately leads to an apparent dead end. When that situation arises we are faced with two choices, continue to plod forward with the hope that science will eventually discover a way around the impediment, *or,* return back to the fork and reconsider the alternate path. Unfortunately, the more Science invests in a particular path, the more difficult it is for Science to let go of beliefs that keep them on that path. As Toynbee suggests, the cultural—and scientific—mainstream inevitably clings to fixed ideas, beliefs that no longer serve us on our mission. Even when confronting a dead end, the scientific discoveries acquired on that path are important contributions to our collective knowledge.

The path that Science is currently navigating has inadvertently brought us to our current moment of global crisis. Since the Modern Scientific Revolution, starting with the publication of Copernicus's observation that the Earth orbits the sun in 1543, Science has perceived of the universe as a physical machine that operated on the mechanical principles later defined by Newtonian physics. In the Newtonian worldview, the Universe is defined by its material reality and its operation could be understood through *reductionism,* the process of taking matter apart and studying its bits and pieces. Knowledge of the universe's parts and how they interact would enable science to predict and control nature. This notion of control is contained within *determinism,* the belief that with knowledge of something's parts, we can predict its behavior.

The reductionist approach to understanding the nature of the universe has provided valuable knowledge that has enabled us to fly to the moon, transplant artificial hearts and read the genetic code. However, applying this science to world problems has hastened our demise. It is a simple fact that society cannot sustain itself by continuing to adhere to its current worldview. To extricate ourselves from the problems we face, we must appeal to a "new" science, one that offers the *new thinking* needed to generate intelligent responses to our global challenges.

Leading edge research is currently questioning fundamental assumptions long held as dogma by conventional science. New science curricula must be developed to accommodate challenges to the following three conventional tenets of biomedical research:

1.   Life operates according to Newtonian mechanics;

2.   Life is controlled by genes, and,

3.   Life arose through neo-Darwinian evolution.

In contrast to conventional reductionism, a new science curriculum would be based upon holism, the belief that an understanding of Nature and the human experience requires that we transcend the parts to see the whole. Though materialism has engendered the idea that we are disconnected from and above nature, the new vision emphasizes that life represents an integration and coordination with both a physical and an immaterial universe. The resolution of our global crisis will be solved through an integration of both reductionist and holistic principles.

The accumulated knowledge of scientists has been assembled into a hierarchical construction resembling a multi-tiered building. Each level of the building is built upon the scientific foundation provided in the supporting lower levels. Each floor of the building is classified as a scientific subspecialty.

The foundation of the "Science" building is Math. Upon math, we assemble the building's second level, Physics. Built upon physics is the building's third level, Chemistry. Chemistry serves as the platform of the next tier, Biology. Built upon biology is the building's current top floor, Psychology.

Curriculum renovations would not only strengthen Science's foundation, they also provide for Noetic Science, a new scientific tier. Hopefully, as one ascends through the curriculum, the integration of the evolving sciences, from tier to tier, will provide them with the mastery to enable humans to thrive on this planet.

Fundamental to a new scientific curriculum is the foundation offered by Math. Mathematical laws are absolute, certain and indisputable, while those of other sciences are to some extent debatable and in constant danger of being revised by newly discovered facts. As Einstein once remarked, "...there is another reason for the high repute of mathematics: it is mathematics that offers the exact natural sciences a certain measure of security which, without mathematics, they could not attain." Before Newton could derive his principles of physics he first had to create its mathematics: differential calculus.

The emphasis of the new math program is on Fractal Geometry and Chaos Theory. Geometry is the science of structure in space, the way the different parts of something fit together in relation to each other. For centuries our math has been used to isolate and divide the universe into separate measurable components that allowed us to focus on the nature of the individual parts.

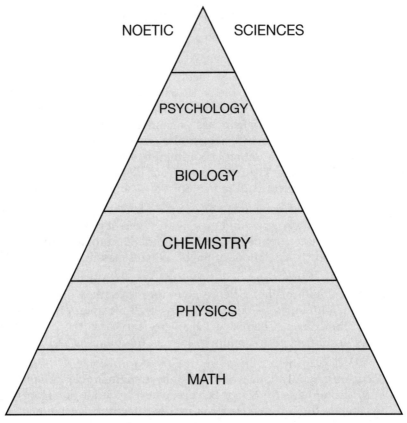

NOETIC / SCIENCES

PSYCHOLOGY

BIOLOGY

CHEMISTRY

PHYSICS

MATH

The Structure of Science

Formerly we emphasized Euclidian geometry, the math involved with cones, cubes and parabolas whose points and shapes we mapped on graph paper. While we use Euclidian geometry to construct our material world, it is a math that does not readily relate to nature. A mountain is not really an inverted cone. When we were children, we drew "Euclidian" trees that were composed of cylindrical trunks crowned with spheres. Though representative of a tree, it is not the shape of a natural tree.

Fractals are a modern version of geometry, officially defined in 1983 by IBM scientist Benoit Mandelbrot. It is actually a simple mathematics based upon an equation involving addition and multiplication, in which the result is entered back into the original equation and solved again. Repetition of the equation inherently provides for a geometry expressing self-similar objects that appear at higher or lower levels of the equation's magnitude. The organization at any level of nature, like nested Russian dolls, reflects a self-similar pattern to organizations found at higher or lower levels of reality. For example, the structure and behavior of a human cell is self-similar to the structure and behavior of a human, which in turn is self-similar to the structure and behavior of humanity. This math substantiates the ancient wisdom implied in the axiom, "As above, so below."

Fractal geometry provides for structures resembling those of the natural world, such as mountains, clouds, plants, and animals. The dynamics of fractal structures are directly influenced by Chaos Theory, a math that is concerned with the nature by which small changes may cause unexpected final effects. Chaos theory concerns the processes by which the flap of a butterfly's wing in Asia may influence the formation of a tornado in Oklahoma. When chaos theory is combined with fractal formulae, the math further defines the behavioral dynamics observed in our physical reality — from weather patterns to human physiology; from social patterns to market prices on the stock exchange.

This new math offers profound insights into the operation of the universe. Information acquired by studying a process at any particular level of nature can be applied toward an understanding of knowledge of self-similar events at other levels of nature. A study of cells enables us to understand the behavior of a human. The behavior of cells within a human can provide us with the behavioral patterns needed by humans to learn to survive as a coherent civilization. Fractal geometry emphasizes that the observable physical universe is derived from the integration and interconnectivity of all of its parts.

Fractal geometry and chaos mathematics are fundamental to constructing modern physics, science's "first floor." A century ago, a creative minority launched a radical new view of how the universe works. Albert Einstein, Max Planck and Werner Heisenberg, among others, formulated new theories concerning the underlying mechanics of the universe. Their work on Quantum Mechanics revealed that the universe is derived from a holistic entanglement of immaterial energy waves — and not from an assembly of physical parts as suggested by Newtonian physics. Quantum mechanics shockingly reveals that there is no true "physicality" in the universe; atoms are made of focused vortices of energy, miniature tornados that are constantly popping into and out of existence. Atoms are not made of physical matter as we have perceived it; consequently, neither are the molecules, cells or humans made from them.

Newtonian physics emphasizes *separatism,* while quantum physics stresses *holism.* Atoms as energy fields interact with the full spectrum of invisible energy fields that comprise the universe; atoms are intimately entangled with each other and the field in which they are immersed.

A fundamental conclusion of the new physics acknowledges that the "observer creates the reality." As observers, we are personally involved with the creation of our own reality! Physicists are being forced to admit that the universe is a "mental" construction. Pioneering physicist Sir James Jeans wrote, "the stream of knowledge is heading towards a non-mechanical reality; the universe begins to look more like a great thought than like a great machine. Mind no longer appears to be an accidental intruder into the realm of matter...we ought rather hail it as the creator and governor of the realm of matter."

Quantum mechanics was acknowledged as the best scientific description of the mechanisms creating our universe eighty years ago. However, some branches of science rigidly cling to the prevailing Newtonian, matter-oriented, worldview, simply because it "seems" to make better sense out our existence. This is probably the first time in history that scientists have refused to believe what their reigning theory says about the world. To grapple with the contradictions, most physicists have chosen an easy way out: they restrict quantum theory's validity to the subatomic world. Renowned theoretical physicist David Deutsch wrote, "Despite the unrivalled empirical success of quantum theory, the very suggestion that it may be literally true as a description of nature is still greeted with cynicism, incomprehension, and even anger." (Folger, 2001) However, quantum laws *must* hold at every level of reality. We can no longer afford to ignore that fact. We must learn that *our beliefs, perceptions and attitudes about the world create the world.*

Quantum physics advances have provided a new foundation for Chemistry, the building's second floor. While conventional chemistry has focused upon the atomic elements as miniature Newtonian solar systems composed of solid electrons, protons and neutrons, our new chemistry is Vibrational Chemistry, based upon quantum mechanics, and it emphasizes that atoms are made of spinning immaterial energy vortices such as quarks.

Traditionally, we emphasize the particulate character of atoms, resembling the ball and stick models built in chemistry lab courses. However, the assembly and interaction of molecules cannot be predicted by matter-based principles of Newtonian physics. Chemical mechanics and behaviors are derived from constructive and destructive interference patterns of entangled energy waves. The new chemistry is concerned with the role of vibration in creating molecular bonds and driving molecular interactions. Energy fields, such as those derived from cell phones or from thoughts, entangle with and influence chemical reactions. Vibrational Chemistry defines the mechanisms that mediate mind-body connections.

Science's third floor, Biology, is built upon a foundation of Physics and Chemistry. Biology, like chemistry, has been investigated using a reductionist philosophy; organisms are dissected into cells, and cells into molecular parts, to gain understanding as to how they work. The new biology perceives of cells and organisms as integrated communities that are physically and energetically entangled within the environment.

The new holism endorses James Lovelock's hypothesis that the Earth and the biosphere represent a single living and breathing entity known as Gaia. Our careless disregard for Nature's holism and our insistence that we are here to "dominate and control Nature" has unwittingly led us to injure and damage the very environment that gives us life. Gaian Physiology would represent a course designed to reacquaint us with our connection to the planet and to our ancient role as the Garden's caretakers.

Central to the new biology is the emerging science of Epigenetics. Epigenetics, which literally translates as "control above (epi-) the genes," provides for a second genetic code that controls the activity and programming of an organism's DNA. This new hereditary mechanism describes how behavior and gene activity are controlled by an organism's perception of its environment.

The fundamental difference between the old view of DNA as containing the entire genetic code, and epigenetics, is that former notion endorses *genetic determinism*, the belief that genes predetermine and control our physiologic and behavioral traits. In contrast, epigenetics reveals that our perceptions of the environment, including our consciousness, actively control our genes. Through epigenetic mechanisms, applied consciousness can be used to shape our biology and make us "masters" of our own lives.

Rather than endorsing a Darwinian evolution based upon random mutations and a struggle for survival, a new sense of Fractal Evolution defines the biosphere as a cooperative communal venture among all living organisms. Rather than invoking competition as a means of survival, the new view of evolution is one driven by cooperation among species and with their physical environment. A change in our perception, from a life based upon competition to one of cooperation is vital to our survival.

The fractal character of evolution reveals that the patterns of life are reiterated throughout nature. Applying the principles of biopolitics used among the cells of our trillion-celled bodies to human civilization would readily support a healthy thriving world of seven billion people, allowing us to live in harmony. As Toynbee suggested, humanity is an evolving living organism in which every human is a constituent "cell." We must own that every human being counts, for each is a member of a single organism. When we war, we are warring against ourselves.

143

Holistic revisions in the supporting sciences of physics, chemistry and biology provide for a radically remodeled fifth tier, Psychology. For centuries, our materialistic perspective dismissed the immaterial mind and consciousness as an epiphenomenon of the mechanical body. We believed that the action of genes and neurochemicals, the hardware of the central nervous system, were responsible for our behaviors and our dysfunctions.

The foundation of quantum mechanics, vibrational chemistry and epigenetic control mechanisms provide for a profoundly new understanding of psychology. It is now recognized that the environment, in conjunction with the perceptions of the mind, controls the behavior and genetics of biology. Our life experiences are recorded as the programmed perceptions constituting the mind. Rather than being "programmed" by our genes, our lives are controlled by our perceptions of life experiences.

The switch from Newtonian to quantum mechanics changes the focus of psychology from physiochemical mechanisms to the role of energy fields. The new psychology is an Energy Psychology. Energy psychology deals with the software of programming consciousness rather than focusing on the physiochemical hardware that mechanistically expresses behavior. Energy psychology directly impacts subconscious programming rather than trying to manipulate genetics, physiology and behavior.

An informative and important course on Conscious Parenting would emphasize the vital role that parents play in programming their child's genes and behaviors. Understanding this new science will enable parents to provide developmental experiences that will enhance the health, intelligence and happiness of their children. Fundamental perceptions have the power to program the subconscious mind. Primal life-shaping experiences are primarily downloaded between fetal development and the first six years of a child's life. Dysfunctional-programmed perceptions, like computer files, can be edited and rewritten using non-invasive energy psychology healing modalities.

This new pyramid only strengthens the conventional sciences; it forms the foundation for a new tier, an all-encompassing field of Noetic Science. Investigations of the cell's brain, its membrane, reveal that the community of cells comprising each human is distinguished by unique clusters of protein markers on the cell surfaces. No two humans are the same and no two humans display the same sets of membrane surface proteins. The membrane protein receptors on the cell's surface are literally antennas that receive and respond to a precisely defined spectrum of environmental "energy waves." Consequently, the individuality of each human is defined by the unique spectrum of extracellular environmental signals received by their "self-receptors." Simply put, our identities are environmental vibrtions that play through our cells; we are not in our bodies.

These environmental signals precede and transcend our earthly life. Life experiences perceived by the body are incorporated into our personal information fields. Our lives are connected to an energy information pattern comprising our environmental field. The information spectrum represents an invisible moving force, which many refer to as a soul or spirit, that is in harmonic resonance with our physical bodies. This spiritual realm is the creative force behind our conscious minds. Noetic Science recognizes that there is a larger, more encompassing Noetic Consciousness from which the spirit is derived.

By integrating and balancing the awareness of our Noetic Consciousness into our physical consciousness, we will be empowered to become true creators of our life experiences. When such an understanding reigns, we and the Earth will once again have the opportunity to create the Garden of Eden.

The first half of Modern Science was preoccupied with reducing our world to separate bits and pieces. These efforts have provided information that has enabled humans to look out into the deepest regions of the universe and peer into the inner workings of a single atom. While the technology derived from reductionist science is miraculous in its nature, our use of it is destroying our civilization.

New science recognizes that life is more than the study of its individual parts. The revised curriculum balances our historic reductionist perspective with the evolving concepts of holism. By focusing on the power of interactive, autopoetic communities, whether they are comprised of energy waves, chemicals, cells or humans, we will be able to realize the peace inherent in our oneness.

As human beings engaged in the great work of re-creating our selves, our species and our planet, our mission is to seek creative responses to the challenges before us. Traditionally, reductionist science has sought resolutions by delving deeper into the material fabric of nature. In contrast, new science directs our attention to the heretofore-invisible matrix of entangled immaterial forces that shape and energize our world. Our holistic pursuit compels us to pull back from studying the trees, and own the scope and magnitude of the forest. From that perspective, we are obliged to recognize the power Noetic Consciousness plays in shaping our lives, our world and our challenges. This new life-sustaining awareness echoes the words of physicist R. C. Henry in his recent essay in *Nature*, "The Universe is immaterial—mental and spiritual. Live and enjoy." (Henry, 2005)

Pamela W. Smith & Christopher T. Smith:

A New World of Medical Knowledge

Nowhere else is the value of optimism more cherished than in the health-care world. When all looks grim—when all of the test results portend a dire prognosis—it is only optimism, a hope for a better outcome, that sustains patients and motivates caregivers. Optimism is the driving force that keeps us from giving up when the chips are down.

Most would agree that there is a strong relationship between psychological constructs, like optimism, and health. The wonderfully human tendency to take a favorable or hopeful outlook in the face of adversity has been shown, time after time, to aid in the healing process by shortening the recovery period and easing pain. The well-documented placebo effect is a prime example of one's expectations of a favorable outcome actually contributing to that result. Assuming an optimist's attitude is a positive coping mechanism that goes a long way toward helping patients become proactive in their efforts to become and remain healthy.

There is no doubt that the field of medicine has surmounted some of humankind's worst maladies. The accomplishments are many and really quite astounding. Death from infectious disease has lessened dramatically in the industrialized world. The fact that body parts can either be replaced with surgical implants or transplanted from other human beings

Pamela Wartian Smith, MD, MPH, spent her first twenty years of practice as an emergency room physician with the Detroit Medical Center. She is currently director of the Center for Healthy Living and Longevity and founding director of the Fellowship in Metabolic, Anti-Aging, and Functional Medicine. An internationally known speaker on the subject of Metabolic, Anti-Aging, and Functional Medicine, she is the author of six best-selling books and codirector of the Master's Program in Medical Sciences with a concentration in Metabolic and Nutritional Medicine at the University of South Florida College of Medicine.

Christopher Todd Smith, MIS, holds a master's degree in interdisciplinary studies from Wayne State University and is the director of research at the Center for Healthy Living in Michigan and Florida.

smacks of science fiction. Vaccines have proven miraculous in their effectiveness. Deadly epidemics are becoming a thing of the past.

The production of truly new and useful drugs has waned in the last twenty-five years, however, and the incidence of certain disease processes such as heart disease, cancer, depression, and diabetes is persistent or on the rise. Ultra-resistant germs have evolved, which even the most powerful of antibiotics cannot put down. We seem to be playing catch up with Mother Nature as she unleashes a new variant of influenza every year. The so-called Golden Age of medicine is long past.

Yet most people remain optimistic that medical science will eventually prevail. Optimism in the realm of medicine is that hopeful confidence that something good, or even great, will be the result of our efforts toward health. In spite of medicine's shortcomings and perhaps in celebration of its grand accomplishments, the time has arrived to give cause for a renewed optimism in what medicine can do for humanity. We now stand at the threshold of the next "Golden Age" of medicine. This new and optimistic era of health care is being ushered in by the newest medical specialty known as "metabolic/anti-aging medicine."

Metabolic medicine/anti-aging medicine is the newest and fastest growing medical subspecialty. It is designed to look at the root causes of a health problem and not just treat or mask symptoms. This new systemic approach to assessing and treating the patient is born of the recent advances in the area of genomic mapping via the Human Genome Project and other scientifically sound advances in gene testing, blood and urine tests, and saliva testing. Testing, conducted before an individual begins to take a medication, to determine if that particular medication will work is now being developed; this testing can also help patients avoid drastic side effects or suboptimal results. How the whole body actually functions on a biochemical and even molecular level is the underpinning of this new and exciting medical subspecialty.

With this new wealth of knowledge available, it is now also possible to individualize medical care. Prior to this new era of medicine, one's high blood pressure, for example, would have warranted receiving a medication to lower blood pressure according to a protocol. This means that everyone got the same basic treatment for a given disease process. But now there are new metabolic and functional medicine tests designed to customize patient treatment. Because of the progress made in this type of testing, most treatment plans can now be based on many more parameters of the individual patient. Factors such as nutritional and hormonal status as well as age, gender, weight, diet, and physical activity can be taken into account to tailor the treatment specifically to that person. One size does not fit all!

Furthermore, we now know that our health status is not totally dictated by our genetic heritage. For many diseases, inheritance is only 20 percent of the cause, while 80 percent is the result of the patient's environment, which includes lifestyle, food choices, exercise habits, and stress levels. In other words, if your father or grandfather had diabetes and your mother or grandmother had Alzheimer's disease, you are not destined to develop these illnesses. If you place your body in an environment in which you have good sleep hygiene, eat nutritious foods, have a healthy exercise program, and mitigate your stress, you may be able to prevent activation of the gene that causes the disease. If you have already turned on the genes responsible for a pathological process, metabolic medicine can often address the underlying metabolic imbalances in order to treat the disease and not just mask the symptoms.

The following are a few examples of how this works.

First, let's say you have depression. Yes, you may need to take an antidepressant. Now, using a metabolic/anti-aging approach, we may be able to find the cause of your depression by measuring the nutritional building blocks of your neurotransmitters such as serotonin, dopamine, and norepinephrine. Testing may reveal that you do not have enough of a certain nutrient for your body to manufacture one of your neurotransmitters and this is why you have the depression. In this situation, giving you the nutrient or helping your body make the nutrient will then aid the body in manufacturing the neurotransmitter. Monitoring your neurotransmitter levels in this way can also help the doctor guide your medication selection. Many of the medications that are used for depression target a particular neurotransmitter. If it is known which neurotransmitter you are deficient in, then it is easier for the physician to choose the right medication for you.

Second, perhaps you have hair loss. Women, for example, may have hair loss due to any of the following reasons: deficiency of biotin (a B vitamin), low progesterone levels, abnormal thyroid levels, abnormal cortisol levels, or elevated DHT (dihydrotestosterone) levels. All of these deficiencies and imbalances can be treated by looking at the cause of the problem. There are other etiologies of hair loss, but, as with the previous, if the cause of the problem can be fixed, then the hair loss may resolve.

Third, insomnia is a common problem in modern life. In the Western world, more than sixty million people have insomnia. When you do not get enough sleep, it increases your risk of heart disease, diabetes, weight gain, and hypertension (high blood pressure). When you sleep poorly, your body does not have the time it needs to repair itself, which is a normal function of sleep. Most physicians agree that the average adult needs between seven and nine hours of sleep each night to detoxify the body, conserve energy, and maintain proper immune, neurological, and cognitive function. Now the science is here to look at the possible causes of poor sleep hygiene. Stress is a common cause. The level of cortisol (a hormone released during stress reactions) in your body can be measured by a simple saliva test and then normalized through metabolic treatments to address the cause of your insomnia. Hormonal imbalances are another common cause of insomnia. For women, low progesterone levels can be the origin of the insomnia, as can low estrogen levels. For men, low testosterone levels can affect sleeping pattern. For both men and women, other hormonal imbalances can be the foundation of a problem with falling asleep or waking up in the middle of the night. Abnormal DHEA (dehydroepiandrosterone) levels, abnormal thyroid levels, low melatonin levels, and low growth hormone levels can be the culprits. Something as simple as eating foods to which you are allergic, for example, gluten, can cause insomnia. Excess intake of caffeine, alcohol, additives found in chocolate, and spicy foods can create an etiology of sleeplessness. Likewise, a nutritional deficiency in copper, iron, magnesium, niacin, vitamin B6, or tryptophan may be the origin of your sleep disturbance. Again, in metabolic/anti-aging Medicine, the basis of the problem can be identified by new testing methods and, in many cases, treated.

This is not "Star Trek" medicine. Metabolic/anti-aging medicine is here today. If you are interested in seeing a doctor or other practitioner that is fellowship trained or has a master's degree in this field of medicine, look at the websites www.worldhealth.net or www.metabolic-anti-agingspecialist.com.

As you can see, there is great cause for optimism in today's world for what medicine has to offer, now and in the future.

DAWSON CHURCH:

Rewiring Your Brain for Optimism

In 1972, a young woman named Nancy was diagnosed with cervical cancer. By the time of her diagnosis, the cancer had metastasized to Stage 4, having spread to other places in her body. Her doctor gave her only a few months to live. She decided to leave her job, and spend the last of her days at home, finding as much peace as she could discover within herself.

Every morning Nancy felt called to take a long hot bath. She would lie in the tub for hours, in a dreamlike state, thinking the most positive thoughts she could imagine. She said to herself, "My body created this thing. It can un-create it too." She imagined little white stars floating down from heaven and washing through her body. Each time one of the stars touched a cancer cell, the sharp points of the star ruptured the cancer cell. Nancy began to feel stronger and more energetic. She began attending a meditation circle at a local church. She took long walks in the Sierra mountains where she lived.

Her thoughts began to shift, from impending death, to plans for the future. One day, after three months, she lay in her bath, the stars drifting through her mind and body, and realized that there were no more cancer cells for them to puncture. She felt vibrantly healthy. Nancy made an appointment with her physician, who was astonished to find that her body was free of cancer. "I already knew," she told me, ten years after all this occurred.

Dawson Church, PhD, is an award-winning author whose best-selling book *The Genie in Your Genes,* (www.GenieBestseller.com) has been hailed as a breakthrough in the field of epigenetics. He has published numerous scientific papers, with a focus on the remarkable self-healing mechanisms now emerging at the intersection of emotion and gene expression. He trains organizations to apply these breakthroughs for optimal health and athletic performance. His online resource is one of the most-visited complementary medicine sites on the Web. www.EFTuniverse.com

You See It When You Believe It

Nancy's story is one of many stories of healing from a book called *Soul Medicine* (www.SoulMedicine.net) that I was privileged to coauthor with my mentor Norm Shealy, MD, PhD. Dr. Shealy is a Harvard-trained neurosurgeon and founding president of the American Holistic Medical Association. We investigated hundreds of cases of so-called miraculous cures, and looked for the themes that were common to them all. We also looked for the qualities of an effective healer, and how you can work in a grand collaboration with your doctor, psychologist, life coach, and alternative medicine practitioner, to create a customized health plan that will support you in living the longest and healthiest life possible. Though you'll read some amazing statements in this article, it is based on hard science, published in peer-reviewed medical and psychological journals.

One of the discoveries Dr. Shealy and I have taken away from our extensive research is this: *You can't see it till you believe it.* Literally.

The old idea that you have to *see it before you believe it* is limited and often misleading. Until you believe that a possibility might exist, your brain is wired in such a way as to *exclude you seeing that possibility*, even if it's squirming and prancing before your very eyes in Glorious Technicolor. An intriguing example comes from accounts of the visit by Ferdinand Magellan to Tierra Del Fuego in 1520. He and his crew rowed ashore in dinghies, and were greeted by the indigenous crowds. The natives could not figure out where Magellan and his men had come from, despite a clear view of the masts and hulls of the sailing ships bobbing nearby in the bay. They pointed to the sky, wondering if these strange men had dropped from the heavens. Having never seen anything larger than a canoe, they had no wiring in their brains to comprehend the vision of a large oceangoing vessel.

Before you chuckle at their ignorance, consider one of scores of scientific studies that have been designed in order to examine human perception. This particular study examined the behavior of 148 British college students at a pub. Everything seemed normal to those students as they entered the pub: the tables and chairs, the bartender, the bottles, and the drinks. They ordered their favorites, and soon the effects of alcohol began to show up in their behavior. They became tipsy, with slurred speech and impaired balance.

Unbeknownst to the experimental group, their drinks contained absolutely no alcohol. The researchers had substituted tonic water for the alcohol. Because the students believed the drinks were alcoholic and would produce certain effects, those effects were produced. When those who had been served fake alcohol were confronted with the truth, some of them swore that the researchers were mistaken, that they must have been drinking real alcohol. Beliefs create behavior.

One of the scientific explanations for this phenomenon is that human beings have more neurological wiring to tell their senses what to perceive than the amount of wiring that runs from the senses to the brain. In fact, there are about ten times as many neural bundles running *from* your brain *to* your sensory organs than run in the opposite direction. In my book *The Genie in Your Genes* (www.GenieBestseller.com), I summarize some of the many scientific studies that show the distortions of perception that this wiring scheme produces.

Figure 1. – Good or evil? Reality doesn't change, though our perception may.

You might yourself have seen graphic images that appear to be one object, in which another is cleverly hidden. The image in figure 1 is one such example. At first, you can see only the obvious word. But when the belief is implanted in your mind, by telling you that another word exists, suddenly you are able to see it. In a cooking class, you might be tasting a stew, and a gourmet chef points out a subtle flavor. Once you understand how to attune your taste buds, you perceive the flavor. You might be looking at a cloud when a friend tells you they see a horse shape there. Till they pointed it out, you did not see it. When they tell you, suddenly the horse becomes obvious. Believing is seeing.

The path to a happy future for you, me, and the rest of humankind is blocked by three great obstacles: beliefs, Mother Nature, and the skeptical tendencies within science. Now that we've looked at the role of belief, let's take a look at the next two and how they influence our ability to create optimistic belief systems for ourselves.

Anecdotal Reports and Medical Advances

Skepticism dominates in many fields, to the detriment of human well-being. In the field of medicine, innovations take an average of thirty years to go from laboratory to clinic. What stands in the path of progress is a belief system that requires reams of proof before any innovation is admitted, rather than an open-minded willingness to examine the evidence for healing. Ideas that run counter to the prevailing wisdom are often viciously attacked. This impedes objective assessment of their value while their evidence base is small, and prevents them from developing an evidence base large enough to compete with established treatments.

There are fields like computing, in which the opposite is true. Improvements are eagerly seized on and immediately implemented, resulting in rapid progress. Competitors strive vigorously to beat each other at making the fastest progress. Moore's law states that the processing power of computers doubles every two years. The digital watch on my wrist contains more computing power than the huge room-sized mainframe computers of the 1980s. Such progress is possible to minds that constantly scan the present moment for evidence of improvement, that believe in unseen potentials for change, and then optimistically search for ways to develop them. This mind-set, which is taken for granted in the world of technological innovation, is worse than absent in the field of medicine. It's actively opposed. Instead, a skeptical, pessimistic mind-set prevails. One physician told me that, while studying at Stanford Medical School, he treated a patient who had a miraculous recovery much like the earlier story of Nancy. He introduced the other students in his class to the patient, and the group made excited plans to discuss the phenomenon with their professor during grand rounds.

The day arrived, and the students told the professor about the amazing case. His face twisted into a sneer and he dismissed the whole matter by spitting out a single word: "Anecdotal." He then went on with his lecture, unperturbed. The students realized that such events were not welcome in that class, and never brought them up again, even if they occurred. As Winston Churchill once observed, "Most men stumble over the truth at some time in their lives. They then pick themselves up and proceed as if nothing had happened!"

Intel is the company that invented the microprocessor, the chip that lies at the heart of every electronic device from your smart phone to your car. Andy Grove, Intel's former CEO, is scathing in his comparisons of the computer field with the medical field. He says the latter creates "conformity of thoughts and values," which leads to "more sameness and less innovation." In the famous words of physicist Max Planck, science progresses "funeral by funeral" as an old generation with fixed beliefs dies off, and a new generation replaces it.

Another inspiring story comes from Patti, who used EFT to help her become cancer-free. EFT, short for Emotional Freedom Techniques, is a stress-reduction technique that is used by many millions of people worldwide. It involves remembering stressful events, and then tapping with the fingertips on twelve acupressure points. While it can be learned in a few minutes, it's extremely powerful, and has been used successfully to reduce the anxiety that accompanies much disease. Patti wrote, "My doctor diagnosed me with advanced terminal breast cancer. He advised an aggressive course of surgery, chemotherapy, and radiation. I've worked around the health field a long time. I know how terrible the quality of life is for people on this program. He told me I had four months, max, to live. I decided to try EFT instead; I'd used it for minor things.

I saw [EFT founder] Gary Craig several times, and I tapped on myself almost every day, often many times a day. When I went back eight months later, the doctors could find no trace of cancer in my body. They found scar tissue there instead. He advised me that this would be a great time to have surgery to remove the scar tissue, and then a course of radiation. I laughed. I'd already decided not to. He got pretty mad at my decision."

Patti tells her story on-camera in the DVD *EFT for Serious Diseases* on the EFT website (www.EFTuniverse.com), and it's very moving to witness how this courageous woman was able to improve her life so radically in so short a time with a simple self-help technique.

A humane and progressive medical system would mine these stories for clues as to why Nancy and Patti recovered when their physicians gave them terminal diagnoses. Scientists would scour the accounts of survivors to determine the factors common to their survival, and look for ways to apply these lessons to improve the lives of other patients. Instead, such anecdotes are usually met with the kind hostile skepticism typified by that Stanford professor. They do not conform to the prevailing paradigm of medical belief, and so they are dismissed. In this way, lifesaving discoveries that might improve the lives of millions of people are delayed for decades, and sometimes lost forever.

Helping Veterans with PTSD

Andy Grove also lambastes the denial of funding and promotion to risk takers, which can result in "more sameness and less innovation." I've seen this firsthand at the Iraq Vets Stress Project, which offers help to veterans with PTSD (posttraumatic stress disorder). It's a network of about two hundred researchers, therapists, and life coaches who offer free or low-cost help to veterans and their family members. At the Stress Project, we use EFT, the same method that helped Patti, as well as associated methods from the field of energy medicine. We've tested our work in several pilot studies as well as full-blown randomized controlled trials, and the results have been remarkable. We've found that 86 percent of veterans who enter our program with "clinical," or full-blown PTSD symptoms, are in the normal range after just six sessions of EFT. We've then followed their progress for as long as three years, and find that they don't relapse. Their families are usually awed by the changes they see in their loved ones, and overjoyed at their progress.

Yet even with these results and this evidence, adoption of such techniques by health-care systems has been very slow, and we've been turned down for every government grant we've applied for. We're hoping it doesn't take thirty years to implement them, and several U.S. Congress members have held hearings on why such a successful method is unavailable to the majority of veterans. You can hear some of the congressional testimony at the website of the Iraq Vets Stress Project (www. StressProject.org). Yet for the moment, the old paradigm rules, skepticism prevails, and hundreds of thousands of veterans continue to suffer from PTSD, blocked from effective treatment by a system that values conformity above innovation.

How You're Hardwired for Pessimism

Changing your default settings from pessimistic paranoia to optimistic happiness is very difficult. Your brain is wired to worry. Your brain is the pinnacle of Mother Nature's creation. She's perfected it during the course of millions of years of evolution. Consider your distant primate ancestors, living in the Great Plains of Africa. Those who were the most paranoid were the most likely to survive, and pass on their genes to their progeny. They were pessimists, always wondering when the next tiger would jump out of the bushes, the next snake slither out of the grass, the next tribe attack without warning. Pessimism worked very well for their survival. By successfully imagining future possible threats, they were able to foresee incipient peril, and avoid it.

By way of contrast, the tribes that were full of easygoing optimists were more likely to die out. Their laid-back attitude might have make them much more pleasant companions, but their lack of anticipation of danger was a drawback that made them unlikely to survive in those circumstances. In a world full of real tigers, lions, and snakes, they were the first to die out, and their genes were less likely to be passed on to subsequent generations. Generation by generation, the most paranoid pessimists survived.

Today, you and I, the end result of this process, are wired for worry, even though predators have vanished from our daily existence. Worry is hardwired into the very structure of our brains. The main business of the limbic system in the middle of our brains is to assess the environment and respond to threats. The amygdala, an almond-shaped part of the midbrain, is like a scout, scanning the horizon for danger. The hippocampus, another midbrain structure, is like a military analyst, filing away images of every possible threat.

When information comes into the hippocampus, existing images are retrieved and compared to the incoming data, to find out if this input matches any stored memories of previous threats to our survival. If it is perceived to be threatening, a signal is sent downstream to the base of the brain, which governs all of our automatic functions such as respiration, circulation, digestion, and reproduction. Our bodies go into high gear to ready themselves to respond to the threat. If we have the ability to calm ourselves, our thinking brain, the big lobes at the front of our head, can stop the signal traveling down the spine. It can reason, for example, "That wasn't gunfire, it was a car backfiring." If we aren't able to interrupt the signal, our bodies gear up for the fight-or-flight (FF) response.

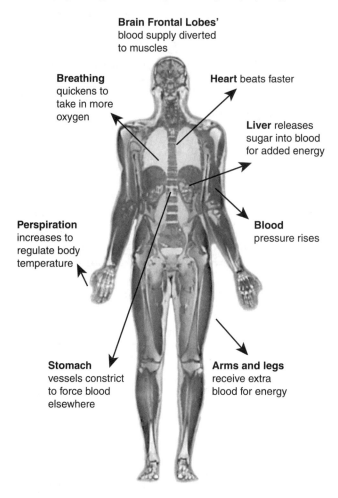

Figure 2. – What fight-or-flight looks like in your body.

Stress Kills

Though it was fantastically useful for our ancestors, enabling them to survive, the FF response is killing us today. When I say "killing us," I'm not speaking figuratively, but literally. Worry kills.

Here's how. With no real predators to discover, our neurological threat-assessment machinery busies itself with imaginary ones. We watch news reports of disasters that have no bearing whatsoever on our daily lives. We obsess about potential problems, most of which will never materialize. In a world without real tigers, we fill our minds with paper tigers.

The problem with this way of functioning is that your body has no way of telling that the paper tiger in your mind is not a real threat. It responds to the image of a paper tiger with the same surge of adrenaline, the same tensing of the muscles, the same speed-up of the heart rate, and the same dumping of sugar into the bloodstream that would be required if a real tiger leaped out of the bushes.

One of my fields of study is the hormonal, neurological, and genetic changes that occur when we worry, or fall into negative and pessimistic thoughts. In a series of studies and papers, in collaboration with researchers at several universities and institutions, I've begun to help map the changes that occur at the most fundamental levels of molecular biology. One place that change shows up right away is in your nervous system. I've hooked up scores of people to machines that measure the balance between the stress-responsive part of the nervous system and the relaxation-inducing part. When you have a negative thought, your body goes into stress in a microsecond. Consider the image below. It shows the neural patterns of a person feeling anger, and one feeling appreciation. The angry person has a pattern that looks like the jagged peaks of a craggy mountain range; the loving person has one that looks like a calm expanse of rolling hills.

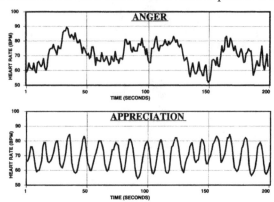

Figure 3. – Anger EEG readout of Heart Rate Variability (above). Appreciation EEG readout of Heart Rate Variability (below).

When you're in that angry state, your body also produces greater amounts of stress hormones like adrenaline (epinephrine) and cortisol. To obtain the precursors to build these stress hormones, your body strips molecules from the hormones that repair your cells and help them stay young and healthy. That's why stressed people age faster; the cell repair hormones that their bodies require are being cannibalized to produce stress hormones instead.

The results of stress also show up in the genes that contain the code to build those hormones. One graphic way of illustrating this is to look at the faces of identical twins. Since these twins have an identical genetic code at conception, you might assume that they have very much the same health history and aging profile. They should have exactly the same genetic pre-disposition to disease, and live the same number of years.

Figure 4. Identical (monozygotic) twins in childhood.

In practice, this does not happen. Identical twins die, on average, more than ten years apart. One may get cancer while the other does not. Figures 4 and 5 show you twins at different stages of their lives; you can see that they look more and more different as they age, and the results of stress show up in their lives. In one much-discussed example, researchers measured the biological age of a set of identical twin women in their late thirties. One twin had a fairly easy life. The other did not; her husband developed Huntington's disease and she was his caregiver. He became abusive as his disease progressed. He eventually died, and by then she'd gained a lot of excess weight, and started smoking. The researchers who measured the cellular age of the two women were stunned to find out that the stressed twin was biologically ten years older than the unstressed twin, even though their chronological age was identical.

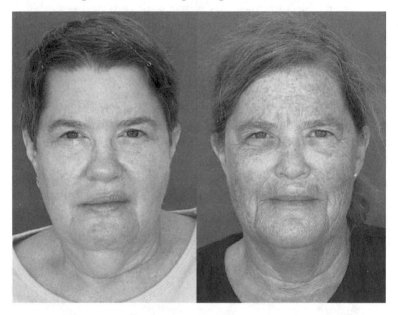

Figure 5. Fifty-year-old monozygotic twins may show marked external physiological differences.

Stress, worry, and pessimism affect your body at the most basic levels. High levels of the stress hormone cortisol are associated with many diseases, and accelerated aging. They are difficult to escape. Have you ever been upset about a problem and tried to talk yourself out of worry? You probably failed, because that worry is located at that basic FF survival level of functioning. Survival trumps thinking every time. When you're stressed and worried, your thinking mind is unable to intervene. Under extreme stress, up to 70 percent of the blood drains from our frontal lobes, the conscious executive part of our brains. Neuroscientist Joseph LeDoux calls this, "The hostile takeover of consciousness by emotion." When 70 percent of the blood has drained out of your forebrain, your intelligence level drops precipitously. That's why your grandmother told you, "Never make a decision when you're upset!" Stress can even trigger genetic diseases like cancer; in the photo below, one identical twin developed leukemia and the other did not. The only major difference in their lives that physicians could find was that the sick twin had suffered the stress of a tonsillectomy at the age of six months.

*Figure 6. Identical (monozygotic) twins. at age six. One developed
leukemia at age two, while the other did not.*

The fact that strong feelings hijack our best conscious intentions is
why most attempts to change human behavior simply fail. Our survival
imperative is biologically hardwired. We go on vacation and relax, and
vow to stay relaxed when we return to work. But we don't. We go to a
church conference, or a weekend meditation retreat, and come back on
Sunday night feeling full of love for our fellow human beings. By Monday
noon, we're ready to send them before a firing squad.

So pep talks, New Year's resolutions, religious vows of chastity,
inspirational books, scriptural admonitions, and motivational talks rarely
stick. They're overwhelmed by the strength of the survival imperative.
When our midbrains are stimulated, we can't talk ourselves out of our
worry, negative thinking, lusts, spiteful words, angry retaliation, resentment, and impulsive behavior.

That's the bad news. The good news is that it's possible to rewire your
brain, just as you might update the wiring in your house. You could take
out all the old wiring in a building and install new and better wiring. So,
too, can you rewire your old patterns of thought and behavior. You can
literally change your brain.

The idea that we can actually reshape the neural networks in our
brains is a relatively recent scientific breakthrough. In 2000, a research
physician named Eric Kandel won the Nobel Prize for Medicine for
showing that neural pathways can rewire themselves. Not only was this

a revolutionary discovery, but also the speed of the neural process was astounding to physiologists who believed that our brains were static in adulthood. Kandel showed that in as little as *one hour* of repeated stimulation of a neural pathway, the number of connections could *double*. So as you practice the violin, you build new neural pathways that facilitate that skill. As you learn a new language, you quickly lay down new neural grids. As you think pessimistic or optimistic thoughts, you grow the neurons required to be that way automatically. In order to change, you have to deliberately feel optimism whenever you automatically feel pessimism. That sounds like a crazy assignment, and it runs counter to the survival skills you inherited from hundreds of generations of ancestors. How do you do it?

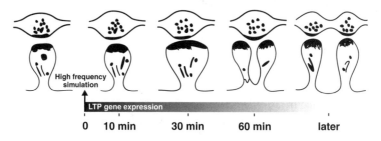

Figure 7. – Within an hour of gene expression in response to environmental stimulation, one synaptic connection has become two.

At the Iraq Vets Stress Project, we work with veterans who have had years, sometimes decades, of debilitating PTSD. Their survival behaviors are deeply engrained in their behavior and their biology. Yet with EFT, they're able to set themselves free from a lifetime of suffering in just a few sessions. It's been an amazing process for me to watch, and to realize that PTSD is reversible. We've learned a lot about how to shift even long-held behaviors, and how to grow the new neural pathways that will lead to optimism and inner peace. We've learned how to help people believe it before they see it, and to make the changes in belief and behavior that are required to produce the evidence. I hope by now you've become intrigued by the possibility of rewiring your own brain in this way. In the final section of this chapter, I share with you some of the practical methods you can use to shift your habitual ways of thinking and behaving.

The Mechanics of Rewiring Your Brain

What are some of the things you can do to grab hold of the best innovations in wellness and use them to improve your health right now? I'm always on the lookout for practical discoveries, and I've discovered a few simple methods that are safe, require no training, don't need fancy and expensive technology, don't require belief, and make use of the body's innate self-healing systems.

These practices can make a big difference in your stress level, and some of them take only a minute or less. The very first time you do them, they will start to rewire your neural net for happiness and optimism. You will feel the difference in your body immediately. Try them now, even as you read each one. Test them by rating how happy you feel on a scale of 0 to 10 right now, and again after you try them. They require no prior experience, practice, training, gadgets, or belief in order to be effective. If that sounds too good to be true, believe it anyway! I've tested thousands of people, read many papers in peer-reviewed medical and psychology journals, and published research of my own that attests to the amazing results that can be achieved by a few easy-to-learn Quick Fixes. Here they are:

Quick Fix #1: Slow your breathing to ten seconds per breath. A breathing rate of ten seconds per breath will instantly make you feel calmer. That's a five-second inbreath, followed by a five-second outbreath. If you perform the addition, that's six breaths per minute. This breathing rate has been found to balance the relaxation part of the nervous system, called the parasympathetic, with the stress part, called the sympathetic. In the illustration of the brain waves of the angry person and the appreciative person, a pattern like that of the appreciative person can be attained by this pace of breathing. When you start breathing at the rate of six breaths per minute, your body calms down automatically, because it knows that you can't be facing any real threats if you're breathing so calmly. If you have a thought or a situation that makes you feel stressed, slow your breathing to six breaths per minute, and your body will recognize that the thought (paper tiger) is not an objective survival problem (real tiger). Every time you do this, you add a few more connections to the wiring in your brain that programs it to treat thoughts as neutral input, not as alarm bells that turn on the entire machinery of stress everywhere in the body. You break down cortisol and start making cell repair hormones. Feel how different you feel once you breathe at this slow pace. Do this every time you think a stressful thought.

Quick Fix #2: Relax your tongue on the floor of your mouth. Our tongues are usually tense, touching the roof of our mouths. When you think a highly stressful thought, your jaw clenches and your tongue becomes rigid. But when you pair that thought with a loose, relaxed tongue, you tell your body that the thought is not reality. That breaks the association between the thought, and the alarm response in the body. You then build a few more neural connections to reinforce the fact that the thought is not a command to your body to go into high gear to avoid a predator. You can't get angry while your tongue is loose on the floor of your mouth. Try it! You simply can't do it. So whenever you feel stressed, relax your tongue, and your whole body will automatically relax along with it.

Quick Fix #3: Imagine a big white space behind your eyes. This brings your brain state from a predominance of beta waves, fast brain rhythms that are associated with anxious "monkey mind," to a predominance of alpha waves. Alpha waves are associated with being alert, but still relaxed and calm. Beta waves are associated with cortisol and stress genes, while alpha waves are associated with cell repair. Just picture a big white space behind your eyes, and you'll feel calmer, no matter what stressful signals are coming from the environment around you, or from your own unruly thoughts.

Quick Fix #4: Tap acupressure points on your skin with your fingertips. Acupressure points are places of very low resistance on the surface of your skin. They have about one two-thousandth of the electrical resistance of the surrounding skin. This low resistance means that signals can travel through them much more easily than they can travel through areas of high resistance. Tapping on your skin generates a type of electrical energy called piezoelectricity. That's the kind of electricity generated by mechanical friction, such as the mechanical "clicker" used to light a gas oven. When you generate this electricity by tapping on these low-resistance points, the current travels more easily through your body. Tapping sends a calming signal to your body, even when you're in the mist of "stink think." It tells your body that the stink think isn't really a threat to your existence. Earlier, you met Patti, who recovered from terminal cancer using EFT, the most popular form of acupoint tapping. You can download the instructions for how to use EFT from the EFT website EFTuniverse.com and be up and running within thirty minutes. Try it, and you'll be amazed at the results. If it can help veterans with chronic clinical PTSD, it can help you.

An Optimistic You in a Happy World

I am a great fan of techniques like mindfulness meditation, contemplation, and prayer. They also reduce stress and, over time, they can rewire your neural net. Research has shown that Tibetan Buddhist monks who are accomplished meditators have more neurons in the parts of their brain associated with happiness than non-meditators possess. These techniques require practice, however, sometimes for years. They may also require religious faith, which you might or might not possess. By comparison, the four simple Quick Fixes I've given here can de-stress you in a few seconds, without any need for belief, faith, or practice. They're triage, designed for use in difficult situations, while the more demanding techniques form a solid lifetime platform for stress reduction. You need both.

In the last few years, I've restructured my life to enable me to spend most of my time promoting simple stress-reduction techniques. I believe it's the activity through which I can do the most social good. If millions more people learn to reduce their stress levels, we can have a more positive future as a species. A healthier, happier human race means a more optimistic future for me, my three children, my community, my country, and the world. Optimism is good for us all. Have the compassion for yourself to practice these methods of reducing your stress level. It's possible for you to enjoy a much happier life. Can our species make the jump to joy in our lifetimes? Believe it, and you'll see it!

ALBERT EINSTEIN:
On Freedom

I know that it is a hopeless undertaking to debate about fundamental value judgments. For instance if someone approves, as a goal, the extirpation of the human race from the earth, one cannot refute such a viewpoint on rational grounds. But if there is agreement on certain goals and values, one can argue rationally about the means by which these objectives may be attained. Let us, then, indicate two goals which may well be agreed upon by nearly all who read these lines.

1. Those instrumental goods which should serve to maintain the life and health of all human beings should be produced by the least possible labor of all.

2. The satisfaction of physical needs is indeed the indispensable precondition of a satisfactory existence, but in itself it is not enough. In order to be content men must also have the possibility of developing their intellectual and artistic powers to whatever extent accord with their personal characteristics and abilities.

The first of these two goals requires the promotion of all knowledge relating to the laws of nature and the laws of social processes, that is, the promotion of all scientific endeavor. For scientific endeavor is a natural whole the parts of which mutually support one another in a way which, to be sure, no one can anticipate. However, the progress of science presupposes the possibility of unrestricted communication of all results and judgments — freedom of expression and instruction in all realms of

Albert Einstein (1879–1955), genius physicist and philosopher, is best known for his theories of relativity, which transformed the field of physics. His work earned him the appellation "the father of modern physics" and led to him winning the Nobel Prize in physics in 1921. German by birth, he fled Nazi Germany in 1933 and subsequently became an American citizen, teaching at the Institute for Advanced Study in Princeton, New Jersey, until his death. His writing was far-ranging, from hundreds of scientific and nonscientific papers to books offering his views on religion, politics, science, and society. In 1999, *Time* magazine named him Person of the Century.

intellectual endeavor. By freedom I understand social conditions of such a kind that the expression of opinions and assertions about general and particular matters of knowledge will not involve dangers or serious disadvantages for him who expresses them. This freedom of communication is indispensable for the development and extension of scientific knowledge, a consideration of much practical import. In the first instance it must be guaranteed by law. But laws alone cannot secure freedom of expression; in order that every man may present his views without penalty there must be a spirit of tolerance in the entire population. Such an ideal of external liberty can never be fully attained but must be sought unremittingly if scientific thought, and philosophical and creative thinking in general, are to be advanced as far as possible.

If the second goal, that is, the possibility of the spiritual development of all individuals, is to be secured, a second kind of outward freedom is necessary. Man should not have to work for the achievement of the necessities of life to such an extent that he has neither time nor strength for personal activities. Without this second kind of outward liberty, freedom of expression is useless for him. Advances in technology would provide the possibility of this kind of freedom if the problem of a reasonable division of labor were solved.

The development of science and of the creative activities of the spirit in general requires still another kind of freedom, which may be characterized as inward freedom. It is this freedom of the spirit which consists in the independence of thought from the restrictions of authoritarian and social prejudices as well as from unphilosophical routinizing and habit in general. This inward freedom is an infrequent gift of nature and a worthy objective for the individual. Yet the community can do much to further this achievement, too, at least by not interfering with its development. Thus schools may interfere with the development of inward freedom through authoritarian influences and through imposing on young people excessive spiritual burdens; on the other hand schools may favor such freedom by encouraging independent thought. Only if outward and inner freedom are constantly and consciously pursued is there a possibility of spiritual development and perfection and thus of improving man's outward and inner life.

Amit Goswami:
Quantum Optimism

The metaphysics on which we base our perception of the world today is pessimistic. The metaphysics of scientific materialism that is now the foundation of all our sciences and social systems recognizes only the existence of matter, which necessarily limits our choices and therefore our ability to solve the planetary crises facing the human race. The material world provides only one kind of experience: sensing. The human faculties of feeling, thinking, and intuiting are left out of this scientific model. (As identified by Carl Jung, people exhibit four psychological preferences in perceiving the world: sensing, feeling, thinking, and intuiting.)

Quantum physics, the new science, makes it possible to recognize that there are four universes for our experiences: the physical, the vital, the mental, and the supramental. The physical, we sense. The vital, we feel. The mental, we think. The supramental, we intuit. In this way, quantum physics helps us put together the entire human experience within one science. When we call upon these resources as well as the concepts of the new science, solutions to the drastic problems occurring in all our social institutions and systems suddenly become possible. We enter the realm of quantum optimism.

Amit Goswami, PhD, is a physicist, pioneer of "science within consciousness," and author of groundbreaking books, which have been translated in sixteen languages. His books include *Quantum Mechanics*, used in universities throughout the world; *The Self-Aware Universe*, presenting a new paradigm of science based on the primacy of consciousness; *The Visionary Window*, demonstrating how science and spirituality can be integrated; *The Quantum Doctor*, integrating conventional and alternative medicine; and *How Quantum Activism Can Save Civilization*. As a practitioner of spirituality and transformation, he terms himself a "quantum activist." He is featured in the films *What the Bleep Do We Know!?* and *The Quantum Activist*. www.amitgoswami.org. Photo credit: bluedot productions

Waves of Possibility

The word "quantum" was used in 1900 by Max Planck to describe a discrete quantity of energy. The true implication of the concept, however, became clear only with the work of Einstein five years later and Niels Bohr in 1913. Both of these physicists suggested something that seemed quite impossible at the time. Einstein suggested that light is both wave, as was well known at that time, and particle. Waves spread out, unlike particles, which travel a trajectory. Bohr suggested that when an electron jumps from one atomic orbit to another, it does not go through the intervening space. This implies discontinuous movement, a phenomenon that cannot be explained by Newtonian physics. Later developments indicated that even matter is both wave and particle. The waves, it was explained, are not ordinary waves. They are waves of possibility.

Here is the crunch. There is no material interaction that could ever transform these possibilities into actual events of experience. The question occurs then: how can waves become actual events/particles that we see when we measure these waves? This problem became the absolutely impossible problem to solve within the philosophy of scientific materialism that people still believe in, which says that everything is matter and material interaction.

The Hungarian mathematician John von Neumann suggested that a nonmaterial consciousness chooses out of the possibilities the actuality that we see. This could be the solution to the dilemma because it is a fact that our choice, our looking, does convert possibility to actuality. But there is an objection to this, too. Philosophically, this solution is untenable because how does a nonmaterial consciousness interact with something that is material? It became a question of finding an intermediary that serves as a signal that involves the exchange of energy. But no such energy exchange ever takes place—a physical law.

The solution that I suggested in 1989 is that consciousness is the ground of being, and matter is possibility of consciousness itself. When consciousness chooses, it chooses from itself, which does not require a signal, does not require an exchange of energy. Consider how spiritual, how mystical this statement is. Consciousness as the ground of being is the fundamental concept that all spiritual traditions accept.

Changing by Choosing the New

As we make decisions, as we focus on certain things, as we direct our consciousness in certain directions—that is what precipitates the particular outcomes. In a single quantum event, we cannot avoid the idea that we can choose the new; we can create so that a completely new actuality comes to pass. This is quantum optimism. The new science tells us that we can always choose the new and, therefore, change.

When politicians and anybody else are talking about change, they should understand that real change is impossible under the aegis of scientific materialism. In fact, the implicit influence of scientific materialism has hampered our creativity. Innovation is at an all-time low in America, a country that is supposed to be a hotbed of creativity. The idea that we are material machines, that we don't have free will, has hurt us. It has not only taken away our creativity, it has also removed values and ethics from our behavior.

We can see the loss of creativity in all fields of human endeavor. Consider the field of medicine. The biggest innovations that are going on in medicine right now belong to the field of alternative medicine. Alternative medicine tells us there are nonmaterial energies to which we have access. For example, there is vital energy, *qi*, the energy associated with our feelings. It is this vital energy that heals in such procedures as acupuncture or homeopathy. But the medical profession has been extremely reluctant to look into anything nonmaterial because scientific materialism is entrenched in the belief system on which the profession operates. The medical field cannot deny that acupuncture and homeopathy work, however. As a result, these modalities are legal, but they have to function in impaired ways. For example, insurance companies do not usually cover these treatments. If we just accepted alternative medicine in an integrative way to complement allopathic medicine, the cost of medicine would immediately and substantially decrease. This is especially true for chronic diseases, which constitute some 80 percent of all our diseases.

Do Be Do Be Do

The new science does not deny the benefits of having the material universe but, rather, recognizes that the constant shift between doing (making material representations of the subtle energies) and being (in undivided consciousness and its possibilities, in a state that depth psychologists call "the unconscious") is how we draw the best of our creative ideas into manifestation and make rapid change. Alternating doing and being, "do be do be do," is the key.

It is in the unconscious state of being that the power of quantum processing comes about. When we are in the "be" state, when we are not doing anything, then we are not choosing from the possibilities making actuality. Possibilities exist as waves. What happens when we are being rather than doing is that the waves expand and become a bigger reservoir of possibilities. Who wouldn't want the chance of choosing from a bigger reservoir of possibilities? But by living a do-do-do kind of life, we ignorantly do not allow the possibility waves to grow.

CHAPTER TWENTY-ONE

This has to change. The immediate benefit of alternating between being and doing is that our creativity will go up by a substantial amount. We will be able to solve problems that may seem insoluble to us. Consider the current drastic situation of economic meltdown. The old-fashioned economic style of consumerism based on scientific materialism is not working. This kind of situation requires a shift in the context of the problem. This is what materialists do not understand. The shift in the context of the problem is impossible to achieve through the Newtonian scientific method (you can think of it as a mechanistic model of creativity) that materialists use for problem solving. It ignores the fundamental strength of human creativity, which is quantum processing. Therefore, every idea is tried out one by one. This is inefficient when a plethora of often-conflicting ideas is required to solve the problem, as in the case of our economic meltdown. With quantum processing, you get to look at many possibilities at once. In the Newtonian scientific method, you get to look at only one possibility at a time. That is such a limitation. Innovation that can solve real problems in real time just cannot happen in that way. We've got to use quantum creativity, the power of quantum or unconscious processing to regain our innovative culture.

I am optimistic because many experiments in different areas of science have now demonstrated signal-less communication, the so-called nonlocal phenomena, which supports the concept of consciousness as the ground of being. One prediction we have is the interaction of consciousness outside of material interaction, which is called downward causation. Characteristics such as quantum nonlocality and discontinuity (as mentioned earlier regarding the quantum leaping movement of electrons) are special because material interaction (called upward causation) cannot even simulate them. So whenever we have discovered discontinuity or quantum nonlocality, we have actually discovered the causal power (called downward causation) of consciousness.

An example of creative quantum discontinuity is spontaneous healing without medical intervention. This is such a fantastic example of a sudden movement that one cannot deny it. People have long recognized such leaps in the creative process. There is a stage in creativity when insights suddenly arrive. Nonlocal communication such as telepathy is another example.

If it's true that consciousness is nonlocal, capable of nonlocal downward causation, then there should be brain-to-brain electrical information transfer. This has been demonstrated in some two-dozen objective experiments going all the way to the pioneering experiment by the Mexican neurophysiologist Jacobo Grinberg. This is an amazing verification of quantum nonlocality. If this does not open our eyes to new ideas, what will?

Moving from the Problem Space to the Solution Space

What makes me optimistic is that when you take this new science seriously, if consciousness is the ground of being, it can contain not only material possibilities, but also other possibilities that we experience. As noted earlier, scientific materialism only grants us one kind of experience — sensing — while the new science embraces all four universes and all four experiences: the physical, the vital, the mental, and the supramental. When we apply this idea to economics, for example, we open up vital economics, mental economics, and supramental economics. We can address not only our material needs but also our needs for exploring these subtle domains, which are still relatively unexplored. That will revolutionize and solve the current difficulties of our material economics, where matter is the only need that we satisfy through economic transactions.

This illustrates the optimism to be found in the new science. In the old paradigm thinking, we have crises and we cannot solve the crises. With the new science, we immediately start seeing solutions. All of a sudden, we have moved from the problem space to the solution space.

Accessing the vital, the mental, and the supramental requires self-transformation, which begins with moving out of a materialistic worldview into a quantum worldview.

In my case, I went on the path of discovery and the discoveries themselves were part of my transformative experience. For example, the whole journey started for me at a conference where I was giving an invited talk. I spent the whole day being jealous of how other people were presenting much better than I. I got so upset by all this jealous energy that I finished an entire packet of Tums. The conference center was on Monterey Bay and, seeking relief from my upset, I went outside. Looking out at the water, a thought suddenly came to me — this was a discontinuous thought, no doubt, a creative quantum leap experience. The thought was: why do I live this way?

I realized that my personal life and my professional life had become totally disconnected. My professional life had absolutely nothing to do with real problems of real people — nothing to do with economics, nothing to do with politics, nothing to do with healing, nothing to do with spirituality, even nothing to do with real liberal arts education. I didn't want to live like that; I didn't want to work like that.

That's what began the journey. Soon after, I found the quantum measurement problem to solve and the solution came as an insight. This creative experience has set me on my way for a long time now.

The answer comes as insight and then you manifest the insight in your work, sometimes in other aspects of your life. For example, one of my insights was that consciousness is the ground of being, and that this is the new paradigm, the metaphysical basis of everything. With that insight, I also immediately felt that the manifestation of it in scientific papers and books and even the change of paradigm was only part of the manifestation. The manifestation had to happen within people as well. The idea came to me that I must participate in transforming myself and to do that I had to integrate the new paradigm. Integration naturally entails self-transformation, for that is the only way you can integrate the outer and the inner. The outer experience is quite objective and we can do it in a dispassionate way. When it comes to the inner experience, however, we've got to meet all of our experience that happens internally, not only thinking but also feeling.

For the first time in my life, I became aware that it is important to integrate feelings and thinking. We have a preponderance of negative emotions in our brains, in our brain circuits, so we easily respond in a negative way. I began to ask in every situation: how do I respond in a positive way? The finding startled me because there was no way I could respond positively all the time unless I made a positive emotional brain circuit in my own brain. We cannot overcome our brain circuits just by thinking. That takes the work of self-transformation. So I began this arduous work. Yes, self-transformation is arduous, but the reward is absolutely amazing. Negative becomes balanced with positive, and you can open yourself up to creativity as much as you want, to spirituality as much as you want.

The Return of Optimism

If two million people did this in a collective way — self-transformation as a collective enterprise — then we could change the entire morphogenetic field that makes the brains of the human race. The resulting changes in the human brain would be nonlocal — that is, outside of space and time — so they could be shared by future people and by the entire human race. This is the reason I am super optimistic.

When you look at global nonlocal connection, one thing can be quite puzzling. If we are nonlocally in communication with everybody, then the amount of communication would be astronomical, beyond the capacity of the brain. So there must be constraint. Three physicists — Einstein, Podolsky, and Rosen — actually discovered this constraint a long time ago. They found that only when two objects interact locally do they become correlated, and then later on they will still be correlated and correlate in such a way that communication is possible. But local interaction begins the whole thing. So how do we locally interact with two million people?

Now look at how wonderfully synchronistic the movement of consciousness is. At the same time that we have developed quantum physics and the idea of quantum nonlocal communication, we have the Internet, which is a local device by which we can connect as many people as we want. So we have a local brain. The local interaction gives us the capacity for nonlocal communication and nonlocal transformation. That will produce changes in our brains and consequent changes in the morphogenetic field, also nonlocal. These nonlocal changes are outside of space and time, so anyone in the future can benefit from the changes.

The new science also gives us a new theory of evolution. The dominant theory, Darwin's determination, is a pessimistic theory of evolution. That's all you can get if you start with a pessimistic physics like Newtonian physics. In physics based on consciousness, however, if you develop a new biology that is also based on consciousness, you get the idea of one complete evolution, and that will bring optimism back. What does evolution do? It takes us further and further in terms of the capacity for the positive. That is evolution. Evolution is very positive. It takes us toward better utilization of the energies of love, better ability to live by ethics, better ability in ecology, and better ability to respond to spiritual matters. That is our future.

Tales of Optimism

STEVE JOBS:

Stay Hungry, Stay Foolish

I'm honored to be with you today for your commencement from one of the finest universities in the world. Truth be told, I never graduated from college and this is the closest I've ever gotten to a college graduation.

Today I want to tell you three stories from my life. That's it. No big deal. Just three stories. The first story is about connecting the dots.

I dropped out of Reed College after the first six months but then stayed around as a drop-in for another eighteen months or so before I really quit. So why did I drop out? It started before I was born. My biological mother was a young, unwed graduate student, and she decided to put me up for adoption. She felt very strongly that I should be adopted by college graduates, so everything was all set for me to be adopted at birth by a lawyer and his wife, except that when I popped out, they decided at the last minute that they really wanted a girl. So my parents, who were on a waiting list, got a call in the middle of the night asking, "We've got an unexpected baby boy. Do you want him?" They said, "Of course." My biological mother found out later that my mother had never graduated from college and that my father had never graduated from high school. She refused to sign the final adoption papers. She only relented a few months later when my parents promised that I would go to college.

This was the start in my life. And seventeen years later, I did go to college, but I naïvely chose a college that was almost as expensive as

Steve Jobs, wizard inventor, cofounded (with Steve Wozniak) the Apple computer company, which went on to produce such innovative products as the Macintosh, the iMac, and the iPhone. He is cited as primary or co-inventor in over 230 awarded patents or patent applications. He epitomizes (and, in fact, helped define) the idiosyncratic, individualistic Silicon Valley entrepreneur, with an emphasis on both function and elegance in the design of his products. After acquiring the computer graphics division of Lucasfilm, he created Pixar Animation Studios and remained CEO until its sale to Disney in 2006. This chapter is the commencement speech he gave in 2005 at Stanford University.

Stanford, and all of my working-class parents' savings were being spent on my college tuition. After six months, I couldn't see the value in it. I had no idea what I wanted to do with my life, and no idea of how college was going to help me figure it out, and here I was, spending all the money my parents had saved their entire life. So I decided to drop out and trust that it would all work out OK. It was pretty scary at the time, but looking back, it was one of the best decisions I ever made. The minute I dropped out, I could stop taking the required classes that didn't interest me and begin dropping in on the ones that looked far more interesting.

It wasn't all romantic. I didn't have a dorm room, so I slept on the floor in friends' rooms. I returned Coke bottles for the five-cent deposits to buy food with, and I would walk the seven miles across town every Sunday night to get one good meal a week at the Hare Krishna temple. I loved it. And much of what I stumbled into by following my curiosity and intuition turned out to be priceless later on. Let me give you one example.

Reed College at that time offered perhaps the best calligraphy instruction in the country. Throughout the campus, every poster, every label on every drawer was beautifully hand-calligraphed. Because I had dropped out and didn't have to take the normal classes, I decided to take a calligraphy class to learn how to do this. I learned about serif and sans-serif typefaces, about varying the amount of space between different letter combinations, about what makes great typography great. It was beautiful, historical, artistically subtle in a way that science can't capture, and I found it fascinating.

None of this had even a hope of any practical application in my life. But ten years later when we were designing the first Macintosh computer, it all came back to me, and we designed it all into the Mac. It was the first computer with beautiful typography. If I had never dropped in on that single course in college, the Mac would have never had multiple typefaces or proportionally spaced fonts, and since Windows just copied the Mac, it's likely that no personal computer would have them.

If I had never dropped out, I would have never dropped in on that calligraphy class and personals computers might not have the wonderful typography that they do.

Of course it was impossible to connect the dots looking forward when I was in college, but it was very, very clear looking backwards ten years later. Again, you can't connect the dots looking forward. You can only connect them looking backwards, so you have to trust that the dots will somehow connect in your future. You have to trust in something—your gut, destiny, life, karma, whatever—because believing that the dots will connect down the road will give you the confidence to follow your heart, even when it leads you off the well-worn path, and that will make all the difference.

My second story is about love and loss. I was lucky. I found what I loved to do early in life. Woz and I started Apple in my parents' garage when I was twenty. We worked hard and in ten years, Apple had grown from just the two of us in a garage into a $2 billion company with over 4,000 employees. We'd just released our finest creation, the Macintosh, a year earlier, and I'd just turned thirty, and then I got fired. How can you get fired from a company you started? Well, as Apple grew, we hired someone who I thought was very talented to run the company with me, and for the first year or so, things went well. But then our visions of the future began to diverge, and eventually we had a falling out. When we did, our board of directors sided with him, and so at thirty, I was out, and very publicly out. What had been the focus of my entire adult life was gone, and it was devastating. I really didn't know what to do for a few months. I felt that I had let the previous generation of entrepreneurs down, that I had dropped the baton as it was being passed to me. I met with David Packard and Bob Noyce and tried to apologize for screwing up so badly. I was a very public failure and I even thought about running away from the Valley. But something slowly began to dawn on me. I still loved what I did. The turn of events at Apple had not changed that one bit. I'd been rejected but I was still in love. And so I decided to start over.

I didn't see it then, but it turned out that getting fired from Apple was the best thing that could have ever happened to me. The heaviness of being successful was replaced by the lightness of being a beginner again, less sure about everything. It freed me to enter one of the most creative periods in my life. During the next five years I started a company named NeXT, another company named Pixar, and fell in love with an amazing woman who would become my wife. Pixar went on to create the world's first computer-animated feature film, *Toy Story*, and is now the most successful animation studio in the world.

In a remarkable turn of events, Apple bought NeXT and I returned to Apple, and the technology we developed at NeXT is at the heart of Apple's current renaissance, and Lorene and I have a wonderful family together.

I'm pretty sure none of this would have happened if I hadn't been fired from Apple. It was awful-tasting medicine, but I guess the patient needed it. Sometimes life's going to hit you in the head with a brick. Don't lose faith. I'm convinced that the only thing that kept me going was that I loved what I did. You've got to find what you love, and that is as true for work as it is for your lovers. Your work is going to fill a large part of your life, and the only way to be truly satisfied is to do what you believe is great work, and the only way to do great work is to love what you do. If you haven't found it yet, keep looking, and don't settle. As with all matters of the heart, you'll know when you find it, and like any great relationship it just gets better and better as the years roll on. So keep looking. Don't settle.

My third story is about death. When I was seventeen, I read a quote that went something like "If you live each day as if it was your last, someday you'll most certainly be right." It made an impression on me, and since then, for the past thirty-three years, I have looked in the mirror every morning and asked myself, "If today were the last day of my life, would I want to do what I am about to do today?" And whenever the answer has been "no" for too many days in a row, I know I need to change something. Remembering that I'll be dead soon is the most important thing I've ever encountered to help me make the big choices in life, because almost everything — all external expectations, all pride, all fear of embarrassment or failure — these things just fall away in the face of death, leaving only what is truly important. Remembering that you are going to die is the best way I know to avoid the trap of thinking you have something to lose. You are already naked. There is no reason not to follow your heart.

About a year ago, I was diagnosed with cancer. I had a scan at 7:30 in the morning and it clearly showed a tumor on my pancreas. I didn't even know what a pancreas was. The doctors told me this was almost certainly a type of cancer that is incurable, and that I should expect to live no longer than three to six months. My doctor advised me to go home and get my affairs in order, which is doctors' code for "prepare to die." It means to try and tell your kids everything you thought you'd have the next ten years to tell them, in just a few months. It means to make sure that everything is buttoned up so that it will be as easy as possible for your family. It means to say your good-byes.

I lived with that diagnosis all day. Later that evening I had a biopsy where they stuck an endoscope down my throat, through my stomach into my intestines, put a needle into my pancreas and got a few cells from the tumor. I was sedated, but my wife, who was there, told me that when they viewed the cells under a microscope, the doctor started crying, because it turned out to be a very rare form of pancreatic cancer that is curable with surgery. I had the surgery and, thankfully, I am fine now.

This was the closest I've been to facing death, and I hope it's the closest I get for a few more decades. Having lived through it, I can now say this to you with a bit more certainty than when death was a useful but purely intellectual concept. No one wants to die, even people who want to go to Heaven don't want to die to get there, and yet, death is the destination we all share. No one has ever escaped it. And that is as it should be, because death is very likely the single best invention of life. It's life's change agent; it clears out the old to make way for the new. Right now, the new is you. But someday, not too long from now, you will gradually become the old and be cleared away. Sorry to be so dramatic, but it's quite true. Your time is limited, so don't waste it living someone else's life. Don't be trapped by dogma, which is living with the results of other people's thinking. Don't let the noise of others' opinions drown out your own inner voice, heart, and intuition. They somehow already know what you truly want to become. Everything else is secondary.

When I was young, there was an amazing publication called *The Whole Earth Catalog,* which was one of the bibles of my generation. It was created by a fellow named Stewart Brand not far from here in Menlo Park, and he brought it to life with his poetic touch. This was in the late Sixties, before personal computers and desktop publishing, so it was all made with typewriters, scissors, and Polaroid cameras. It was sort of like Google in paperback form thirty-five years before Google came along. I was idealistic, overflowing with neat tools and great notions.

Stewart and his team put out several issues of *The Whole Earth Catalog,* and then when it had run its course, they put out a final issue. It was the midseventies and I was your age. On the back cover of their final issue was a photograph of an early morning country road, the kind you might find yourself hitchhiking on if you were so adventurous. Beneath were the words, "Stay hungry, stay foolish." It was their farewell message as they signed off. "Stay hungry, stay foolish."

And I have always wished that for myself, and now, as you graduate to begin anew, I wish that for you. Stay hungry, stay foolish.

Tavis Smiley:

The Substance of Things Hoped For

CHAPTER
23

The book of Hebrews declares that "Faith is the substance of things hoped for, the evidence of things not seen." There are three things in life that I think sustain us. I call them the three F's: faith, family, and friends.

I don't know how people survive, let alone thrive, without having an abiding faith in something bigger and beyond them. Faith is what makes this universe work.

I believe the ultimate compliment is to have someone put faith in your ability to deliver. People do not necessarily put their confidence in you or believe in you because the evidence is there for them to do so. Rather, they are doing it in light of the biblical definition of faith: the substance of things hoped for and the evidence of things not seen. In other words, people often have put faith in us simply because they believe in us, not because they have evidence to support their belief. It's easy to bet on Tiger Woods and on Michael Jordan in their respective sports if you've seen them play before, because the evidence abounds that they are the best at what they do. Faith is not really a factor here. Let me tell you about faith.

I ran for a seat on the Los Angeles City Council in 1991. I was a twenty-six-year-old kid who had never run for public office before. My opponent was the incumbent, and early on I realized that I was going to be vastly outspent. But I just campaigned harder, and the closer it got to election day, the more it appeared that I had a reasonable chance of

Tavis Smiley, talk show host, author, political commentator, and philanthropist, hosts the late-night television talk show *Tavis Smiley* on PBS and *The Tavis Smiley Show* from Public Radio International (PRI). His prime-time TV specials *Tavis Smiley Reports* included going behind the scenes with Secretary of State Hillary Clinton and traveling to the streets of New Orleans to mark Hurricane Katrina's fifth anniversary. He is the author of fourteen books, including *How to Make Black America Better* and the *New York Times* best-seller *What I Know for Sure: My Story of Growing Up in America*. www.tavistalks.com

forcing a runoff with the incumbent, although there was never any evidence suggest I could beat her. I was running a "faith" campaign.

As we neared the end of the campaign, with literally just weeks to go, I ran out of money. My funds were so depleted that my campaign manager and my staff had not been paid in weeks. I didn't have the money to print any more brochures or lawn signs. I was completely dry.

My mother apparently had talked to someone on my campaign staff and found out that I had run out of money. She had enough faith in me (and was crazy enough) to go down to her bank and mortgage *her house* to get me the additional money that I needed to finish my campaign.

Fortunately, I overheard someone on my staff share this news with another campaign staff person. When I caught up with my mother, she was actually on her way to the bank to get the money. I had to stop her from going through with it. But I cannot tell you how moved to tears I was that my mother thought enough of me and had enough faith in me to mortgage her house on my behalf. My mother has always believed in me, and the myriad ways she has demonstrated this have helped me to develop into the person I am today.

Having just one person truly believe in you is one of life's greatest and most precious gifts.

If more of our young people had someone who really believed in them, who demonstrated unwavering faith and trust in them, I think they would be capable of achieving great things. More often than not, our young people deliver what is simply ordinary because we adults don't expect the extraordinary. Nor do we give them the proper tools to perform at a high level. In this respect, there is much that we adults can do to help advance our young people on their journey through life.

Sometimes you have to believe with all your heart in someone else, and conversely have someone believe in you in exactly the same way. We owe this to each other, as African Americans, and we owe it especially to our young people.

Hope

During my senior year at Indiana University, I came to Los Angeles to do an internship with Tom Bradley. It actually took me nine months, from January until September 1985, of writing, calling, and faxing his office, as well as using my student aid money to fly twice to Los Angeles to try (unsuccessfully) to meet with him, before he finally granted me an internship.

The unpaid internship lasted for one semester, from September through December of 1985. Through the course of my internship, I got to know the mayor fairly well, and when my internship was over, he told me he would hire me as a member of his staff once my studies were completed if I was interested. I returned to Bloomington, Indiana, to complete my degree, and one year later I packed up everything I owned into my Datsun 280Z and drove out west to Los Angeles to work for Mayor Bradley. When I arrived in Los Angeles, I discovered that the city's economy had taken a downturn, making it necessary to impose a mandatory hiring freeze on all employment opportunities. As a result, he didn't have a job to give me. The best advice he could give me at that point was to stick around until the hiring freeze lifted and he would bring me on staff right away.

The hiring freeze ended up lasting over a year. I found myself stuck in Los Angeles, without money, without family, and without a job. I was ashamed to admit to my college buddies back home that my situation had taken a turn for the worse. Especially since I had bragged to them about my success in landing a job right out of college.

I had received an eviction notice to move out of my apartment. I looked for work wherever I could. The truth of the matter was that I couldn't find any job, not even a menial one. I was denied employment at McDonald's because I was "overqualified." No one would hire me even for a manual-labor, minimum-wage job.

When I thought I could not go any further, I reluctantly called my mother. I broke down in tears, crying and sobbing like a baby. I explained to her that I was coming home because I could not make it in Los Angeles. I could hear Gladys Knight and the Pips warming up: "LA proved too much for the man. He couldn't take it. So he's leaving the life he's come to know." I had given it everything I had, but things weren't working out and I was at my wits' end.

My mother said to me, "Honey, you can always come home. You'll always have a bedroom here at the house, and all I want is for you to be happy. Come home, stay as long as you like, regroup, and do whatever you need to do. We are your family—we're here for you, and we'll always be here for you." I thanked my mother for her words of comfort, although I was very disappointed in myself. I did not want to go back to Indiana with my tail between my legs.

When I finished talking to my mother, I made it into the shower. In the midst of my tears, I reconciled myself to the fact that it was time for me to go home. "Things cannot get any worse for me," I thought. At that very moment, a massive earthquake hit the city of Los Angeles. I started slipping and sliding in the shower with soap and water flying everywhere. All of a sudden, the voice of the Lord spoke to me and said, "Things can always get worse; they can get *much* worse."

Hearing the voice of God made me realize that as long as I was alive and had breath in my body, there would always be hope. There are times when hope is the only thing we have to cling to. I didn't have a job, I didn't have any food, and I didn't have any money, but I always had hope.

I managed to make it out of the shower in one piece, and right away my phone rang. It was my friend Harold Patrick, calling to see if I was all right. When I answered the phone, I was still upset and trying to process all that had taken place. Harold became concerned about me and rushed over to my apartment. We ended up having a long conversation about my circumstances and my feelings about leaving Los Angeles and returning to Indiana.

Harold listened to what I had to say. Then he replied, "I will support you in whatever decision you make. But I want you to know that I am not going to give up on you until forty-eight hours after you have given up on yourself. I want to give you enough time to change your mind. I have great expectations for your future. I believe in you; you are the hope of my dreams. I'm going to be here for you." I was extremely moved by his words.

As I thought about God's message in the shower and Harold's unshakable belief in me, I saw in that moment my own sense of hope-lessness through the lens of the blood, sweat, and rears of my ancestors and the sacrifices they had endured to pave the way for those coming behind them. We became the hope of *their* dreams, and the purpose for which many of them gave their lives. I thought, "I have a whole lot of nerve giving up on anything." Here I was talking about giving up hope and going back home to Indiana because I didn't have a job, because I was being evicted from my apartment. How could I compare my situation with the experiences of my ancestors who had survived the journey to America on slave ships, survived the institution of slavery, and lived through segregation?

Those two back-to-back moments that morning in 1987 set me straight about what it meant to be hopeful. Since that day, I have never taken hope for granted. There is always hope, and hope springs eternal. Whether we have money or not, whether we have good health or not, and whether our mates walk out on us or not, we need to latch on to hope and never let it go.

Garrison Keillor:

The People, Yes

CHAPTER
24

Barry told me I ought to go cover Kennedy's speech and I rode over to the Minneapolis Auditorium on a chartered bus that was packed, girls sitting on laps, boys crushed together in the aisle. I crushed myself into them and stood pressed against a girl's back, a solid mass of people swaying on the turns. I joined the crush streaming into the hall and climbed up under the rafters as the mighty Wurlitzer played "Happy Days Are Here Again" and sat through the prelims, all the little frogs getting their moment in the spotlight, and Senator Eugene McCarthy was introduced and then Hubert, who got a long ovation but not too long, and then Orville Freeman got behind the lectern and introduced John F. Kennedy and out he came, covered in glory, and the place almost came loose from its moorings. In that shining moment, standing, grinning, drenched in applause, the whistles and the cheers, he truly seemed to rise to meet our hopes for him. I sort of knew the rap against him—he had dodged the issue of McCarthyism, his father's shady fortune had bought the nomination, the grandma of the Democratic Party, Eleanor Roosevelt, couldn't stand him because he wasn't Adlai Stevenson—but there in the flesh, he was thrilling to us Democrats, a plain people; he was the first politician with movie hero presence and he had the elegant dignity of someone who has always known who he is, unlike the herky-jerky Nixon of the mawkish Checkers speech and the weird marionette arms. Kennedy was classy, not overeager like so many politicians, who were tuned a half step sharp and didn't know how to play the crowd. They could do Earnest and Hortatory with the three obligatory jokes at

Garrison Keillor is the host and writer of *A Prairie Home Companion,* the radio show that began in 1974 and continues today, drawing more than four million listeners each week on 590 public radio stations. He is the author of more than a dozen books, including *New York Times* best-sellers *Love Me, Lake Wobegon Summer 1956, Wobegon Boy,* and *Lake Wobegon Days,* and the editor of the anthology *Good Poems.* A member of the Academy of American Arts and Letters, he lives in St. Paul, Minnesota.

the beginning and some Keening and Baying at the end and the Hands High Touchdown pose, but he had more keys on his piano. He had black keys and they didn't. There was playfulness in him; he didn't just preach about freedom, he performed it. (Did the GIs die in the snowy forests of Belgium so we could be like Nixon, the prisoner of his own demons? I didn't think so.)

Kennedy was a new man, a man of our time, not one of the old jowly guys who peered at TV cameras as if they were bombs and read from prepared texts and struck the old ritual poses, kissed the symbolic baby, ate the ceremonial hot dog, waved the flag, decried godless communism, posed with other jowly guys. Kennedy was an improviser. He stood there and grinned and soaked up the applause and then joked about Ted Williams having announced his retirement from the Red Sox at the age of forty-two — Kennedy was forty-three — "It shows that perhaps experience isn't enough." Huge laugh — and he tipped his hat to Hubert as a worthy opponent (more applause) and went on to his speech. I remember he quoted Dante — politicians didn't quote Dante then, any more than they'd pose in a little black beret with a cigarette dangling from their lower lip. Kennedy made you believe that at one time in his life he'd sat down and read the *Inferno,* that he lived in a house with books on the shelves and didn't care if you knew it, that he might have enjoyed Italy and knew about more than politics. He shared our disdain for the dull-witted bullies of the world who lord it over the meek and lowly. He was a liberating man. I didn't care that he was rich and Catholic. So what? It felt as if a great loosening was coming and a jazzier spirit was in the air. And we'd have a President for whom we felt admiration. So I was a Democrat. Republicans were those fraternity boys on University Avenue, the Dekes engaged in the manly pursuit of drunkenness and fart lighting, maintaining their antique Greek culture, the annual Pajama Parade and the Tunic Tswirl where the frat houses sang their raccoon songs and Sno Week with the Lennon Sisters and the Glenn Miller Band on the bill, a bunch of gladhanders and blowhards, scions of car dealers, who devoted more attention to their hair than to what lay beneath it.

I walked back to campus from his speech. At eighteen, I was deeply into my family's history and I felt a connection between Kennedy and my family's New England roots, which I was just then hugely proud of, having recently learned about them. The reference to Dante was, "We have all made mistakes. But Dante tells us that divine justice weighs the sins of the cold-blooded and the sins of the warm-hearted on different scales. Better the occasional faults of a party living in the spirit of charity than the consistent omissions of a party frozen in the ice of its own indifference." To me this spoke volumes about the cold legalism of fundamentalist Christianity, which was its dark side — the bright side was the evangelical spirit and the gospel of Jesus Christ who came to free us from bondage —

but then there was the cold literalist judgmental schismatic side and the gimlet-eyed bluenosed martinets who would expel you into outer darkness if you departed from orthodoxy by so much as a quarter inch. My New England ancestors were warmhearted. Joseph Crandall was an associate of Roger Williams who founded the first Baptist church in America in Providence in 1639. Roger Williams had grown up in England when Puritans were burned at the stake and came to Massachusetts Bay Colony where he found the Puritans to be just as intolerant as the people who had incinerated them back in England. He founded Rhode Island as a haven for people of all beliefs, including Indians. Roger Williams made Indian languages the great scholarly enterprise of his life. And my ancestor was there with him. And then there was Prudence Crandall who opened a school for young women in Canterbury, Connecticut, in 1831. When she admitted a colored girl the following year, all of the decent white families pulled their children out, whereupon Prudence opened a school for young colored women, the first in the country, which was shut down by a mob. She was a Quaker. She married a Baptist clergyman named Calvin Philleo and they moved to Kansas and she kept on teaching and was a staunch advocate of equal rights for women until she died in 1890. Mark Twain once spoke admiringly of Prudence Crandall and I was as proud of her as I could be, my ancestor who stood up to a mob for what she knew to be right. Maybe the rest of us Keillors were just clerks and farmhands and parking lot attendants but at one time we stood for something. So did Kennedy.

In the Great American Divide between the cold avengers and the sons of liberty, the paranoid and the happy entrepreneurs, the bullies and the defenders of justice, he was over on the side of the warm-hearted, and that was his mystique, no mystery about it.

I remember I walked in silence across that high narrow bridge over the Mississippi gorge and up the empty street behind Walter Library and thought about Kennedy and the Crandalls and the University and my ambitions to be a writer, which seemed to be all tangled up together in a ball, and was overjoyed a few weeks later when he beat Nixon. And then his heroic inauguration, his good speech with some nobility in it, and the heroic performance by Robert Frost of "The Gift Outright" — what a good country to be able to sense the difference between Nixon and Kennedy, even by a narrow margin. He stood in the light and he was worthy of our ideals. I never met him or his wife or children. I never was fascinated by their Kennedyness, only by him as President. Under his sway, I signed up for the Don Fraser for Congress campaign in 1962, which knocked off a crusty old Republican in Minneapolis and was managed by Don's wife Arvonne, a short peppery woman who personified for me the Democratic-Farmer-Labor party, open-hearted, perpetually hopeful, honest to a fault, and the mother of us all. I was in Eddy Hall on November 22, 1963, when

I heard the President had been shot. I was an announcer at the University AM radio station, KUOM, and was sitting in the record library when the secretary, Bobbie, came in and told me. I walked to the United Press teletype in the hall closet and saw the first fragmentary bulletins, all caps, DALLAS, NOV. 22 (UPI) — THREE SHOTS WERE FIRED AT PRESIDENT KENNEDY'S MOTORCADE IN DOWNTOWN DALLAS. — I stood reading this in stunned silence, the teletype clacking away, and there was something about the President's limp body being carried from the car, and the word *fatally* appeared, and I took the paper into the studio where an actor was reading Tolkien's *The Hobbit* on a show called *Your Novel* — he glanced up in alarm and I handed him the bulletin and he said, in a rather grand voice, "I have just been handed a news bulletin —" and I went back to the record library and got a record of, I think, a Spanish Mass and we played the *Benedictus*. And then Tchaikovsky's *Pathétique*. There was no need for us to read more news, everybody knew the news. Who killed him was never clear and either one read the conspiracy literature or one did not. I didn't. I never could bring myself to visit the assassination museum at the schoolbook depository in Dallas. Nothing I read later about Kennedy and his life essentially changed how I felt about him the night I walked back to campus from his speech in October 1960.

One day in the Scholar Coffeehouse, a kid strummed a twelve-string guitar and everyone sang, without prompting, *Deep in my heart, I do believe that we shall overcome someday.* With all our hearts. Underneath the thin patina of coolness, we were all church kids. We'd read the prophets, heard the gospel, were exalted by the thought of being soldiers for the Lord and setting the prisoners free. Kennedy didn't live to see it, but it was done in his spirit.

A couple years after he died, the Mississippi River rose in the spring and there were urgent flood warnings on the radio. One afternoon I put on warm clothes and took the bus to St. Paul and crossed the Wabasha Bridge to the West Side where people were at work filling sandbags and building dikes to save the low-lying houses. It was foggy, and then it began to rain. An army of hundreds of volunteers hard at work, men and women, drawn up in assembly lines, holding the sacks and filling them and passing them in a chain to the dike. It got dark. Nobody left. The Red Cross brought around sandwiches and coffee. We rested and went back to work. Trucks brought in more sand and bags. A couple of front loaders worked at anchoring the dikes with earthen banks. It felt like wartime. I worked until after midnight and lay down in the back of a truck under a tarp and slept until daybreak and got up stiff and cold and they brought us more sandwiches and coffee and I got back in the gang and worked until noon. Someone said the flood would crest that evening. Someone worried about the dike bursting. A man said, "When they go, they go slow, they don't go sudden." I wasn't sure about that, but I stayed because everyone else stayed. I sort of collapsed in the afternoon and was going to go home but slept a couple hours on a tarp in somebody's front yard and when I woke up, there was water in the street, people wading through it, some men with muddy overalls, pitched emotion in the air, though nobody said much. We had put so much into beating back the flood, and we kept working—shovel, fill, tie, and pass, shovel, fill, tie, and pass— and felt privileged to be there doing it. I could hear the river boiling by and slabs of ice heaved up on the dike and National Guardsmen patrolling and when people couldn't stand up any longer, they sat down and ate baloney sandwiches and drank coffee. And got back up.

I went home in the morning. It was so overwhelming, I sat on the bed and cried. For the relief of getting out of those mud-crusted clothes and standing under a hot shower, but also for what I'd seen, the spirit of all those workers caught up in the job of saving their neighbors' houses. Forget all the jabber and gossip, all the theoretical balderdash and horsefeathers, here is reality: the river rises up in its power and majesty, and the people rise up in theirs, and while one can do only so much, you must do that much, and we did. None of the news reports captured the reality of that event, which was the spirit of the crowd, of which I was one. An experience that warms a Democrat's heart, a scene from *Grapes of Wrath*, or the crossing of the Red Sea. The People, yes.

By God, no matter what Republicans say, the people of this country really do care about each other. We are not a cold people. By God, when John F. Kennedy said, "Ask what you can do for your country," he spoke to this country's heart and conscience.

Mitch Albom:

Happiness

CHAPTER
25

T he Reb opened his eyes.

He was in the hospital.

It was not the first time. Although he often hid his ailments from me, I learned that in recent months, staying upright had become a problem. He had slipped on the pavement and cut open his forehead. He had slipped in the house and banged his neck and cheek. Now he had fallen getting up from his chair and slammed his rib cage against a desk. It was either syncope, a temporary loss of consciousness, or small strokes, transient attacks that left him dizzy and disoriented.

Either way, it was not good.

Now I expected the worst. A hospital. The portal to the end. I had called and asked if it was all right to visit, and Sarah kindly said I could come.

I braced myself at the front entrance. I am haunted by hospital visits and their familiar, depressing cues. The antiseptic smell. The low drone of TV sets. The drawn curtains. The occasional moaning from another bed. I had been to too many hospitals for too many people.

For the first time in a while, I thought about our agreement.

Will you do my eulogy?

I entered the Reb's room.

Mitch Albom is a best-selling author, journalist, screenwriter, playwright, radio and television broadcaster, and musician. His books have sold over twenty-eight million copies, been published in forty-two languages worldwide, and been made into Emmy Award-winning television movies. *Tuesdays with Morrie,* which spent four years on the *New York Times* best-seller list and became the most successful memoir ever published, is the chronicle of his time spent with a beloved former professor who was dying of ALS (Lou Gehrig's disease). He wrote the book as a labor of love, to help pay Morrie's medical bills. www.mitchalbom.com

"Ah," he smiled, looking up from the bed, "a visitor from afar..." I stopped thinking about it.

* * *

We hugged—or, I should say, I hugged his shoulders and he touched my head—and we both agreed that this was a first, a hospital conversation. His robe fell open slightly and I caught a glance at his bare chest, soft, loose flesh with a few silver hairs. I felt a rush of shame and ooked away.

A nurse breezed in.

"How are you doing today?" she asked.

"I'm dooooing," the Reb lilted. "I'm dooooing..."

She laughed. "He sings all the time, this one."

Yes, he does, I said.

It amazed me how consistently the Reb could summon his good nature. To sing to the nurses. To kid around with the physicians. The previous day, while waiting in a wheelchair in the hallway, he was asked by a hospital worker for a blessing. So the Reb put his hands on the man's head and gave him one.

He refused to wallow in self-pity. In fact, the worse things got for him, the more intent he seemed on making sure no one around him was saddened by it.

As we sat in the room, a commercial for an antidepressant drug flashed across the TV screen. It showed people looking forlorn, alone on a bench or staring out a window.

"I keep feeling something bad is going to happen...," the TV voice said.

Then, after showing the pill and some graphics, those same people appeared again, looking happier.

The Reb and I watched in silence. After it ended, he asked, "Do you think those pills work?"

Not like that, I said.

"No," he agreed. "Not like that."

* * *

Happiness in a tablet. This is our world. Prozac. Paxil. Xanax. Billions are spent to advertise such drugs. And billions more are spent purchasing them. You don't even need a specific trauma; just "general depression" or "anxiety," as if sadness were as treatable as the common cold.

I knew depression was real, and in many cases required medical attention. I also knew we overused the word. Much of what we called "depression" was really dissatisfaction, a result of setting a bar impossibly high or expecting treasures that we weren't willing to work for. I knew people whose unbearable source of misery was their weight, their baldness, their lack of advancement in a workplace, or their inability to find the perfect mate, even if they themselves did not behave like one. To these people, unhappiness was a condition, an intolerable state of affairs. If pills could help, pills were taken.

But pills were not going to change the fundamental problem in the construction. Wanting what you can't have. Looking for self-worth in the mirror. Layering work on top of work and still wondering why you weren't satisfied — before working some more.

I knew. I had done all that. There was a stretch where I could not have worked more hours in the day without eliminating sleep altogether. I piled on accomplishments. I made money. I earned accolades. And the longer I went at it, the emptier I began to feel, like pumping air faster and faster into a torn tire.

The time I spent with Morrie, my old professor, had tapped my brakes on much of that. After watching him die, and seeing what mattered to him at the end, I cut back. I limited my schedule.

But I still kept my hands on my own wheel. I didn't turn things over to fate or faith. I recoiled from people who put their daily affairs in divine hands, saying, "If God wants it, it will happen." I kept silent when people said all that mattered was their personal relationship with Jesus. Such surrender seemed silly to me. I felt like I knew better. But privately, I couldn't say I felt any happier than they did.

So I noted how, for all the milligrams of medication he required, the Reb never popped a pill for his peace of mind. He loved to smile. He avoided anger. He was never haunted by "Why am I here?" He knew why he was here, he said: to give to others, to celebrate God, and to enjoy and honor the world he was put in. His morning prayers began with "Thank you, Lord, for returning my soul to me."

When you start that way, the rest of the day is a bonus.

* * *

Can I ask you something?

"Yes," he said.

What makes a man happy?

"Well..." He rolled his eyes around the hospital room. "This may not be the best setting for that question."

Yeah, you're right.

"On the other hand..." He took a deep breath. "On the other hand, here in this building, we must face the real issues. Some people will get better. Some will not. So it may be a good place to define what that word means."

Happiness?

"That's right. The things society tells us we must have to be happy — a new this or that, a bigger house, a better job. I know the falsity of it. I have counseled many people who have all these things, and I can tell you they are not happy because of them.

"The number of marriages that have disintegrated when they had all the stuff in the world. The families who fought and argued all the time, when they had money and health. Having more does not keep you from wanting more. And if you always want more — to be richer, more beautiful, more well known — you are missing the bigger picture, and I can tell you from experience, happiness will never come."

You're not going to tell me to stop and smell the roses, are you?

He chuckled. "Roses would smell better than this place."

Suddenly, out in the hall, I heard an infant scream, followed by a quick "shhh!" presumably from its mother. The Reb heard it, too.

"Now, that child," he said, "reminds me of something our sages taught. When a baby comes into the world, its hands are clenched, right? Like this?"

He made a fist.

"Why? Because a baby, not knowing any better, wants to grab everything, to say, 'The whole world is mine.'

"But when an old person dies, how does he do so? With his hands open. Why? Because he has learned the lesson."

What lesson? I asked.

He stretched open his empty fingers.

"We can take nothing with us."

* * *

For a moment we both stared at his hand. It was trembling.

"Ach, you see this?" he said.

Yeah.

"I can't make it stop."

He dropped the hand to his chest. I heard a cart being wheeled down the hall. He spoke so wisely, with such passion, that for a moment I'd forgotten where we were.

"Anyhow," he said, his voice trailing off.

I hated seeing him in that bed. I wanted him home, with the messy desk and the mismatched clothes. I forced a smile.

So, have we solved the secret of happiness?

"I believe so," he said.

Are you going to tell me?

"Yes. Ready?"

Ready.

"Be satisfied."

That's it?

"Be grateful."

That's it?

"For what you have. For the love you receive. And for what God has given you."

That's it?

He looked me in the eye. Then he sighed deeply.

"That's it."

QUEEN NOOR:

A Leap of Faith

King Hussein was one of the world's most eligible bachelors. Families in Jordan, not to mention other countries in the region, would delight at the thought of having a daughter marry the King; the advantages of such a union would be enormous. During an official visit to the United States, shortly after his third wife's death, the King had traveled to Texas and had come away with the impression that every single young woman in the community had been paraded in front of him as if, he said later, they were competing to be the next Grace Kelly. The idea of material or social advantage deriving from one's choice of husband was not something that I would have considered under any circumstances, let alone now. My generation married for love.

I agonized over my decision for the next two weeks, trying to work out in my mind whether I should question his judgment in considering me to be the right choice for him and for the country. Although none of his previous wives had been born in Jordan either, what might be the negative implications for him in the Arab world if he married me? Would it matter that I was born in the United States? Was I suitable? I had lived an independent life, traveled in many different countries. I had a free, open spirit. Would I have the self-discipline necessary to make a good wife for a king? The responsibility was daunting. And what about my own role?

HM Queen Noor is an international public servant who, since marrying King Hussein of Jordan in 1978, has actively promoted cross-cultural exchange and understanding of Arab, Muslim and Western relations, and conflict prevention and recovery issues such as refugees, missing persons, poverty and disarmament. Her peace-building work has focused on the Middle East, the Balkans, Central and Southeast Asia, Latin America and Africa. Her work in Jordan and the Arab world has concentrated on human security issues through pioneering programs in the areas of poverty eradication and sustainable development, women's empowerment, human rights, microfinance, health, conservation, and culture, many of which are best practices models for the developing world. www.KingHusseinFoundation.org, www.NoorAlHusseinFoundation.org

I had always worked, not only out of necessity, but also because it was important to me to contribute to society.

It concerned me that I had not spent that much time talking to King Hussein about my life before Jordan. I knew how the international media could pick apart public figures. And I wanted Hussein to be wise about his choice. I did not want him to ever have to pay a price for choosing someone that might further complicate his life. On a more personal level, I wondered where I would find the strength for the difficult times that were bound to come. Would I be able to cope? My mind was ablaze with questions and worries.

I also had to think through what little I knew about the King, and sort through all the rumors and the gossip about his personal life. I will not deny that the idea of being his fourth wife, or anybody's fourth wife, was troubling to me. He had told me about his first, eighteen-month marriage to Sharifa Dina Abdel Hamid (who became Queen Dina), a distant Hashimite cousin seven years older than he with whom he had a daughter, Alia; his second marriage in 1961 was to a young Englishwoman, Antoinette Gardiner, who became Princess Muna. They had two sons, Abdullah and Feisal, and twin daughters, Zein and Aisha. He divorced Muna after eleven years to marry Alia Toukan, from a Palestinian family, who died tragically after four years. If I accepted his proposal, I would be stepmother to his eight children, including Queen Alia's very young children. That seemed an enormous responsibility, but in my idealistic view it was one that I could gladly embrace.

* * *

I already had tremendous personal respect for him and admiration for all he stood for and was trying to achieve. The gossip and rumors aside, I knew the man as he really was, full of character, decency and conviction. I was also deeply attracted to him. Still, I knew that this would be no ordinary union.

I had an incomplete picture of what the future might be, but I knew that no matter what happened, I would always have my work and the contributions I could make to the country to see me through. The King had let me know in so many words that he was offering me a partnership. That realization, too, helped me make up my mind. I had a job to do for a country I already loved and an extraordinary man as a partner. Together we could make a difference.

"Shall I call your father?" he asked me again on May 13, eighteen days after he had first proposed. We were at Hashimya in the early afternoon, having just put the children down for a nap. I looked at him across the room, seeing the sincerity in his gaze, hearing the certainty in his voice. My mother was right about those eyes. "Yes," I said.

* * *

"Slightly amazed" were the words my father used to describe the moment when he picked up the phone in his kitchen in his house in Alpine, New Jersey, and heard King Hussein say in his deep, rich voice: "I have the honor to ask for the hand of your daughter in marriage." The last encounter my father knew about was our March audience with King Hussein and the invitation he had extended for me to inspect Hashimya. "I thought it was just for lunch," he blurted out. My mother was equally stunned when we telephoned her afterward on the secure phone in the King's radio room in Hashimya. I told her that I was in love and going to marry the man with the beautiful eyes. There was silence on the line until she collected herself and said how happy she was for me. Both of my parents counseled me to carefully consider my decision, knowing nothing of my long internal debate. Their loving concern meant a great deal to me. Rather than considering prestige or any kind of benefit that might accrue to them at any level, they were focused on my personal happiness. They both liked King Hussein very much but were apprehensive about the challenges I would face as his wife.

My mother did not like the idea of me living so far away, and she expressed her concern that our culturally different backgrounds might prevent us from finding a common language. I told her about our long conversations and that I had never met anyone easier to talk to. My father's anxieties were more political. He wondered whether I was ready to handle the Byzantine ways of a royal family and court. He was also concerned about my safety, given the turbulence in the Middle East. Threats to the King's life were well documented, and he feared I would face the same danger.

* * *

With great effort I concentrated on repeating the simple marriage vows that I had been practicing in Arabic. Looking at the King, I said, "I have betrothed myself to thee in marriage for the dowry agreed upon." He replied, "I have accepted thee as wife, my wife in marriage for the dowry agreed upon." We sealed our vows by clasping our right hands and looking at each other. No rings were exchanged, The sheikh conducting the ceremony recited verses from the Quran; then we walked into an adjoining room, where we were joined by our families and guests shouting, "*Mabrouk*, congratulations!"

Looking now at the pictures of us that appeared on the front page of newspapers around the world, I see a young woman flushed with optimism and hope, smiling with all her heart at a handsome bearded man who is responding in kind. The rest of my wedding day is a jumble of memory fragments: our struggle to cut the wedding cake—no one had pointed out that the bottom layer was cardboard; our impatience to leave the reception to be alone; and our walk to the front courtyard of the

Palace, where we adroitly avoided the elaborately decorated Excalibur to leap into Hussein's car and escape to the airport for our precious refuge in Aqaba.

I invited all eight children to join us in Aqaba for the few days we were there before leaving for our honeymoon in Scotland, I wanted them to feel part of our new life together as soon as possible, I knew it would not be easy. Three mothers were involved. Some of Hussein's older children were fully grown adults, and the youngest, Ali, was only two. But all the children adored their father, and with this common denominator I had every hope we might succeed in creating a loving, secure, nurturing family spirit. Our brief Aqaba idyll was great fun as far as I was concerned. In spite of the differences in their ages, the children seemed to enjoy one another's company tremendously. There was a lot of laughter, teasing, and games. No doubt they were all checking me out, but I felt very easy and at home in their midst.

* * *

It had been on our first night in Aqaba, when my new husband and I were watching the news on television, that I heard the announcement that he was giving me the title of Queen. I do not know why he had not told me himself. Perhaps he wanted to surprise me. I was the only person, it seems, in Jordan and the Western world who was not fixated on what title I would have. The newspapers had been filled with conjecture ever since our engagement had announced. There had also been concerns that, as an American, I might not be accepted in the region, but there was no Arab outcry, as far as I knew, about our marriage, nor any I was aware of from Jordanians. As a Halaby, I was considered an Arab returning home rather than a foreigner.

Our departure for our honeymoon in Scotland was further delayed by graduation day at Jordan University. My husband always handed out the diplomas to all the graduating students, so two days after our marriage we returned to Amman for what would be our first public event. I was quite nervous, not knowing what to expect. There was tremendous excitement when we arrived at the university and great warmth in the way we were received. I knew that the outpouring of affection for me, including the photos of me throughout the city and on cars and buses, was in fact for Hussein, and I was very touched by it—but also conscious that I should not take that affection as an entitlement: I had to earn it in my own right.

One contribution I did make was simply instinctive. I had become so conscious of the issue of the King's security that every time we went out in public, beginning with the graduation at Jordan University, I would try to subtly position myself to protect him in relation to the crowds. Our children would do the same in later years, but at the beginning of our marriage I reflexively found myself contributing to his front line of protection.

As Hussein and I prepared to leave for Scotland, I was filled with a sense of happiness and calm. I felt life had no boundaries, that every dream and goal was possible. I had committed my life to my husband and to Jordan, with all its demands and responsibilities, its frustrations and setbacks, its victories and disappointments. I had taken a leap of faith, and faith has richly rewarded me.

DAVID SEDARIS:

Memento Mori

For the past fifteen years or so, I've made it a habit to carry a small notebook in my front pocket. The model I currently favor is called the Europa, and I pull it out an average of ten times a day, jotting down grocery lists, observations, and little thoughts on how to make money, or torment people. The last page is always reserved for phone numbers, and the second to last I use for gift ideas. These are not things I might give to other people, but things that they might give to me: a shoehorn, for instance — always wanted one. The same goes for a pencil case, which, on the low end, probably costs no more than a doughnut.

I've also got ideas in the five-hundred-to-two-thousand-dollar range, though those tend to be more specific. This nineteenth-century portrait of a dog, for example. I'm not what you'd call a dog person, far from it, but this particular one — a whippet, I think — had alarmingly big nipples, huge, like bolts screwed halfway into her belly. More interesting was that she seemed aware of it. You could see it in her eyes as she turned to face the painter. "Oh, not now," she appeared to be saying. "Have you no decency?"

I saw the portrait at the Portobello Road market in London, and though I petitioned hard for months, nobody bought it for me. I even tried initiating a pool and offered to throw in a few hundred dollars of my own money, but still no one bit. In the end I gave the money to Hugh and had him buy it. Then I had him wrap it up and offer it to me.

"What's this for?" I asked.

David Sedaris, preeminent humor writer, is the author of collections of personal essays such as the best-selling *Me Talk Pretty One Day* and *Dress Your Family in Corduroy and Denim,* among other books. Seven million copies of his books are in print and they have been translated into twenty-five languages, including Estonian, Greek, and Bahasa. His essays appear frequently in the *New Yorker* and are heard on Public Radio International's *This American Life.*

CHAPTER TWENTY-SEVEN

And, following the script, he said, "Do I need a reason to give you a present?"

Then I said, "Awwwww."

It never works the other way around, though. Ask Hugh what he wants for Christmas or his birthday, and he'll answer, "You tell me."

"Well, isn't there something you've had your eye on?"

"Maybe. Maybe not."

Hugh thinks that lists are the easy way out and says that if I *really* knew him I wouldn't have to ask what he wanted. It's not enough to search the shops; I have to search his soul as well. He turns gift-giving into a test, which I don't think is fair at all. Were I the type to run out at the last minute, he might have a valid complaint, but I start my shopping months in advance. Plus I pay attention. If, say, in the middle of the summer, Hugh should mention that he'd like an electric fan, I'll buy it that very day and hide it in my gift cupboard. Come Christmas morning, he'll open his present and frown at it for a while, before I say, "Don't you remember? You said you were burning up and would give anything for a little relief."

That's just a practical gift, though, a stocking stuffer. His main present is what I'm really after, and, knowing this, he offers no help whatsoever. Or, rather, he *used* to offer no help. It wasn't until this year that he finally dropped a hint, and even then it was fairly cryptic. "Go out the front door and turn right," he said. "Then take a left and keep walking."

He did not say "Stop before you reach the boulevard" or "When you come to the Czech border you'll know you've gone too far," but he didn't need to. I knew what he was talking about the moment I saw it. It was a human skeleton, the genuine article, hanging in the window of a medical bookstore. Hugh's old drawing teacher used to have one, and though it had been ten years since he'd taken the woman's class, I could suddenly recall him talking about it. "If I had a skeleton like Minerva's...," he used to say. I don't remember the rest of the sentence, as I'd always been sidetracked by the teacher's name, Minerva. Sounds like a witch.

There are things that one enjoys buying and things that one doesn't. Electronic equipment, for example. I hate shopping for stuff like that, no matter how happy it will make the recipient. I feel the same about gift certificates, and books about golf or investment strategies or how to lose twelve pounds by being yourself. I thought I would enjoy buying a human skeleton, but looking through the shop window I felt a familiar tug of disappointment. This had nothing to do with any moral considerations. I was fine with buying someone who'd been dead for a while; I just didn't want to wrap him. Finding a box would be a pain, and then there'd be the paper, which would have to be attached in strips because no one sells rolls that wide. Between one thing and another, I was almost relieved when told that the skeleton was not for sale. "He's our mascot," the store manager said. "We couldn't possibly get rid of him."

In America this translates to "Make me an offer," but in France they really mean it. There are shops in Paris where nothing is for sale, no matter how hard you beg. I think people get lonely. Their apartments become full, and, rather than rent a storage space, they take over a boutique. Then they sit there in the middle of it, gloating over their fine taste.

Being told that I couldn't buy a skeleton was just what I needed to make me really want one. Maybe that was the problem all along. It was too easy: "Take a right, take a left, and keep walking." It took the hunt out of it.

"Do you know anyone who *will* sell me a skeleton?" I asked, and the manager thought for a while. "Well," she said, "I guess you could try looking on bulletin boards."

I don't know what circles this woman runs in, but I have never in my life seen a skeleton advertised on a bulletin board. Used bicycles, yes, but no human bones, or even cartilage for that matter.

"Thank you for your help," I said.

* * *

Because I have nothing better to do with my time than shop, I tend to get excited when someone wants something obscure: an out-of-print novel, a replacement for a shattered teacup. I thought that finding another skeleton would prove difficult, but I came across two more that very afternoon—one a full-grown male and the other a newborn baby. Both were at the flea market, offered by a man who specializes in what he calls "the sorts of things that are not for everyone."

The baby was tempting because of its size—I could have wrapped it in a shoe box—but ultimately I went for the adult, which is three hundred years old and held together by a network of fine wires, There's a latch in the center of the forehead, and removing the linchpin allows you to open the skull and either root around or hide things—drugs, say, or small pieces of jewelry. It's not what one hopes for when thinking about an afterlife ("I'd like for my head to be used as a stash box"), but I didn't let that bother me. I bought the skeleton the same way I buy most everything. It was just an arrangement of parts to me, no different from a lamp or a chest of drawers.

I didn't think of it as a former person until Christmas Day, when Hugh opened the cardboard coffin, "If you don't like the color, we can bleach it," I said. "Either that or exchange it for the baby."

I always like to offer a few alternatives, though in this case they were completely unnecessary. Hugh was beside himself, couldn't have been happier. I assumed he'd be using the skeleton as a model and was a little put off when, instead of taking it to his studio, he carried it into the bedroom and hung it from the ceiling.

"Are you sure about this?" I asked.

The following morning, I reached under the bed for a discarded sock and found what I thought was a three-tiered earring. It looked like something you'd get at a craft fair, not pretty, but definitely handmade, fashioned from what looked like petrified wood. I was just holding it to the side of my head when I thought, *Hang on, this is an index finger.* It must have fallen off while Hugh was carrying in the skeleton. Then he or I or possibly his mother, who was in town for the holidays, accidentally kicked it under the bed.

I don't think of myself as overly prissy, but it bothered me to find a finger on my bedroom floor. "If this thing is going to start shedding parts, you really *should* put it in your studio," I said to Hugh, who told me that it was his present and he'd keep it wherever the hell he wanted to. Then he got out some wire and reattached the missing finger.

* * *

It's the things you *don't* buy that stay with you the longest, This portrait of an unknown woman, for instance. I saw it a few years ago in Rotterdam, and rather than following my instincts I told the dealer that I'd think about it. The next day, I returned, and it was gone, sold, which is maybe for the best. Had I bought it myself, the painting would have gone on my office wall. I'd have admired it for a week or two, and then, little by little, it would have become invisible, just like the portrait of the dog. I wanted it, I wanted it, I wanted it, but the moment it was mine, it ceased to interest me. I no longer see the shame-filled eyes or the oversized nipples, but I do see the unknown woman, her ruddy, pious face, and the lace collar that hugged her neck like an air filter.

As the days pass, I keep hoping that the skeleton will become invisible, but he hasn't. Dangling between the dresser and the bedroom door, he is the last thing I see before falling asleep, and the first thing I see when opening my eyes in the morning.

It's funny how certain objects convey a message—my washer and dryer, for example. They can't speak, of course, but whenever I pass them they remind me that I'm doing fairly well. "No more laundromat for you," they hum. My stove, a downer, tells me every day that I can't cook, and before I can defend myself my scale jumps in, shouting from the bathroom, "Well, he must be doing *something*. My numbers are off the charts." The skeleton has a much more limited vocabulary and says only one thing: "You are going to die."

I'd always thought that I understood this, but lately I realize that what I call "understanding" is basically just fantasizing. I think about death all the time, but only in a romantic, self-serving way, beginning, most often, with my tragic illness and ending with my funeral. I see my brother squatting beside my grave, so racked by guilt that he's unable to stand. "If only I'd paid him back that twenty-five thousand dollars I borrowed," he says. I see Hugh, drying his eyes on the sleeve of his suit jacket, then crying even harder when he remembers I bought it for him. What I *didn't* see were all the people who might celebrate my death, but that's all changed with the skeleton, who assumes features at will.

One moment he's an elderly Frenchwoman, the one I didn't give my seat to on the bus. In my book, if you want to be treated like an old person, you have to look like one. That means no face-lift, no blond hair, and definitely no fishnet stockings. I think it's a perfectly valid rule, but it wouldn't have killed me to take her crutches into consideration.

"I'm sorry," I say, but before the words are out of my mouth the skeleton has morphed into a guy named Stew, who I once slighted in a drug deal.

Stew and the Frenchwoman will be happy to see me go, and there are hundreds more in line behind them, some I can name, and others I'd managed to hurt and insult without a formal introduction. I hadn't thought of these people in years, but that's the skeleton's cleverness. He gets into my head when I'm asleep and picks through the muck at the bottom of my skull. "Why me?" I ask. "Hugh is lying in the very same bed. How come you don't go after him?"

And the skeleton says, "You are going to die."

"But I'm the one who found your finger."

"You are going to die."

I say to Hugh, "Are you sure you wouldn't be happier with the baby?"

For the first few weeks, I heard the voice only when I was in the bedroom. Then it spread and took over the entire apartment. I'd be sitting in my office, gossiping on the telephone, and the skeleton would cut in, sounding like an international operator. "You are going to die."

I stretched out in the bathtub, soaking in fragrant oils, while outside my window beggars were gathered like kittens upon the heating grates.

"You are going to die."

In the kitchen I threw away a perfectly good egg. In the closet I put on a sweater some half-blind child was paid ten sesame seeds to make. In the living room I took out my notebook and added a bust of Satan to the list of gifts I'd like to receive.

"You are going to die. You are going to die. You are going to die."

"Do you think you could alter that just a little?" I asked.

But he wouldn't.

Having been dead for three hundred years, there's a lot the skeleton doesn't understand: TV, for instance. "See," I told him, "you just push this button, and entertainment comes into your home." He seemed impressed, and so I took it a step further. "I invented it myself, to bring comfort to the old and sick."

"You are going to die."

He had the same reaction to the vacuum cleaner, even after I used the nozzle attachment to dust his skull. "You are going to die."

And that's when I broke down. "I'll do anything you like," I said. "I'll make amends to the people I've hurt, I'll bathe in rainwater, you name it, just please say something, anything, else."

The skeleton hesitated a moment. "You are going to be dead…some day," he told me.

And I put away the vacuum cleaner, thinking, *Well, that's a start.*

Cornel West:
Teachable Moments

Some entertainers are also blessed to be profound teachers. I think of the genius of Bob Dylan. Dylan came to mind not long ago when I was at the airport on my way to Germany. I was at the gate talking to Mom on the cell when I noticed a brother patiently waiting to approach me. When I hung up, he came over and, with a sweet sincerity, said, "Professor West, my name is Winston, and I've only wanted to meet two people in my life. Frederick Douglass and you. I'll never meet Frederick, but thank God today I can meet you."

"Well, thank you, my dear brother," I said. "That's a mighty compliment."

"I don't want to take up too much of your time, professor," Winston went on to say, "but I do have to tell you this: I've played drums for Bob Dylan for years. We travel the world together, and sometimes your name comes up. Both Bob and I love and respect you. Once, when I mentioned you to Bob, he said something I'll never forget. 'Cornel West,' said Dylan, 'is a man who lives his life out loud.'"

"Lord, have mercy!" I said. "I've never heard that formulation before. Tell Brother Dylan that I love him as well, and that even though he doesn't know me personally, he sure-enough knows my heart."

Dylan's heart rests in his vocation. He is a white bluesman par excellence. His voice is born out of that vocation, informed by a vision rooted in reaching and teaching as many people as possible.

Cornel West, educator and philosopher, is the Class of 1943 University Professor at Princeton University. Known as one of America's most gifted, provocative, and important public intellectuals, he is the author of the contemporary classic *Race Matters,* which changed the course of America's dialogue on race and justice; and the *New York Times* best-seller *Democracy Matters.* He is the recipient of the American Book Award and holds more than twenty honorary degrees. www.cornelwest.com

Reaching and teaching is my greatest joy as well, especially lighting a fire in the minds of young people. Every year at Princeton I insist on teaching freshmen. I want to be part of their academic lives, knowing that connecting with them at an early juncture might move their stories in a positive direction.

In my freshman seminar on "The Tragic, The Comic, and The Political," we read works such as Plato's *Republic,* Sophocles's *Antigone,* Dante's *Inferno,* Shakespeare's *Hamlet,* essays by Kant and Hume, fiction by Dostoyevsky, Kafka, and Nathanael West, and plays by Ibsen, Chekhov, Hansberry, Lorca, Williams, O'Neill, Soyinka, and Beckett. The course focuses on the never-ending activity of paideia — deep education — and the problem of evil. Freshmen begin with a sense of trepidation in the face of this formidable parade of great texts.

How does my freshman seminar in humanities differ from those of my colleagues? My lens as a bluesman is to begin with the catastrophic, the horrendous, the calamitous and monstrous in life. So Plato's discussion of death that inaugurates the *Republic,* Hamlet's discussion of Yorick with the grave diggers in Shakespeare's classic play, or Gregor's transformation into a huge, foul vermin in Kafka's *The Metamorphosis* initiates us into the traumatic coping with "humando" — with burial, death, and the worms waiting for us in the soil. In this way, the tragicomic sensibilities of a bluesman are an essential feature of the rich humanist tradition.

Initially, students are quite shaken with this stress on the fragility of their lives and the inevitability of their own death. Yet as they examine these great texts and see the centrality of death and rebirth, of learning how to die to learn how to live, they are initiated into paideia. I consider this a lifelong initiation in deep education, a priceless contribution to their lives and to my life as a teacher. In fact, my enthusiastic teaching itself at my beloved Princeton is a living testimony to the sheer transformative power of paideia.

Teachable moments do not just happen in the classroom. They are shot through everyday life and take place in a variety of contexts. To be teachable is to muster the courage to listen generously, think critically, and be open to the ambiguity and mystery of life. For example, I began as a fierce critic of black leaders Reverend Jesse Jackson, Reverend Al Sharpton, Minister Louis Farrakhan, Bishop T. D. Jakes, and Barack Obama. But after breaking bread with all five and spending countless hours in rich dialogue, I realized how short-sighted I had been. All five men had much to teach me, and I certainly had a deep love for each of them. We vowed to continue the conversation for the rest of our lives. Of course, it mattered that we disagreed deeply on many subjects. But what mattered more was the mutual love and respect that came out of those meetings.

There was another impromptu meeting that took me by surprise. I was at Reagan Airport in DC, munching on a hot dog in the waiting area, when I looked up to see Supreme Court Justice Clarence Thomas and his beloved wife standing nearby.

I approached the justice and said, "It's a pleasure to meet you. I just spoke at a school where you had spoken and given encouragement to young students."

"Thank you. It's a pleasure to meet you too, Professor West. I do have to say, though, you've uttered some awfully harsh words about me."

"Yes, they were based on principle and had nothing to do with personal attacks."

"I do welcome criticism and wish we had more time to discuss our differences. Please feel free to visit my home."

With that, we hugged and went our separate ways. It is this spirit of breaking bread that I cherish.

One of my grand moments of being taught took place during the presidential campaign of my dear brother Bill Bradley. During the Iowa primary, I met the Boston Celtic star Bill Russell. His wisdom blew me away. I shall never forget his profound and poignant words. He told Brother Bradley and me "to absorb wounds with dignity and turn defiance into determination and to win with integrity." If ever there was a grand bluesman in sports, it was Bill Russell.

I also cherish historical links and historical continuity. Like my favorite philosopher Gadamer, tradition is central to my understanding of vocation. But it is a tradition of critique and resistance. At its best, it is a tradition of bearing witness to love and justice.

As a freshman at Harvard, I experienced such a historical link in this grand tradition when attending the lectures of Shirley Graham Du Bois, the widow of W. E. B. Du Bois, the greatest black scholar ever to walk the streets of America.

Yet the story of another such witness both alarmed and troubled me.

It was 1990, and I was walking with John Hope Franklin, the second most famous black scholar, in the hills of Bellagio, Italy. We were attending a conference put together by the prophetic figure Marian Wright Edelman for poor black children. Above us, the sky was a baby blue. Below us, Lake Como was comforting and calm. Professor Franklin, a man of quiet dignity with an enchanting smile, was in a reflective mood.

"Cornel," he said, "let me tell you a story that I rarely share. It's about me and W. E. B. Du Bois."

"Wow. Did you know him well?"

"No one knew him *that* well, but my first encounter with him was extraordinary."

"What was it like?"

"I was at a hotel in North Carolina in 1938. I recognized W. E. B. Du Bois sitting in the lobby. He was reading a newspaper. I approached him with great respect and anticipation.

"'Dr. Du Bois,' I said, 'good morning, sir. My name is John Hope Franklin.'

"Du Bois did not react. His eyes remained fixated on the newspaper to the point that he didn't even acknowledge my presence. No matter, I wasn't about to leave. After all, this was the great W. E. B. Du Bois.

"'Dr. Du Bois,' I reiterated, 'I am named after John Hope, the president of Atlanta University.'

"Still, no reaction. But, Cornel, I could not imagine leaving without some interaction. So one last time, I said, 'Sir, I am a Harvard graduate student in the same program that awarded you your PhD.'

"After several long seconds of silence, Du Bois gave me a quick cursory glance. A glance, mind you, not a word. I slowly walked away."

As I looked into the eyes of John Hope Franklin, I could see inner tears of deep disappointment. The incident might have occurred a half-century earlier, but Professor Franklin made it feel like it happened yesterday.

My gut reaction was, if it had been me, I would have rhetorically slapped Du Bois upside the head and said, "You can at least take a second to say hello." But on further reflection, I recognized that he was who he was—an intellectual freedom fighter and an elitist. I have come to realize that everybody's who they are, and not somebody else. And I believe that Professor Franklin, though his heart was broken, reached the same conclusion. The happy footnote to this story is that years later Du Bois and Franklin became friends. Did Du Bois ever realize whom he failed to acknowledge that morning in North Carolina? We will never know.

What does it mean to be an educated person? Academic accolades and doctoral degrees are one measure of education, but life experience and selfless service are another. One of the most moving experiences I have ever had took place at the 2009 commencements at Morehouse and Spelman. Both events took place on the same day at these historical black institutions where education and empowerment are rooted in the unique brotherhood and sisterhood that comes from a tradition of excellence.

In the morning over four hundred young, brilliant black men graduated in pomp and circumstance. At various moments, they placed the academic hoods over each other's heads. As I reflected on my time spent with precious young black men in prisons, on blocks of the 'hood, or just in trouble, tears flowed from my eyes. Listening to the valedictorian's speech and the honoring of those who were graduating was a deeply humbling moment.

In the evening over five hundred young, brilliant black women graduated. Just before I was about to give the commencement address, the Spelman College glee club broke into beautiful song filling our hearts with the powerful Negro spiritual "I Can't Tarry" — "I've got to keep running, running, running as I ascend to the kingdom." Tears again flowed from my eyes. I thought of the powerful new wave of national and global leaders distinctively black and female.

What a blessing to bear witness to these students' glorious achievements. I am their servant and I can't tarry.

* * *

My story, like all of our stories, is a work in progress. At several junctures and in several ways, it breaks down. That's because, as a cracked vessel, I break down. I try to love my crooked neighbor with my crooked heart. I try to rid myself of prejudices, but always fall short.

I often talk about how all of us live on the edge. Catastrophes are a constant part of our lives on the planet. Disease is always a threat — disease of the body and mind. Staying sane in this world of ours is no easy task. You could lose it. I could lose it. Any of us could. To retain peace of mind and equanimity of spirit is no easy task. As the product of an oppressed, resilient, joyful people, I take refuge in my heritage. My heritage sees life through a tragicomic lens. The comedy is not without dire consequences and the tragedy is not without soul-saving humor.

I am encouraged by the ascendancy of President Barack Obama for whom I worked tirelessly — from campaigning in the cold days of Iowa through over twenty events in a two-day marathon in the swing state of Ohio. As he aspires to be the black Lincoln, I intend to be a blacker Frederick Douglass.

I am encouraged that racism, deep-seated and long-lasting, did not overpower the worthiness of his cause. I am blessed to have lived long enough to see the end of the age of Reagan, the era of conservatism. Barack stepped out on faith and landed on something solid. I hope that the age of Obama is the age of empowering everyday people rather than a recycling of neo-liberal mediocrity. Like all of us, he's got to keep on steppin' too. He'll need all the faith in the world. I believe that faith is that fiduciary dimension in the human condition where we admit that we can't live on doubt. We can't survive on arguments. Logic won't do it. To get up in the morning and do the monumental tasks that face us, our labor is best fueled by love. That's the only way we can move forward —

with decency and dignity. That's the only way we can turn our devotion to others.

Meanwhile, the empire continues to wobble and we all continue to waver. There are declines in our culture and decay in our hearts. As the Spinners said, we need a mighty love. We need a mighty healing. I look back at my life, knowing that without that healing love—from my grandparents and parents, from my brother and sisters, from my children and the women I have been blessed to know—I would have spun out a long time ago. This broken vessel would have plain collapsed.

So I say, thank you, Jesus.

I say, thank you, Lord.

I say, thank you for the breath in my lungs and the strength in my loins. May that strength endure so that I can serve you. And in serving you, may I serve others, especially the least of these.

Everyday Optimism

Brian Tracy:
You Are Remarkable

Y ou are a remarkable person who has extraordinary qualities. You have more talent and abilities than you could use in one hundred lifetimes. What you can do with your life from this day forward is limited only by your own imagination.

Your brain contains about one hundred billion neurons, each of which is connected to as many as twenty thousand other cells in a complex network of ganglia and dendrites. This means that the possible thoughts and combinations of thoughts that you could think would be equal to the number one followed by eight pages of zeros; this number is greater than all the molecules in the known universe.

Dr. Wayne Dyer, a well-known author and speaker on the topic of self-development [see chapter 3], says, "Each child comes into the world with 'secret orders.'" This means that you were born with a unique destiny at a certain time and place, under certain circumstances, in a special situation. You are put on this earth to do something wonderful with your life, something that no one else but you can do.

You are unique in every sense. There is no one in the world, in all of human history, with the special combination of talents, abilities, knowledge, experience, insights, feelings, desires, ambitions, hopes, or dreams that you have. And there never will be.

Your greatest satisfaction and joy in life will come when you have the wonderful feeling that you are realizing your full potential and becoming everything you are capable of becoming. The only question is, "Are you an optimist or a pessimist?" Do you see the glass as half full or half empty?

Brian Tracy is the best-selling author of *Create Your Own Future, The Power of Charm,* and *Reinvention: How to Make the Rest of Your Life the Best of Your Life,* among numerous other books. One of the world's most popular and influential speakers on personal and professional development, he addresses more than a quarter of a million people every year. www.briantracy.com

CHAPTER TWENTY-NINE

The Highest-Paid Work

What is the highest-paid, most important work in America? Some people think that the answer is sports, show business, Fortune 500 CEO, or something else. The fact is that the most important work of all is "thinking." The better you think, the better decisions you make. The better decisions you make, the better actions you take.

The better actions you take, the better results you get. In the long run, and in the short run, the quality of your thinking largely determines the quality of your life. All truly successful, happy people are good thinkers.

Today, you are essentially a knowledge worker. The greater the quality and quantity of knowledge that you have acquired, the more tools you will have at your disposal to shape your thinking, hone your decisions, and ensure that you get better results. Fortunately, thinking critically is a learnable skill. You can get better at it by doing it more often.

Thinking Skills for the Twenty-First Century

There are a series of thinking skills that you must master in order to succeed in a world of turbulence and rapid change. I call them the Seven Rs.

1. **Reevaluating.** This occurs when you take a time-out to reexamine all the details of your life, especially when your life has changed dramatically. You'll know it is time to reevaluate when you experience stress, resistance, frustration, failure, disappointment, or difficulties of any kind. When you are chronically irritable, angry, or unhappy with your work or personal situation, it's a sign that it's time for you to stand back and reevaluate the situation based on the way it is today.

2. **Rethinking.** The quality of your thinking is largely determined by the quantity of the information you have with which to work. In rethinking, you make every effort, as Harold Geneen of ITT said, to "get the facts." You ask as many questions as you possibly can about the person, problem, or situation so that you can make your decisions based on fact rather than emotions.

3. **Reorganizing.** The purpose of organizing any personal or business situation is to ensure the smoothest possible functioning. As time, people, and situations change, especially in a turbulent world, you must carefully and continually examine your current ways of living, working, and doing business. Be prepared to organize and reorganize processes, procedures, and activities to increase the smoothness of operations and the efficiency of your work or personal life.

4. **Restructuring.** Because there is never enough time or money for everything that you want to be, have, and do, you must economize. Restructuring involves moving time, money, and resources away from lower-value areas of activity to higher-value areas.

5. **Reengineering.** This popular management tool is aimed at simplification, continually looking for ways to reduce the complexity or number of steps in any process.

6. **Reinventing.** This is one of the most exciting and revolutionary ways of thinking you will ever learn. Reinventing yourself involves drawing a line under your past and imagining what you would or could do if you were starting over today, in any area, with a clean slate.

7. **Regaining Control.** When you experience a major change or a transition in your life, you may often feel like a small boat that has just hit a squall. You sometimes feel as if you are being pitched up and down physically and emotionally. In the midst of turmoil you will sometimes revert to the "fight or flight" reaction, alternately wanting to attack or withdraw. You will feel as if you are on an emotional roller coaster. It is at this time, more than at any other, that you must regain control of yourself, your feelings, and your actions.

Six Stages of Regaining Control

Psychologist Elisabeth Kubler-Ross identified several stages a person goes through when grieving the death of a loved one, especially a spouse or child. But people also go through several similar stages when they experience an unexpected setback or reversal in their work or personal life.

1. *The first of these stages is denial.* "I don't believe it! This can't be happening!" is a common reaction in this stage. Denial — the refusal to face the inevitable and unavoidable reality of the situation — causes much mental anguish and unhappiness.

2. *The second stage of dealing with a death or setback is anger.* Once it is clear that the event has occurred, the person reacts with anger toward the person or situation he considers responsible for what has happened.

3. *Closely following anger is the third stage, blame.* The individual who has suffered a traumatic event or a loss of some kind immediately blames someone or something else for what has happened. His conversation with himself and others becomes an explanation of why and how he is innocent and why and how someone else is to blame for his unhappiness.

4. *Once you have gone through denial, anger, and blame, the next stage in dealing with death or traumatic events is guilt.* You begin to feel that you did

or failed to do something that led to or contributed to the problem. Feelings of guilt soon turn into feelings of negativity, inferiority, and depression. You may feel like giving up or feel sorry for yourself. It becomes easy to slip into self-pity and self-reproach.

5. *The true antidote to denial, anger, and blame is accepting responsibility.* It is only when you accept responsibility for your situation and for the way you respond to what has happened to you that you can deal with the problem and take control of the situation.

6. *One of the most powerful tools that you can use to regain control of your mind is called reframing.* The way you feel about any situation is largely determined by your explanatory style—by how you interpret the event to yourself, in either a positive or negative way.

Resurgence

Once you have accepted responsibility, reinterpreted the negative event in a positive way, and taken complete control of your mind and emotions, you are ready to resume your upward journey. As Napoleon Hill said, "The only real cure for worry is purposeful action toward a predetermined goal."

You accept what has happened as inevitable and irreversible. You refuse to waste a minute worrying about the past or something that cannot be changed. Instead, you

focus on the future, on the almost unlimited number of possibilities and opportunities open to you to create a wonderful life for yourself.

Questions for Reflection

1. In what one specific area of your life should you take some time to completely reevaluate your situation based on the reality of today?

2. How could you reorganize your life or work so that it is more in harmony with what you want and what makes you happy?

3. How could you restructure your life or work so that you are spending more time doing the things that bring you the greatest rewards?

4. How could you simplify your life by delegating, downsizing, consolidating, or eliminating low-value or no-value tasks and activities?

5. If you could wave a magic wand and reinvent your life completely, what changes would you make?

6. In what areas of your life do you need to accept complete responsibility so that you can start moving forward?

7. What one action are you going to take immediately as the result of what you have learned in this chapter?

MERYL STREEP:

Imagined Possibility

If you are all really, really lucky, and if you continue to work super hard, and you remember your thank-you notes and everybody's name; and you follow through on every task that's asked of you and also somehow anticipate problems before they even arise and you somehow sidestep disaster and score big. If you get great scores on your LSATS, or MSATS, or ERSATS, or whatever. And you get into your dream grad school or internship, which leads to a super job with a paycheck commensurate with responsibilities of leadership, or if you somehow get that documentary on a shoestring budget and it gets accepted at Sundance and maybe it wins Sundance and then you go on to be nominated for an Oscar and then you win the Oscar. Or if that money-making website that you designed with your friends somehow suddenly attracts investors and advertisers and becomes the go-to site for whatever it is you're selling, blogging, sharing, or net-casting. And success—shining, hoped-for but never really anticipated success—comes your way, I guarantee you someone you know or love will come to you and say, "Will you address the graduates at my college?" And you'll say, "Yeah, sure, when is it? May 2010? 2010? Yeah, sure, that's months away," and then the nightmare begins. The nightmare we've all had and I assure you, you'll continue to have even after graduation, forty years after graduation. About a week before the due date, you wake up in the middle of the night, "Huh, I have a paper due and I haven't done the reading, Oh my god!"

Meryl Streep, actor extraordinaire, has won two Academy Awards, with sixteen nominations, and seven Golden Globes, with twenty-five nominations, making her the most nominated actor in the history of both awards. She is the recipient of a host of other awards for her acting on stage, screen, and television, including the American Film Institute's 2004 Lifetime Achievement Award. Among her stellar performances are the ones for which she won Oscars, *Kramer vs. Kramer* and *Sophie's Choice.* This chapter is the commencement speech she gave in 2010 at Barnard College in New York City.

CHAPTER THIRTY

If you have been touched by the success fairy, people think you know why. People think success breeds enlightenment and you are duty bound to spread it around like manure, fertilize those young minds, let them in on the secret, what is it that you know that no one else knows. The self-examination begins, one looks inward, one opens an interior door. Cobwebs, black, the lights bulbs burned out, the airless dank refrigerator of an insanely overscheduled, unexamined life that usually just gets takeout. Where is my writer friend Anna Quindlen when I need her? On another book tour.

I am very honored and humbled to be asked to pass on tips and inspiration to you for achieving success in this next part of your lives. When I consider the other distinguished medal recipients and venerable board of trustees, the many accomplished faculty and family members, people who've actually done things, produced things, while I have pretended to do things, I can think of about 3,800 people who should have been on this list before me and since my success has depended wholly on putting things over on people. So I'm not sure parents think I'm that great a role model anyway.

I am, however, an expert in pretending to be an expert in various areas, so just randomly like everything else in this speech, I am or I was an expert in kissing on stage and on screen. How did I prepare for this? Well, most of my preparation took place in my suburban high school or rather behind my suburban high school in New Jersey. One is obliged to do a great deal of kissing in my line of work. Air kissing, ass-kissing, kissing up, and of course actual kissing; much like hookers, actors have to do it with people we may not like or even know. We may have to do it with friends, which, believe it or not, is particularly awkward; for people of my generation, it's awkward.

My other areas of faux expertise—river rafting, miming the effects of radiation poisoning, knowing which shoes go with which bag, coffee plantation, Turkish, Polish, German, French, Italian, that's Iowa-Italian from *The Bridges of Madison County*, a bit of the Bronx, Aramaic, Yiddish, Irish clog dancing, cooking, singing, riding horses, knitting, playing the violin, and simulating steamy sexual encounters—these are some of the areas in which I have pretended quite proficiently to be successful, or the other way around. As have many women here, I'm sure.

Women, I feel I can say this authoritatively, especially at Barnard where they can't hear us, what am I talking about? They professionally can't hear us. Women are better at acting than men. Why? Because we have to be, if successfully convincing someone bigger than you are of something he doesn't know is a survival skill, this is how women have survived through the millennia. Pretending is not just play. Pretending is imagined possibility. Pretending or acting is a very valuable life skill and we all do it, all the time. We don't want to be caught doing it, but nevertheless it's part of the adaptations of our species. We change who we are to fit the exigencies of our time, and not just strategically, or to our own advantage, sometimes sympathetically, without our even knowing it, for the betterment of the whole group.

I remember very clearly my own first conscious attempt at acting. I was six, placing my mother's half slip over my head in preparation to play the Virgin Mary in our living room. As I swaddled my Betsy Wetsy doll, I felt quieted, holy, actually, and my transfigured face and very changed demeanor captured on super-8 by my dad pulled my little brother, Harry, to play Joseph, and Dana too, a barnyard animal, into the trance. They were actually pulled into this nativity scene by the intensity of my focus, which my usual technique for getting them to do what I wanted—yelling at them—would never ever have achieved. I learned something on that day.

Later when I was nine, I remember taking my mother's eyebrow pencil and carefully drawing lines all over my face, replicating the wrinkles that I had memorized on the face of my grandmother whom I adored, and made my mother take my picture. I look at it now and, of course, I look like myself now and my grandmother then. But I do really remember in my bones, how it was possible on that day to feel her age. I stooped, I felt weighted down, but cheerful—I felt like her.

Empathy is at the heart of the actor's art. And in high school, another form of acting took hold of me. I wanted to learn how to be appealing. So I studied the character I imagined I wanted to be, that of the generically pretty high school girl. I researched her deeply, that is to say shallowly, in *Vogue*, in *Seventeen*, and in *Mademoiselle* magazines. I tried to imitate her hair, her lipstick, her lashes, the clothes of the lithesome, beautiful, and generically appealing high school girls that I saw in those pages. I ate an apple a day, period. I peroxided my hair, ironed it straight. I demanded brand-name clothes—my mother shut me down on that one. But I did, I worked harder on this characterization really than anyone I think I've ever done since. I worked on my giggle. I lightened it because I thought it sounded childlike and cute. This was all about appealing to boys and at the same time being accepted by the girls, a very tricky negotiation.

Often success in one area precludes succeeding in the other. And along with all my other exterior choices, I worked on my, what actors call, interior adjustment. I adjusted my natural temperament, which tends to be slightly bossy, a little opinionated, a little loud, full of pronouncements and high spirits, and I willfully cultivated softness, agreeableness, a breezy, natural sort of sweetness, even shyness if you will, which was very, very, very effective on the boys. But the girls didn't buy it. They didn't like me; they sniffed it out, the acting. And they were probably right, but I was committed — this was absolutely not a cynical exercise; this was a vestigial survival courtship skill I was developing. And I reached a point senior year when my adjustment felt like me. I had actually convinced myself that I was this person and she me — pretty, talented, but not stuck-up. You know, a girl who laughed a lot at every stupid thing every boy said and who lowered her eyes at the right moment and deferred, who learned to defer when the boys took over the conversation. I remember this so clearly and I could tell it was working. I was much less annoying to the guys than I had been; they liked me better, and I liked that. This was conscious, but it was at the same time motivated and fully felt; this was real, real acting.

I got to Vassar, which forty-three years ago was a single-sex institution, like all the colleges in what they call the Seven Sisters, the female Ivy League, and I made some quick but lifelong and challenging friends. And with their help outside of any competition for boys, my brain woke up. I got up and I got outside myself and I found myself again. I didn't have to pretend. I could be goofy, vehement, aggressive, and slovenly and open and funny and tough and my friends let me. I didn't wash my hair for three weeks once. They accepted me like the Velveteen Rabbit. I became real instead of an imagined stuffed bunny, but I stockpiled that character from high school and I breathed life into her again some years later as Linda in *The Deer Hunter*. There is probably not one of you graduates who have ever seen this film, but it won best picture in 1978 — Robert De Niro, Chris Walken, not funny at all. And I played Linda, a small-town girl with a working-class background, a lovely, quiet, hapless girl, who waited for the boy she loved to come back from the war in Vietnam. Often men my age — President Clinton, by the way, when I met him — mention that character as their favorite of all the women I've played. And I have my own secret understanding of why that is and it confirms every decision I made in high school. This is not to denigrate that girl, or the men who are drawn to her, in any way because she's still part of me and I'm part of her. She wasn't acting, but she was just behaving in a way that cowed girls, submissive girls, beaten-up girls with very few ways out have behaved forever and still do in many worlds.

Now, as a measure of how much the world has changed, the character most men mention as their favorite is Miranda Priestly. The beleaguered totalitarian at the head of *Runway* magazine in *The Devil Wears Prada*. To my mind, this represents such an optimistic shift. They relate to Miranda. They wanted to date Linda. They felt sorry for Linda, but they feel like Miranda. They can relate to her issues, the high standards she sets for herself and others. The thanklessness of the leadership position. The "Nobody understands me" thing. The loneliness. They stand outside one character and they pity her and they kind of fall in love with her, but they look through the eyes of this other character.

This is a huge deal because, as people in the movie business know, the absolute hardest thing in the whole world is to persuade a straight male audience to identify with a woman protagonist, to feel themselves embodied by her. This more than any other factor explains why we get the movies we get and the paucity of the roles where women drive the film. It's much easier for the female audience because we were all brought up identifying with male characters from Shakespeare to Salinger. We have less trouble following Hamlet's dilemma viscerally or Romeo's or Tybalt or Huck Finn or Peter Pan—I remember holding that sword up to Hook, I felt like him. But it is much much much harder for heterosexual boys to identify with Juliet or Desdemona, Wendy in *Peter Pan* or Joe in *Little Women* or the Little Mermaid or Pocahontas. Why, I don't know, but it just is.

There has always been a resistance to imaginatively assume a persona if that persona is a she. But things are changing now and it's in your generation we're seeing this. Men are adapting...about time...consciously and also without realizing it for the better of the whole group. They are changing their deepest prejudices to regard as normal the things that their fathers would have found very very difficult and their grandfathers would have abhorred and the door to this emotional shift is empathy. As Jung said, emotion is the chief source of becoming conscious. There can be no transforming of lightness into dark, of apathy into movement, without emotion. Or as Leonard Cohen says, pay attention to the cracks because that's where the light gets in. You, young women of Barnard, have not had to squeeze yourself into the corset of being cute or to muffle your opinions—but you haven't left campus yet. I'm just kidding. What you have had is the privilege of a very specific education. You are people who may be able to draw on a completely different perspective to imagine a different possibility than women and men who went to coed schools.

How this difference is going to serve you it's hard to quantify now. It may take you forty years, like it did me, to analyze your advantage. But today is about looking forward into a world where so-called women's issues, human issues of gender inequality lie at the crux of global problems from poverty to the AIDS crisis to the rise in violent fundamentalist juntas, human trafficking and human rights abuses, and you're going to have the opportunity and the obligation, by virtue of your providence, to speed progress in all those areas. And this is a place where the need is very great. This is your time and it feels normal to you, but really there is no normal. There's only change, and resistance to it and then more change.

Never before in the history of our country have most of the advanced degrees been awarded to women, but now they are. It's hardly more than a hundred years since we were even allowed into these buildings except to clean them, but soon most law and medical degrees will probably also go to women. Around the world, poor women who used to *be* property now own property. And according to *Economist* magazine, for the last two decades, the increase of female employment in the rich world has been the main driving force of growth. Those women have contributed more to global GDP growth than have either new technology or the new giants India or China. Cracks in the ceiling, cracks in the door, cracks in the Court and on the senate floor.

You know, I gave a speech at Vassar twenty-seven years ago. It was a really big hit. Everyone loved it, really. Tom Brokaw said it was the very best commencement speech he had ever heard, and of course I believed this. And it was much easier to construct than this one. It came out pretty easily because back then I knew so much. I was a new mother, I had two Academy Awards, and it was all coming together so nicely. I was smart and I understood boiler plate and what sounded good and because I had been on the squad in high school, earnest full-throated cheerleading was my specialty so that's what I did. But now, I feel like I know about one-sixteenth of what that young woman knew. Things don't seem as certain today. Now I'm sixty. I have four adult children who are all facing the same challenges you are. I'm more sanguine about all the things that I still don't know and I'm still curious about.

What I do know about success, fame, celebrity—that would fill another speech. How it separates you from your friends, from reality, from proportion. Your own sweet anonymity, a treasure you don't even know you have until it's gone. How it makes things tough for your family, and whether being famous matters one bit, in the end, in the whole flux of time. I know I was invited here because of that. How famous I am, how many awards I've won. While I am overweeningly proud of the work that, believe me, I did not do on my own, I can assure you that awards have very little bearing on my own personal happiness, my own sense of well-being and purpose in the world. That comes from studying the world feelingly, with empathy in my work. It comes from staying alert and alive and involved in the lives of the people that I love and the people in the wider world who need my help. No matter what you see me or hear me saying when I'm on your TV holding a statuette, spewing, that's acting.

Being a celebrity has taught me to hide, but being an actor has opened my soul.

Being here today has forced me to look around inside there for something useful that I can share with you and I'm really grateful you gave me the chance.

You know you don't have to be famous. You just have to make your mother and father proud of you and you already have. Bravo to you. Congratulations.

Holli Thompson:

Our Food, Our Outlook, Our Lives

In my past life, I was a vice president at Chanel in New York and Paris, head of their Fine Watch and Jewelry Division. Does that sound like a dream? It was. I lived in a high-rise New York City apartment and wore head-to-toe Chanel, courtesy of a generous company clothing allowance. My job consisted of, among other things, merchandising a collection of drop-dead gorgeous precious jewelry in Paris and New York. I frequently flew around the country to visit our stores (Hawaii, Beverly Hills, you get the picture), attended chic social events in Manhattan at the "Chanel table," and vacationed at the world's finest luxury spas. I was single, but when the time was right, I met the man of my dreams, my future husband.

He lived in a charming, idyllic, and sophisticated place called Middleburg, a Virginian town where Jackie Kennedy Onassis once owned a home and visited regularly to fox hunt. "Hunt Country" Virginia is home to many other names you might know as well—a place where money is quiet and the people are interesting and fun. Middleburg reminded me of my Princeton upbringing, with farms, horses, and a small colonial town. My new husband and I enjoyed a busy lifestyle there, with me commuting from Manhattan each Friday afternoon.

After about a year of marriage and weekly flights back and forth, I was feeling a bit worn out, and my husband and I wanted to be together. I was also coming to the realization that perhaps it was time for me to move on to something else professionally. I was at the top of my game

Holli Thompson, "the Nutrition Stylist," is a Certified Holistic Health Counselor, Certified Health and Nutrition Coach, and the founder of Nutritional Style, which offers health consultation to assist people in finding their own individual style, based on the principle that what works for one person may not for the next. Formerly a vice president at Chanel in New York and Paris, she is a recognized public speaker and media personality, was recently featured in More magazine, and has appeared on CBS, ABC news, and FOX networks. www.nutritionalstyle.com.

and, yet, I was being called to something else, to give back in some way. Perhaps it was my new stepdaughter, who at age nine filled my weekends with her cousins and lots of fun. Or perhaps I was being called to have my own child before time ran out. I know I was influenced by my husband's life path of service and working in impoverished countries. Whatever the impetus, I tearfully decided to leave my dream job and my dream company, and I set out bravely to pursue motherhood and find my next "act."

I left Manhattan with two Persian cats and wardrobes full of Chanel, and settled in a country home in the middle of a field. Gone were the ringing phones and constant demands and I found myself with time to fill. I bought a "fancy" horse, and then another, and I began to oil paint. I had decided to take some time off, to explore the things I had always wanted to do and to see what emerged. I was happily in love, a new wife and stepmom, and my life was filled with joy.

One intensely hot day in June, we took my stepdaughter and her cousins to the Upperville Horse Show, a picturesque location adjacent to philanthropist Paul Mellon's farm. The sun was blistering and I made sure the young girls drank lots of water but somehow forgot about myself.

Two hours later, I felt a stabbing pain in my head and I grabbed my husband's arm. "Get me out of here, help me," I said, but I don't remember much more. I tried not to let the girls see what was happening, but I was terrified. My husband drove us home, not knowing his new bride thought she was dying. At home, I could tell him and he called for an ambulance. An MRI at the hospital proved inconclusive. One doctor commented, "Some people are not meant to retire," referring to my new nonworking status. I had a migraine, they said, and they sent me home to deal with it.

The migraine cycle continued for months that summer. At one point, my parents came to stay with me, as my husband was traveling overseas. It's difficult to describe the pain of a migraine if you've never experienced one. The pain was so severe that it hurt to lay my head on a pillow, and days would pass with me in a comatose state. In between migraines, on the "good days," I became sensitive to the Virginian countryside and developed what doctors called "allergies."

Over the next several years, my migraines, often triggered by allergies, became a way of life. I sought the advice of a few doctors and was given various medications. Some of them worked temporarily, but the migraine cycles continued. I also developed chronic sinusitis, and became very tired from the continuous use of antibiotics. My low energy made me depressed and a well-meaning doctor suggested antidepressants. Antidepressants led to low energy, the low energy wiped out my fitness program, and I gradually gained weight.

During this time, we were trying to conceive a baby and, joyfully, a year later, I was pregnant, only to miscarry at eleven weeks. Grief-stricken, we decided to go straight to in vitro fertilization. The fertility drugs were a nightmare and basically dropped my hormones to a place of desolation. We conceived right away, only to miscarry again after the fleeting joy of seeing a heartbeat in a sonogram on Valentine's Day. That spring, I was back for more and, determined to give birth to a child, I managed to conceive for just a couple of weeks. Within a year, I had endured three miscarriages. We were exhausted, my hormones were imbalanced, and we still didn't have our baby.

My husband and I knew we couldn't take "trying" anymore. We had both always been open to adoption; his sister had three adopted children, and my mother recalled that even as a child I had wanted to adopt a baby. As we learned more about children overseas, we were drawn to Russia.

Within ten months, I held my new bouncing baby boy on the plane home from Russia. He looked like my husband's brother and my dad. He was alert, very active, and a beautiful boy. There was no doubt that this was our son and somehow he had called us to him.

My new baby was perfect in every way. I was not. My weight was up, my moods were down, my sinus and allergies had not let up, and I still lived in fear of migraines. We had installed blackout drapes in the bedroom of the new home we had just bought, and motherhood, for all its joy, proved exhausting. By this time, I was running my husband's company, because I had, as I put it, failed at "time off."

Having a new baby was unlike anything I had managed or run in the business world, and the endless demands of my long-sought motherhood left me, within a year, with a viral rash and mononucleosis. My doctor recommended rest. I kept going, of course, and I knew that there had to be a way out of this perfect storm of health issues. Looking back and knowing what I now know, I realize how interrelated these ailments were, but at the time I kept moving forward.

One day I was sitting at a lecture next to one of my friends—my first time out in weeks. I had had another sinus infection, the seventh one in a year. She looked at me and asked, "Holli, are you sick again? Have you considered that your immune system is compromised?" There was something about the way she said it that shook me.

I knew I was frequently sick, and my healthy times had become few and far between. But my life was amazing—I truly believed that and I was happy. The idea that my immunity might be compromised scared me to my core.

The next morning, I looked for the phone number of a nutritionist I had heard about. I called an acupuncturist who had success working with migraines. I went to the health food store to grill them about my various ailments and returned home with my first neti pot, an East Indian china teapot used for pouring water in one nostril and out the other, which would become key to my sinus survival at the time.

I was taking my health into my own hands and out of the hands of my many doctors and the fistful of medications I had been taking each morning. I spent the next several months seeking alternative help and, with my doctor, came up with a plan to wean myself off antidepressants, a process that took well over a year and was extremely difficult.

I returned to the nutrition and health books that had been a passion throughout my life but had gotten filed away in the past few years of coping. I ordered more books and read with a vengeance. My life in New York had been a healthy one, but I had to relearn the healthy habits of those days. I came back to the importance of organic foods, avoiding pesticides, and adding in antioxidants in abundant quantities. I began to juice green vegetables and discovered an energetic high from drinking healthy organic veggies. I made morning smoothies that contained my own immune-building protocol of hemp seeds, flax, organic berries, and varying superfoods that boosted my energy.

Thanks to my nutritionist, I confirmed that I was dairy intolerant, something I had known since childhood but never wanted to admit. The memory of my first ice cream sundae and the subsequent nausea flooded back, as did years of trying to eat lasagna and cheeses and always feeling bloated and sick afterward.

Removing dairy was a key piece in my recovery. Years later, after attending nutrition school, I discovered that dairy had been directly related to the chronic inflammation I faced during my years of allergies, sinusitis, and migraines. Subsequently, I gave up gluten and refined sugars, also possible inflammatory foods, and my energy and health continued to improve.

With each small change, my optimism grew. I was finding my way out of this bleak time, and I was learning. I realized the strong connection between food and mood, and how much easier it is to feel optimistic and hopeful when you are healthy. I learned that eating the right foods can actually boost your outlook on life and raise your endorphins. I remembered how vital exercise was to my overall holistic health, and how sometimes what you do *not* eat is just as important as what you do.

I inspired myself to keep going and, with each pound lost and each long walk or trip to the gym, my confidence in the outcome improved. I convinced my husband that I needed to get to a spa, and I chose one in Mexico that I knew would jump-start my fitness and clean eating. I could see light at the end of the tunnel, and I knew that I could get myself back. I could feel it coming.

My road back to health was profound and noticeable to others. People began to see that not only had I lost weight, but also my spirits were high and I had a "glow." My skin became clear, my hair was getting shinier, and my energy was soaring. "What are you doing?" was the common question and I started to share information and tips about my eating and diet with my neighbors and friends.

During this time, as my health improved, I realized I was finally ready for my "next act." It had been years coming, but the problem was I had no idea what it might be. I explored every option I could think of: opening a retail store, starting a jewelry line, selling a friend's jewelry line, going back to corporate, becoming a lobbyist, becoming a fashion stylist, opening an eBay store, selling real estate, and so on. Girlfriends grew exhausted as I ran ideas by them and my husband happily entertained each one with me.

One evening at a dinner with friends, a close friend of mine mentioned that her husband's daughter had gone back to school for nutrition and she began to talk about the school. I nearly leapt across the table, saying, "That's it! I'm going." It made sense; I was passionate about nutrition, had studied it on my own, and had healed my body through my food, but, most important, I wanted to share what I had learned. I wanted to help others realize the power of food, and the profound effect what we put into our mouths can have on our bodies, our minds, and our emotions.

I called the next day and enrolled, and I felt the joy of being in the "flow," realizing I had made the right decision and was connected to a source of inspiration that had propelled me to this moment.

Although my class was not to start for a year, I began formal nutrition education at a gourmet cooking school in Manhattan and began commuting back and forth to New York a couple of times a month. I explored the trendy "raw food" movement, read every book I could get my hands on, and became a raw food chef. I invested in a dehydrator that "cooks" food at 115 degrees, and started my own file of raw recipes.

Within a year, I launched Nutritional Style and began coaching clients. I coached high-powered executives who had no idea how to feed themselves healthy foods, and prominent philanthropists interested in living a long and energetic life. I worked with several moms on their nutrition and taught them how to prepare delicious healthy foods for their families, and I resolved some serious food intolerance issues like my own that would have gone unresolved, perhaps for years, under conventional health care.

CHAPTER THIRTY-ONE

I asked and still ask the question, "What did you eat today?" and I listen. I look for sugars, gluten, dairy, processed foods, and unhealthy fats. I add in whole foods, greens and vegetables, grains, legumes, fruits, and healthy protein. I work with clients on their food's integrity, and encourage them to avoid factory-farmed meat and spend a little extra for meat that has been humanely and organically raised, if they need to eat meat. I let my clients know about the seafood that is high in toxins or overfished, and encourage a sustainable approach to eating.

Gradually, health improves with clean, organic food, and our hope and vision for the future follows. I had watched my own body prematurely age as it carried extra weight and processed antidepressants and allergy medications daily. I had felt the sadness and lack of optimism that the hormonal imbalance of multiple miscarriages can bring and the desolate well of depression due to ill health. But I had also watched my body become younger and more toned from eating healthy foods, saw the natural face lift that happened when I started eating within my own "nutritional style," and felt my moods lift to where medications are no longer necessary.

A few months ago, I gave a talk at a women's event, and a woman raised her hand. She was a self-described couch potato and said she knew what to do for her health but couldn't get herself to do it. She described herself as tired and without "willpower." Her husband was a professional baker and he brought home hard-to-resist cookies and pastries daily. Her skin was dull, her hair was dry, and she was about twenty pounds overweight. She lacked energy to move or exercise.

How could she have had any energy? She was eating processed sugars daily and the temporary highs left her exhausted. She was drinking coffee throughout the day and making poor choices in an effort to get some kind of "lift" from her food. She was depressed and on an antidepressant, and it was obviously not working for her.

She asked me, "What can I do? Just give me one thing to do; I can't do it all." She was clearly in an overwhelmed state.

I recommended she buy herself a beautiful new fruit bowl and that she go to her local organic market and purchase whichever fruits she loved. I asked her to fill the bowl with the fruits and give it a prominent place on her table. I told her, when your husband comes home proudly carrying the evening's cookies, you can, if you must, take just one small one. Eat it, savor the flavor, and enjoy every bite. Then stop and leave the room. If you want more cookies, have a piece of fruit, but pause to enjoy and savor the fruit. If after having your fruit, you are still craving the cookies, have another piece of fruit. In fact, I told her to eat as much fruit as she wanted, knowing that the high fiber would prohibit her from overeating. I asked her to try that for one week.

A week later, the woman called me to set up a one-on-one session to begin working with me. She had done what I said, and realized that the fruit tasted better than the cookie, and she had also felt full and satisfied. Her moods and confidence had improved with just one night of my "Fruit vs. Cookie" program. She woke the next morning feeling something she had not felt for years. *She felt optimistic about her future.*

Empowered by her choices of fruit over the cookie, she began to make better choices during the day as well. She began to substitute salads for her daily processed sandwich, and made lean protein choices with vegetables instead of having pasta several times a week. She realized the significance that food played in her depression and her ultimate outlook on life. Within a few months, she had lost twenty pounds and was riding her bike everywhere. She had signed up for yoga and enthusiastically purchased and cooked whole foods for herself and her husband. Her posture improved, her skin glowed, and she radiated health and happiness. She looked, without a doubt, ten years younger. She was vibrant and sunny and her final step was to discover a new purpose in life. Reconnecting to her love of plants, she went back to school to become a landscape architect.

Making conscious choices about our food each day plays directly into our outlook on life. The smallest choice can fuel a bright outlook and create a ripple effect in the rest of our diet. Many people make the mistake of "all or nothing" and take a small slip-up as license to binge or toss good choices out the window. Once my clients realize that each small victory builds to the next and that backslides are part of life, they relax into the long path to fabulous and vibrant health.

One of my favorite moments is when a client I've been working with over time can't even remember how unhealthy their eating once was. When I share my notes from our first session, they often stare at me in amazement. I remind them of how tired or sick they once were, or how their skin was dull from their daily bag of chips or can of soda. They give a big smile, because optimism and faith in their future has won out. Their daily food choices are now their biggest advocate for a fabulous and passionate life.

With that kind of optimism, who knows what's now possible?

JOHN GRAY:

Guiding Principles for Practical Miracles

CHAPTER
32

I n practical terms, by applying the nine guiding principles you can start making changes in your life that previously seemed impossible for you. Any new skill is easier to learn if we have examples or demonstrations to follow. For easy assimilation of the nine principles, it is helpful to have a vision of possibilities. There are unique benefits that come directly from applying each of the nine guiding principles. While these are some of the benefits, you may experience your own unique benefits and miracles. These are a few examples of changes or practical miracles I have regularly witnessed in my own life and in the lives of participants of my workshops.

1. Believe as if miracles are possible. Using this guiding principle, participants have hope again. With hope they are motivated to make new resolutions. Miraculously, they find that they are able to follow through. They feel the confidence to do things they have been putting off for years. Procrastination no longer holds us back when we believe and experience that the miracle of change can really happen.

2. Live as if you are free to do what you want. Using this guiding principle and applying self-healing techniques in a group or with a healer, in ten minutes, chronic pain and other health problems have miraculously disappeared. After a "miracle healing," whether it be physical or emotional, instead of feeling burdened by your lot in life, suddenly you feel your new freedom to be all that you have the potential to be. With this experience, you gain the support to enjoy life, to "live freely" as if no one is holding you back.

John Gray, PhD, is a certified family therapist and author of the *New York Times* long-running best-seller *Men Are from Mars, Women Are from Venus,* published in 1995, and the numerous subsequent books in the Mars-Venus series on relationships, which together have sold more than fifty million copies in over forty-five languages worldwide. He has appeared on *Oprah,* the *Today Show, Good Morning America,* and *Larry King Live,* among many other shows, and been profiled in *Newsweek, Time, Forbes, USA Today, TV Guide,* and *People.* www.marsvenus.com

"Miracle healings" are not new; they have occurred throughout history. They have been fully documented during the past thousand years in every culture and tradition in the world. Even in the last one hundred years, the scrutiny of the most rigorous scientific research and testing has shown that unexplained immediate recovery from a variety of deadly diseases is a reality.

And miracle healings continue to occur. No educated medical researcher doubts this. The reason some scientists, researchers, and doctors minimize or cringe at the mention of miracle healings is that they can't duplicate or understand them.

Miraculous healing in the past was a hit-or-miss occurrence and thus "nonscientific," simply because people could not explain or replicate it. A few people were healed but most were not. It is important to recognize that just because something can't be understood, it doesn't mean that it didn't happen or doesn't exist.

In my workshops and while studying with healers around the world, I personally have witnessed almost every illness—from such serious diseases and conditions as stage-four cancer, multiple sclerosis, and strokes to such less serious illnesses as chronic back pain, headaches, and hay fever—immediately disappear in a few months. Though history is filled with these kinds of miraculous healings, what is different today is that everyone can experience them with a little instruction and support.

3. Learn as if you are a beginner. These miraculous healings are sustained by making a few significant dietary adjustments. To make these changes, we must open our minds and be willing to experiment and test out the dietary suggestions of the Natural Energy Diet. By using this principle, we are motivated to learn something new, try it, and then discern for ourselves what works for us.

Without dietary changes a healing may not last. Symptoms go away in a healing session, but within a few days they may come back. If we continue to poison ourselves with just a few particular foods, the effect of a healing disappears almost as quickly as it was gained. With a few new insights about drinking and eating, and the practice of self-healing techniques, my clients and workshop participants have been automatically attracted to nutritious foods to rebuild and sustain a healthier body. After a healing takes place, healthy, nutritious food actually tastes better. For this reason, all the suggestions are easy to practice. They are sustained over time because they work immediately. When we try them, we will immediately begin to feel better.

Healing power does not make medicine obsolete in any way. Modern medicine, ancient healing practices, "alternative" medicine, and these new self-healing techniques, when used together in a complementary manner, can create even greater miraculous healings than any singular approach.

As you experience the immediate results of self-healing, you realize how little you really know about your potential to change and become excited about all the new possibilities that now exist. A whole new world opens up when we are willing to learn again as if we are beginners.

4. Love as if for the first time. In relationships, by using this guiding principle, many couples have found that miraculously they are once again falling in love with their partner. They are able to forgive ex-partners and wish them well. The old resentments just melt away into the sunset of the past when we learn how to forgive. Everyone aspires to forgive; but few have learned how to do it. The good intention to forgive is not enough; we must actually learn how to do it.

In the area of relationships, through teaching the ideas contained in *Men Are from Mars, Women Are from Venus,* I first began to notice the accelerated changes of this new age. Couples were finding that in a one-day workshop they were able to open their hearts to rekindle the love they thought was lost. Many marriages were saved. But even when relationships ended in divorce, couples were able to break up with greater love and forgiveness.

Creating lasting love doesn't mean that you will always stay married to the same person; it does mean you will always love that person and wish him or her well. People mistakenly blame themselves for failing in relationships when they get divorced, and yet some people find that after a divorce their lives have become more wonderful. Through forgiveness they were able to love freely again, as if they had never been hurt.

Thousands of couples at the brink of divorce have created lasting love by finding forgiveness and learning the skills for successful communication. When we feel that we are victims of love, this self-pity inevitably prevents us from opening our hearts and trusting love again. Fortunately, this old pain can be healed, and we can begin to love and trust again as if for the first time.

5. Give as if you already have what you need. With an understanding of their new potential for change, many have given up smoking or other unhealthy habits or addictions. Although they may have tried to stop in the past and failed, they are inspired to try again and this time succeed with an understanding of how to remove all addictive cravings. This time, by using this guiding principle, they are armed with a new arsenal of practical techniques, and it is easy to stop.

When you understand what creates miracles, you find that you already have the power to change and then follow through without difficulty and suffering. All that is required is an understanding of your new potential and a few new insights and techniques for awakening and using your inner power.

All addictions ultimately come from being overly dependent on someone or something outside of yourself to be happy. As you experience your inner power to get what you need, then you are not as dependent on others. You are then free to release addictive cravings.

As you give more while taking responsibility for your blocks, you begin to experience that it is through giving that you receive. For most of us, this concept is familiar but still just a concept. One cannot actually experience getting more through giving unless one is already self-sufficient.

If you are dependent on your partner to feel good, then when you give, some part of you needs and hopes to get something in return. Couples who primarily come together to fill up and not to give are always disappointed. The act of giving is eventually not as fulfilling because they are still dependent on receiving before they can feel good. Even when we are needy, giving can be very fulfilling in the beginning of a relationship, because we don't know our partner and we expect to get everything back. We naively expect perfection, which does not exist. Ultimately, instead of feeling energized by giving we become tired, empty, and exhausted. Whenever you feel resentment, it is a sign that you were giving to get something in return rather than giving from a sense of fullness without expectations or demands.

This explains the common perception that you can't really love another unless you first love yourself. Rather than depending on your partner to feel good, view him or her as a good dessert. You — not your partner — are responsible for supplying the important nutrients in your life. By loving yourself and having a fulfilling life first, the extra love your partner provides is an added bonus that you are not as dependent on. When you experience being independent and self-sufficient, you are able to give of yourself freely, not to expect a return, but to enjoy the fulfillment that comes from giving. You are able to give as if you already have what you need.

Women often think that they are giving without expecting something in return, but after a few years of feeling neglected in a relationship, they will complain in counseling, "I have given so much and have gotten nothing in return." The mistake is not in giving to her partner but rather in not taking the time to give to herself so that she is free to give to her partner without demanding more in return.

It is amazing how much more willing men are to give when they are asked for more in a nondemanding or nonresentful manner. It is practically impossible to ask for support in an easy, loving manner when we are not getting what we need. At those times, the secret to enjoying more of what our partner has to offer is first to give to ourselves whatever we need so that we are not dependent or demanding change from our partner.

6. Work as if money doesn't matter. The greatest miracle that I repeatedly observe is how quickly change can occur for people. It is not that every aspect of their life changes or gets better at once, but some significant aspect does. It may be that a woman is overweight, experiencing low energy, feeling deprived in her relationship, and not liking her job. It doesn't all get better at once.

Some will begin to lose weight right away, but others begin to love themselves and their partner more, and then, at a later time, they begin to lose weight or change jobs. Sometimes, before we can make a life change, we first need to make an attitude change. Sometimes when a physical healing does not occur, it is not until we experience an attitude shift about work that the body heals. Using this sixth guiding principle, many people begin to experience their power to create practical miracles.

Although we live in an age of miracles, it is still true that change occurs gradually. It still takes time for the seed to grow into a tree. Everything doesn't change at once. The miracle is that now the blocks to natural change and healing can be easily removed. The seeds of greatness in our hearts now can grow freely at their natural rate into a beautiful tree.

Sometimes before a physical sickness clears up, an emotional issue must be healed. At other times, a physical sickness is miraculously healed, and then the buried emotional issues responsible for that sickness begin to surface. In a similar manner, sometimes a person can make a life change or change of habit first, and then the emotional issues begin to surface in order to be healed. Or, it may be that first the emotional issue becomes healed and released, and then the necessary life change becomes clear, and we are naturally motivated to make the change.

In most cases, when it comes to healing the body, some emotional change must first occur. This explains why some people get a more dramatic physical healing than others do. They come to the healing more emotionally vulnerable and open to being helped or healed. In a similar way, when it comes to being more successful in life, some attitudinal changes need to occur first. By first learning to change our attitude, our power to create outer change in our life dramatically changes.

If every day we go to work because we need the money and not because it makes us feel good, then we are disconnecting from our inner power. By not following our heart and freely choosing our work, we create our own misery and sickness. On the other hand, when we are free to work, not primarily for the money but because it makes us feel good, then our greatest power to change our circumstances comes forward.

This explains why some wealthy people just get richer. They work not because they need the money but to serve others in a way that makes them feel good. When wealthy people get sick or lose their wealth, it is often because they stop working. Since they don't have to work, they lose their motivation to work. As a direct result, they often become soft, lazy, unproductive, unhappy, sick, or experience substance abuse.

More commonly, people spend their lives working for the money so that one day they can retire and stop working. When we work for the money, then, if we make a lot of money or we retire, our tendency is to stop working. This is a particularly common scenario for men. We stop working because we don't have to work anymore, and very quickly we get sick and die. Insurance companies have observed that men tend to die three years after retirement. Having a lot of money and the time to do what we want to do is great if we also have the motivation to continue working in service of others in some meaningful manner.

Rather than seeking to change circumstances to feel good, the secret of creating miracles is first to change your attitude without depending on outer circumstances to change. If we are dependent on a job to pay our bills, then the first step is to begin awakening our power to be more fulfilled with our circumstances the way they are. Once we can appreciate the opportunities we do have, then miraculously new opportunities begin to present themselves that allow us to express more of who we are and to create the opportunity for greater success.

When you work as if money doesn't matter as much, your decisions come from your own set of values and not from those of others. You are free to be yourself and do what your conscience and sense of duty dictates. With this awareness, we can work as if money doesn't matter even though we do need the money to pay our bills. With this attitude shift, we still need money from our work, but the primary reason we work is to express ourselves in service to the world in some meaningful way.

7. Relax as if everything will be okay. Workshop participants often report that life is freer from struggle. Extreme mood swings transform so that we are easily able to manage our ups and downs. As you learn to purify your body and release old toxins, unhealthy cravings are replaced with healthy desires. As you begin to experience your miraculous inner potential, then fear, worry, panic, and anxiety lessen and eventually disappear.

With this amazing transformation, circumstances that would have caused fear or anxiety now generate a sense of relaxed calm and enthusiasm. One feels again (or for the first time) the innocence of a confident young adult ready to leave home and take on the challenges and enjoy the wonders of a new and exciting life.

Grounded in our true selves, we are able to relax in our lives even in the midst of turmoil, helplessness, and uncertainty as if we know with certainty that everything will turn out okay. The ultimate truth is that everything eventually does turn out to be okay. Yes, we experience loss, and, yes, we make mistakes, but by healing our wounds and facing our challenges with an open heart, we discover that every experience offers a growth opportunity to us. Gradually, one learns to remain alert, as if one were in danger, but relaxed, as if everything will be okay. When we approach crises with inner calm, we are much more effective at finding solutions than we would be if we were experiencing anxiety and fear.

8. Talk to God as if you are being heard. Literally within a few hours most participants in my Practical Miracles workshop have a tangible experience that God, or whatever they choose to refer to as their spiritual or guiding source, immediately responds to their requests. Even those who are uncomfortable with using or hearing the word "God" experience the incredible natural energy that is always surrounding us. It is this energy that heals a wound or inspires greatness. Though I personally call this intelligent and responsive energy "God," participants are free to call it by any name.

Suddenly the notion of right or wrong concepts and confusion about God disappear or become irrelevant when you have the direct experience. When the pain you have felt for nine years disappears, you suddenly become a believer, not by someone telling you what is right, but because you have directly experienced it.

With the simple technique of recharging, participants immediately experience this natural healing energy by following a simple procedure for asking for help. Within minutes, a pleasing energy begins to flow into their bodies through their fingertips. Once aware of this energy, they can direct it to release all stress, distress, resistance, and pain in their mind, heart, soul, and body.

By learning to feel this energy, you automatically connect with your true inner potential. The doorway to increasing success is opened. Good fortune and greater competence always comes to those who listen to the whispers of their hearts and follow through with their impulses to change. Many people in my seminars have noticed that when they are more confident and motivated, they experience greater success and good luck in making their dreams come true.

The reason good and loving actions can create good fortune is that they require us to open our hearts, and then miraculous power can be better accessed. It is often easier for those who have tried to do good to feel more of this energy. Sometimes, however, it is more difficult. They have tried so hard in life always to be loving that they have disconnected from their occasional negative feelings. By suppressing negativity, they have lessened their ability to feel altogether.

Without a feeling heart, one cannot experience the energy and begin immediately to benefit from it. Fortunately, there are simple techniques to awaken one's ability to feel fully. Regardless of one's mistakes or history, everyone quickly gets access. It is everyone's birthright and is immediately available when you know where to look.

Good fortune is the nature of life. It is only when we persist in going against our heart that we miss out on all that life is ready to give us. With the ability to open your heart and mind, you gain the power to release struggle in your life and to turn the inevitable dramas and crises into opportunities to leam lessons and to grow stronger.

As you begin to follow your personal dreams, you begin to experience an enormous amount of creativity. With this incredible flow, you realize that you really "don't do it," but that it *happens through you*. At this point, the experience of God and God's miraculous creative power becomes a direct experience, feeling, or perception rather than just a concept. At this point, when you pray, you will know with complete certainty that you are talking to God as if you are being heard, and you will get help immediately.

As you experience this flow, the struggle leaves your life. Whenever people struggle, ultimately it is because they have forgotten or disconnected with the great power or God that works through all of us and in nature. It is as though you have purchased a new car and, instead of starting it up and driving away, you get out and start pushing it on your own.

In my workshops, generally speaking, 90 percent of the audience can easily experience natural healing energy and immediately begin drawing it in. For most people, it is a completely new experience. Some others simply need a little more practice, while yet others need to find their own different approach.

Remember: One way is not for everyone. I do not consider it a failure when someone doesn't have the experience others have. I know people are different and that my way is not the best for everyone. I always say a prayer for them and wish them well, trusting that with this greater awareness of what they want, they will be able to attract it into their life in some other form.

When people use these simple techniques, suddenly God or a higher power is no longer a concept to be thought about or discussed, but a direct experiential reality. Once you can feel God's natural energy flowing in through your fingertips, then you can begin using God's support to heal yourself and those you care about. As you continue to use this energy to change yourself, you can use it to increase creativity, success, and good fortune. This is what was meant in the past by getting the blessings of a saint or a "boon" from the gods. When you can feel this energy, you can direct it and immediately see the benefits.

9. Feast as if you can have whatever you want. By applying easy dietary changes and the self-healing technique of decharging, many over-weight participants have shed unwanted pounds in a few months. Using new techniques, extra weight drops off, as you eat as much as you want. Even when you are overweight, as 70 percent of Americans are, by eating more, you can restore your body to its ideal healthy weight.

Miraculous change doesn't require any sacrifice. To lose weight, boring or tedious exercise regimes are not necessary. I personally lost thirty pounds in two months without any exercise program. Once I regained my healthy weight, I started wanting to exercise my body and use it more. It is no wonder that overweight people have a difficult time sticking to exercise programs. Pushing an unhealthy overweight body to exercise sometimes is an additional strain and is not only unhealthy but also unnecessary. Once you lose your extra weight, you want to cre-ate opportunities to exercise, because it feels good and keeps your body strong and vibrant.

Once you can experience your natural desire, with a little guidance you discover that you can eat as much as you want of the foods that you want without any sacrifice. This wonderful abundant state is created after giving up your addictions to just a few very unhealthy foods.

Putting It All Together

By using each of the nine guiding principles as they fit and work for you, and by regular practice of the natural energy self-healing techniques, you can and will begin to see practical benefits right away. Some people already may be using some of the guiding principles, but, until they find and apply the missing ingredient, they are still blocked from accessing their inner power to create miracles. Some already may be using all of the principles but are not aware of the simple advanced techniques of practi-cal miracles. With one small change, they become unblocked and sud-denly experience the benefits they have been working so hard to achieve.

If you read through the list and panic because you are not already using them, don't despair. All it takes is to make one change in the right direction and you will see remarkable results. It is amazing how quickly the results come when you make the right change for you, which also hap-pens to be an easy change. Change is difficult when you are not accessing your miraculous power. Difficult practices actually block your miraculous power. In the past, difficulty was needed, but now everything has changed, and it is only the easy approaches that work. If something seems too diffi-cult, then look in a different direction. If this approach is right for you, you will experience that the different techniques of practical miracles are not complex or difficult, and they begin working right away.

Robert Kiyosaki:

When Being Wrong Is Right

T he school year had begun. Students and their teachers were still checking each other out in eighth-grade math.

"I give tough tests and I have no mercy," our teacher, Mr. Barber, began. "Either you know the answers or you fail."

I could feel the fear building inside me. I glanced around the room, seeing some of my friends rolling their eyes as if to say "not again." I sat confused. As much as I enjoyed learning mathematics, I hated the pain and pressure from the way it was taught and the stress presented by the teacher. The course was tough enough without him acting so macho. Why didn't he motivate us by making it fun instead of driving us by fear?

Despite these methods, we all passed and proceeded to high school. What we studied that year I don't really remember, but by the time I finished high school I had been through calculus, plane trigonometry, and spherical trigonometry. How much of that math do I use today? None. Today, could I solve those same problems for which I had studied so hard and had gotten the correct answers? No, I have to admit that I couldn't.

Today I don't use much of what I learned after the fifth grade. But that's not to say school didn't leave its permanent mark on me. The fact is, I left school with several behavioral traits I hadn't walked in with. Engraved in my mind was the belief that making a mistake, or "screwing up," got me ridiculed by my peers and often my teacher. School brainwashed me into believing that if a person wanted to be successful in life,

Robert Kiyosaki, author of the runaway best-seller *Rich Dad, Poor Dad,* is an investor, entrepreneur, and educator whose perspective on money and investing flies in the face of conventional wisdom. He has, virtually single-handedly, challenged and changed the way tens of millions of people think about money. The books in the *Rich Dad* series, which includes *Conspiracy of the Rich: The 8 New Rules of Money,* have been translated into forty-five languages and sold more than twenty-six million copies worldwide. He writes a biweekly column, "Why the Rich Are Getting Richer," for Yahoo! Finance and is the founder of the financial education-based Rich Dad Company. www.richdad.com

he or she had to always be right. In other words, never be wrong. School taught me to avoid being wrong (making mistakes) at all costs. And if you did happen to make a mistake, at least be smart enough to cover it up.

This is where all too many people are today—not allowing themselves to make mistakes and thus blocking their own progress. The symptoms of this "disease" are feelings of boredom, failure, and dissatisfaction, although most of us never come to understand why we feel this way. After having it drilled into us for so many years, ifs hard to imagine that being "right" could cause such unhappiness.

In 1981, I had the opportunity to study with Dr. R. Buckminster Fuller. Although I can't quote him exactly, the first lesson I learned from him still sticks in my mind. He told us that humans were given a right foot and a left foot...not a right foot and a wrong foot. We make progress through our lives by advancing first with the right foot, then with the left. With each new step we both move forward and correct the prior step so that we come closer and closer to our destination. Most people, however, are still trying to walk the straight and narrow, avoiding mistakes and thus getting nowhere. What's wrong with the straight and narrow path? Perhaps nothing except the fact that straight and narrow paths simply don't exist in the real world. Not even physicists have ever found anything that is absolutely straight. Only curves have been found. Straight lines exist only in human minds.

In *The Abilene Paradox*, Jerry B. Harvey writes about the "paradox of paradoxes." He explains the universal principle that "unity is plural." Just as "up" cannot exist without "down," or "man" without "woman," a "right" cannot exist without a "wrong." Similarly, people who can only be right eventually wind up being wrong. And people who are willing to risk making mistakes in order to discover what is "wrong" eventually end up knowing what is "right."

In maturing as a businessperson, I have learned to be cautious of people who act as if they have all the right answers. At the same time, I have had to acknowledge my own over-zealous desire to be right. I had to learn that a person who stayed on his right foot too long would eventually end up on the wrong foot—or worse yet, with that foot in his mouth.

Allowing ourselves to be wrong, to make mistakes, isn't easy. Think about how you feel when you hear the words "you're wrong." If you're anything like me, you become defensive and try to think of ways to prove you are right. In my own struggles, as well as in working with thousands of other people on this issue, I continue to be amazed at how terrified we humans can become at the thought of being punished for being wrong. Our efforts to prove ourselves right are often carried to the extreme, destroying marriages, businesses, and friendships.

To finally discover that knowing the wrong answer can be the most powerful beacon we could ever hope to have, shining a brilliant light for us on the right answer, is greatly liberating. But to be able to enjoy the vast benefits of this insight we need to re-think how we handle mistakes; rather than punishing us for them, education should teach us the art of learning.

Our fear of making mistakes is so ingrained in us that we habitually react to our errors in ways that blind us to the real learning in them. Here are four of the most common and destructive "skills" that we have learned for handling those times when we make mistakes. These are the key reactions that stop the learning process:

1. Pretending we did not make a mistake.

The last U.S. President I recall accepting full responsibility for his actions was President John F. Kennedy for his part in the Bay of Pigs incident. Since then there have been such classic statements as "I am not a crook" (Nixon during Watergate) and "I don't remember" (Reagan during the Iran-Contra hearings). These men's avoidance of any responsibility has kept the issues alive and smoldering—as jokes, if nothing else.

It has been shown through other examples that the public demonstrates understanding and compassion for people who commit errors and then acknowledge responsibility for their actions. This seems odd in a world where we are taught to avoid making mistakes. Yet, it seems that each of us continues to be responsive to the wisdom that still lies buried deep within us that, as the poet says, "To err is human; to forgive is divine." Perhaps there is something in the act of forgiveness that makes us remember how we are meant to learn.

Comedian-actor Richard Pryor, after making the "mistake" of freebasing and badly burning his face and upper body, went on national television to come clean about drug use. TV evangelist Jimmy Swaggart admitted to visiting "women of the red-light districts." As a result, both their careers continued and their "wrongs" were put behind them. I cannot say whether they truly learned from their mistakes, but at least they didn't pretend they were not responsible.

2. Blaming something or someone else for the "mistake."

Immediately after the failure of my business in 1979, I blamed my two partners for the money loss. I was very stubborn, refusing to look at the role I had played in my downfall. I continued to dig in my heels and deny my own part in it for two years. I was angry, hurt and broke. It was not until I calmed down that I realized the experience was probably one of the best things that ever happened to me. I am not saying I would want to lose everything again, but I am grateful for the valuable lesson. Had I not lost my money in 1979, I am certain I would have lost it later because

263

of my ignorance. There is the saying that "A fool and his money are soon parted." My mistake allowed me to better understand how I had been a fool, and how to avoid making similar mistakes again.

I know many people who are not successful because they are still consciously or subconsciously blaming other people for things that happened to them. I hear many horror stories about money or romance and how someone "did them wrong." The problem with that point of view is that the source of the mistake continues to lie dormant, just waiting to come to the surface again. One example of this is found with people who divorce and then marry a "different-same" person again and again, because they didn't learn the lesson from the previous marriage. They continue to blame the previous spouse for the failure of their relationship. Had I continued to blame my partners for what I did not know, I am certain I would have made the same mistake again and again, with different partners, until I either got the lesson, gave up, or died broke, frustrated, and bitter.

American society has become "blame-happy," and the term "victim" has become a part of everyday conversation. Courts are jammed up with lawsuits brought on by "victims" wanting compensation for being "wronged." No one can deny that there are legitimate claims, but we also know that the practice of suing has gone to extremes. Doctors have become fearful of delegating any of their duties to other clinicians with whom they work for fear of malpractice suits. This single factor has caused an increase in medical costs and a decrease in insurance benefits.

Similarly, the highest single cost of producing a car in North America is not steel, but insurance. Insurance of all kinds is a hidden cost of every car produced—for a commodity that benefits the consumer in no way.

We could do with fewer victims and with more people willing to learn instead of wanting to blame.

3. Rationalizing the "mistake" instead of learning from it. (Also known as the "Sour Grapes Syndrome.") "Oh, well, I really didn't want that anyway."

The world is filled with people who are always ready with perfect rationalizations about why they are unsuccessful. For a short time after I lost my business, I used the rationalization that I failed because I didn't have an MBA. By clinging to this rationalization I only prolonged my mental poverty and slowed down my comeback.

One of the most prevalent justifications today is, "Oh, the money doesn't matter to me." I often hear it from people who are not winning at the game of financial well-being. Does money really not matter? Let's ask the question another way: is it a mistake to put yourself and your family in the position of not having enough money? At the very least, not having enough money should be interpreted as a "tap on the shoulder," a signal to change something in our lives.

4. Punishing oneself.

Possibly the most destructive behavior of all is the emotional torment people inflict on themselves as retribution for making a mistake.

When asked who is hardest on them, most people will point to themselves. They often do this with an apparent sense of pride and humility. And yet, punishment is one of the most destructive aspects of human behavior there is, whether it is self-inflicted or inflicted by a third party. One reason people are not successful is that they are consciously or subconsciously punishing themselves for something they did in the past. They cannot allow themselves to be successful because deep down inside they do not feel they deserve it. They are punishing themselves by withholding the opportunity to enjoy a successful life.

Truly successful people learn to take full responsibility for their actions; they apologize and do whatever is appropriate to correct their errors. They acknowledge the mistake, seek the lesson, make whatever corrections are required and then move on to become more successful.

Unsuccessful people harbor the emotional pain of self-blame and fail to get the valuable lessons made available to them through their mistakes. Not acknowledging mistakes makes for narrow-minded, self-righteous people who ultimately hinder their own ability to be happy and find financial success.

Always Having to Be Right

Along with denying that we've made a mistake, there are several problems associated with having to be right:

1. Inability to see the future.

The person who has to be right often clings to old information, information which might have been right in the past but is no longer appropriate or true in the present. Most people confuse facts with truths. Prior to Orville and Wilbur Wright's successful flight in a heavier-than-air machine, the "fact" was that humans could not fly and never would fly. While it was a fact at that moment, it was not a "truth." Similarly, prior to the day Roger Bannister broke the four-minute mile barrier, sports physiologists presented dozens of very convincing articles "proving" that such a feat was "humanly impossible."

Most of what we call human knowledge is only information we that we have jointly agreed is "true." Another word for it is "consensual reality," meaning simply that it is knowledge that most people recognize as "true." History is filled with stories of great new ideas or inventions that were ridiculed because society adamantly refused to look beyond consensual reality. Businesses have been destroyed by failing to recognize a new reality that was staring them in the face. Today, changes are coming at a pace never experienced before, making it more hazardous than ever to cling to the notion that "what worked today will work tomorrow."

To learn from mistakes, we need to learn never to say, "That's a crazy idea. It will never work," no matter how crazy it may seem. We need to learn how to at least suspend our belief in consensual reality long enough to listen openly to new ideas and new possibilities. Rigid thinkers cannot hear new ideas as long as they cling to what they believe is "right."

2. No increase in wealth (knowledge).

People who have to be right rarely learn anything new because they are too busy having to be right. It is only when they are willing to be wrong that learning comes alive. Wealth only increases when people learn how to learn from their mistakes. After all, there is very little knowledge in the world that won't be obsolete tomorrow, or next year, or in the next decade. Facts change—and so must our minds.

3. More conflicts.

I remember, as a child, going to our family's Methodist Church. I remember asking my Sunday school teacher what the difference was between our church and the Catholic Church. She told me, "The Methodists are following the right teachings of Jesus and the Catholics are wrong." I was only ten, yet something about that statement struck me as ridiculous. But how ridiculous is it? People cause pain, grief, and bloodshed in the name of needing to prove that they are "right."

Remember the slogan that was so prevalent in the years of the Cold War between the United States and Russia? The saying was "Better dead than Red," and indeed there were many times when our two nations stood on the brink of an atomic holocaust in the name of defending their beliefs.

Again, what most people and most nations insist is "right" or "wrong" is often only their point of view or opinion. Each of us has our own hidden agenda, an opinion that we are right and that anything to the contrary is wrong. We need to learn to think more broadly and to accept that there are probably infinite numbers of answers for every question.

Change in these matters can begin with our educational system, letting go of the belief that students should strive for the ideal of always being "right." It is the need to be "right" and the subsequent neglect of any real understanding that causes conflict between individuals as well as nations. As our planet shrinks, becoming increasingly crowded, "right-wrong" thinking will need to be reevaluated or the world is going to become uncrowded very quickly through global war.

As an ex-Marine and a person who grew up fighting, I've noticed much more peace in my life since I have allowed that other people also have "right" answers. I have greatly lessened my use of the words "right" and "wrong," as well as "good" and "bad." Instead, I try to comprehend different points of view and acknowledge that people differ. I have learned the hard way that opposing points of view don't mean that someone is right and someone else is wrong.

In our schools, however, I am afraid that we are still teaching our children to be narrow-thinkers. We are planting the seeds of war, not peace.

4. Stagnating income.

In most businesses, people are paid for what they know. People who have to be right all the time, as we've already seen, tend to stagnate, sticking tenaciously to the "nests" of what they know instead of taking the risks that would provide them with new knowledge. Since their knowledge never changes, neither does their income. In the worst-case scenario, they are discharged from the company because it has gone on to new technologies or is making a new line of products for which this person's knowledge is no longer useful. We see this every year in the hundreds of thousands of people who are let go or offered early retirement because the knowledge they have no longer serves the company.

5. Dimming futures.

A person who holds onto old ideas finds that his path becomes increasingly narrow. Often frustration and justification increase and opportunities decrease. The world is changing, but the person clings to the ways of the past or waits for the "good old days" to return.

6. Progressive inner blindness.

Growing up in Hawaii, I learned to love diving in the ocean for fish and lobsters. I used to see other divers coming home with octopi caught in the same area. I had never seen one.

One day, I asked a seasoned diver to take me out and show me where the octopus lives. He soon had me looking into a pile of dead coral. He pointed into a hole. I looked and stared as long as I could hold my breath but saw nothing. Then I pushed my spear into the hole. Immediately, an enraged octopus leaped out, scurried along the bottom and disappeared right in front of me. I realized the octopi had always been there, right in front of me, except I could not see them.

It is the same with business and investing. I find it amusing when a person tells me there are no more opportunities out there or that all the good investments are taken. Opportunities are always out there. Over the years, I have noticed that the more calculated risks, mistakes, and corrections I made, the better my "eyesight" became. However, I would have to say too that people who are afraid of making mistakes frequently never see the opportunities, even the ones staring them in the face. The people who can't see call the people who can "sharks" because they are able to take advantage of opportunities that nobody else could see. The real problem is that the person who always needs to be right stops looking in new places.

7. Inability to reap the benefits of "doing poorly."

All too many people become so fixated on doing things right that they spend their entire lives doing nothing at all. This is the typical pattern of "perfectionists;" their own fears of making mistakes literally paralyze them. Progress is made by following the path with "both feet," as Bucky Fuller pointed out. We discover new paths and move forward by taking a new step, looking around to see where it has taken us, then taking another step with which we can both correct our course. Could we ever have built a 747 jet had the Wright Brothers not risked their financial resources and reputations, to say nothing of life and limb, to build and fly their crude heavier-than-air machine? What the history books often fail to tell us is the number of times they failed to get their machine off the ground and the number of times they crashed. Through this seemingly endless series of "mistakes" they made they became the brunt of journalists' jokes. Only their willingness to take these risks carried them forward to success and eventually won them a permanent place in the history books.

8. Personal potential turning to frustration.

I frequently meet people who have great potential but no cash or professional success. The same people seethe with envy and frustration. Much of their frustration stems from being too hard on themselves. They know they have what it takes to get ahead but they won't let themselves make the necessary mistakes and go through the learning curve which leads to personal satisfaction.

"Your son has so much potential," was the statement on the report card I took home. I remember going to school conferences with my parents and every time the teacher said the same old thing: "Robert has lots of potential, but he doesn't apply himself."

Now I understand my teachers' frustrations and my own. How could they expect me to manifest my full potential when I was always being punished for making mistakes? I went through those years knowing there were things I wanted to do and could do; however, I was living my life in the straightjacket of feeling that it was bad to make mistakes, that above all I had to be right. I didn't begin to grow and learn until I threw off that straightjacket and dared to make mistakes.

9. Being increasingly out of pace with the moment.

People who fear making mistakes are slow because they are too cautious; as the world speeds up, such people tend to slow down. This doesn't mean we should be reckless. But once free of the fear of making mistakes, we are much more likely to stay in the race. Asking a person who is afraid of making mistakes to keep up in the modern world is a little like putting a Volvo driver in a high performance Indianapolis 500 race car. The car has all the speed and power necessary to win the race but the driver is conditioned to a slower, more sedate pace. He can't get past his own habits and his cautious outlook on life long enough even to test the car's full potential. Thus, it's the driver and not the car that loses the race.

Successful race car drivers are conditioned to respond with swift but very small incremental corrections, which is the only thing that works at high speed. They know what happens when they don't recognize and acknowledge their mistakes and correct their course accordingly; they end up in the pits — or worse, on the wall.

As much as we may dislike it, our fast pace is a fact of modern life. Whether he's aware of it or not, the person who fears mistakes is constantly resisting this pace. And this resistance only compounds his stress and actually increases his chances of making mistakes. Unable to acknowledge or perhaps even recognize that he is straying off course, he cannot correct his actions and so ends up crashing.

A Major Turnaround Needed

The long-term effect of our grossly inadequate educational system is all too often the erosion of our ability to function well in the real world. All too many of us come away from the system with a lack of self-confidence, drummed into our hearts and minds by what we've failed to learn about the positive side of making mistakes.

We can no longer afford to tolerate an educational program that punishes honest mistakes and fails to design programs that make full use of our natural learning abilities. We must change the course of this antiquated behemoth that is degrading our society, eroding our children's desire for knowledge while causing pain and frustration. True learning can be frustrating enough without a system that makes it worse.

We must find a way to teach through love and kindness so that the "right/wrong" systems of education can be exposed for what they really are: filter systems for rejecting those who won't buckle under and conform to the system. We must have the courage to create new learning environments, where mistakes are applauded and seen as the invaluable source of wisdom that they are. We would prosper both in terms of tapping the full potential of our human resources and in terms of bringing greater happiness into all our lives. We must take this next step in our evolution so that we can finally see that we all benefit exponentially when we reach for the very best in ourselves and support others to do the same.

Martha Stewart:

Ten Essentials for Achieving Success

CHAPTER
34

In 2004, I entered a federal prison camp in Alderson, West Virginia. There, amidst a thousand or so women, were hundreds of young, middle-aged, and older women who had dreams of starting a business when they were released. Many of them came to me to express their passion, their hopes, and their ideas. They were so like the myriad people who write to me with their ideas, seeking guidance, advice, hard facts, and a road map to a successful business.

Two very young women called me over to a picnic table one warm spring evening—there were metal picnic tables with benches at which we sat to talk, to plan, to read, and to eat the few "home-cooked" meals some of us concocted in the microwave ovens. Spread out before them were pages and pages of writing, drawings, calculations; this was their vision statement, their business plan, and the sketches of what their Big Idea would really look like once they were free to build their dream. I studied the plans. They wanted to create and operate a unisex hair salon combined with a café, salad bar, and soul food restaurant in a warehouse district of a large southern city.

Neither had much experience, neither was really a chef or a hairdresser, and neither had any experience running a business. I was astonished at the complexity of the idea, stunned at the expansiveness of the

Martha Stewart, creator of a business empire that encompasses publishing, broadcasting, and merchandising, has been cited by *Time* as one of America's 25 Most Influential People and by *Fortune* as one of the 50 Most Powerful Women in American Business. The author of best-selling books, publisher of the magazine *Martha Stewart Living*, and producer of her own talk show, *Martha*, which is syndicated worldwide, has been awarded numerous other honors and distinctions from the worlds of business, education, television, media, culinary arts, and retail. She is the host of the NBC-TV reality show *The Apprentice* and the founder of Martha Stewart Living Omnimedia. In 2004, she was convicted of obstructing justice and lying to investigators about a stock sale based on insider information from her broker. She served five months in prison, which she writes about here.
www.marthastewart.com

plan, and really pleased that two young dreamers wanted to set out on such an adventure. They were asking for advice, however, and I felt that as the experienced mentor, the entrepreneur with concrete success, I was required to be fair, circumspect, critical, and even blunt. I did not want to dampen their spirits; both still had a long while to spend confined in Alderson. So I arranged to give a talk about starting a business, right there in the speakers' room, underneath the chapel. Using the young women's idea as an example, I spoke about dreams and passion and vision statements and business plans. I encouraged planning, investing, partnering, and careful, thoughtful research.

Expressing my concern that their plan was too ambitious, too expansive, too difficult, too expensive, and maybe even too old-fashioned, I explained that in New York and other metropolitan areas, hair salons were chic havens for beauty, health, personal care, and skin and nail care. Women did not want to eat where they had their hair cut — a fine cappuccino, maybe; a glass of iced tea and a sandwich on the run, okay. I encouraged them to divide the business in two: a restaurant, and a hair salon that catered to male and female customers. This was a better plan — the one-stop shopping plan that many retailers are now starting to develop. I told them which trade journals to read, what fashion magazines to study, and which books to gather to do their research.

When I returned home from Alderson, I had five months of home confinement, and I watched lots of late-night movies. One such movie was *Barbershop*, perhaps the inspiration for the young women's plan. I know that inspiration can be found in many different places. So did the girls.

Their Big Idea reminded me so much of a plan that I had proposed to a group of astute and experienced venture capitalists about five years ago, a group that had helped nurture and finance companies like Netscape, Google, Intuit, and many others. I was so enthusiastic about my idea, so talkative and effusive about its possibilities and its potentially wonderful impact on the world of homemakers. In return, I was stared at and discouraged with words and phrases such as, "It's too ambitious"; "It's too early for such an idea"; "It's too big"; "You're not focused." I used the criticisms and comments to reformulate the idea of Martha Stewart Living Omnimedia, and we are still working on it, still passionate about it.

Being an entrepreneur is not easy, but it is exciting, fun, and amazingly interesting and challenging. Being an entrepreneur requires a person to do more than just "go to work," much more than just "do a job." It requires eyes in the back of one's head; constant learning; curiosity; unflagging energy; good health, or at least a strong constitution that will ward off illnesses; and even the strength and desire to put up with leep deprivation and long hours of intense concentration. To many, these characteristics might sound rather daunting, but among successful entrepreneurs, these are common traits.

The entrepreneurial spirit is alive and well. I see evidence of that fact each and every day. And because so many budding entrepreneurs have so many questions about how to take an idea and make it happen, I decided to write the Martha Rules... My hope is that you will use [them] as a recipe book to make your own success.

Martha Rules

Martha's Rule 1:
What's passion got to do with it?

Build your business success around something that you love—something that is inherently and endlessly interesting to you.

Martha's Rule 2:
Ask yourself, What's the Big Idea?

Focus your attention and creativity on basic things, things that people need and want. Then look for ways to enlarge, improve, and enhance your Big Idea.

Martha's Rule 3:
Get a telescope, a wide-angle lens, and a microscope

Create a business plan that allows you to stay true to your Big Idea but helps you focus on the details. Then remain flexible enough to zoom in or out on the vital aspects of your enterprise as your business grows.

Martha's Rule 4:
Teach so you can learn

By sharing your knowledge about your product or service with your customers, you create a deep connection that will help you learn how best to build and manage your business.

Martha's Rule 5:
All dressed up and ready to grow

Use smart, cost-effective promotional techniques that will arrest the eye, tug at the heart, and convey what is unique and special about your business or service.

CHAPTER THIRTY-FOUR

Martha's Rule 6: Quality is everyday

Quality should be placed at the top of your list of priorities, and it should remain there. Quality is something you should strive for in every decision, every day.

Martha's Rule 7: Build an A-team

Seek out and hire employees who are brimming with talent, energy, integrity, optimism, and generosity. Search for advisors and partners who complement your skills and understand your ideals.

Martha's Rule 8: So the pie isn't perfect? Cut it into wedges

When faced with a business challenge, evaluate or assess the situation, gather the good things in sight, abandon the bad, clear your mind, and move on. Focus on the positive. Stay in control, and never panic.

Martha's Rule 9: Take risks, not chances

In business, there's a difference between a risk and a chance. A well-calculated risk may very well end up as an investment in your business. A careless chance can cause it to crumble. And when an opportunity presents itself, never assume it will be your last.

Martha's Rule 10: Make it beautiful

Listen intently, learn new things every day, be willing to innovate, and become an authority your customers will trust. As an entrepreneur, you will find great joy and satisfaction in making your customers' lives easier, more meaningful, and more beautiful.

GARY ZUKAV:

Creating Authentic Power

"There are many types of bread," Tony said with a flourish of his index finger, giving it a little spin and pointing it upward. "Today we will learn how to bake the most basic kind, but, of course, bake it to perfection." He stood behind his counter in the studio. Cameras moved in and out to catch his every motion and smile.

"There is only one way to bake bread," he continued with a grin. "First, you must want to do it. Second, you must have flour, water, yeast, and salt."

So began another of Tony's delightful cooking courses. Across the city, novice and expert cooks alike took notes, or stood in their own kitchens, following Tony step by step.

"First, mix the yeast, flour, and water, like this." He demonstrated, roughly measuring each ingredient and stirring it in with a wooden spoon. "Then put the dough on a countertop, like this, and begin sprinkling in more flour. Knead the dough as you do, using your hands and arms as well as your fingers, like this." His body rocked rhythmically back and forth as he lovingly kneaded the lump of dough, which was growing softer and more malleable.

"Don't forget to add a little salt, and maybe a little sugar," he continued. "So much of baking is personal taste. Experiment. Let yourself be guided. It's your bread you're baking."

Gary Zukav is a master teacher and the author of four consecutive *New York Times* best-sellers: *The Dancing Wu Li Masters, The Seat of the Soul, The Heart of the Soul,* and *The Mind of the Soul* (the last two coauthored with his spiritual partner, Linda Francis). His latest book is *Spiritual Partnership: The Journey to Authentic Power.* He has been a guest on *Oprah* thirty-four times, and six million copies of his books, in twenty-four languages, are in print. In 1999, he and Linda Francis cofounded the Seat of the Soul Institute, dedicated to assisting people across the world in the creation of authentic power. www.seatofthesoul.com

Creating authentic power is like baking bread. First, you have to want to do it. Then you need to follow the recipe. If you do these things, you'll have lots of opportunities to experiment and be guided by your inner promptings. As with bread, its your own loaf that you are baking. Unlike bread, no one else can bake it for you.

The recipe for authentic power is as simple as the recipe for bread — harmony, cooperation, sharing, and reverence for Life. Those are the ingredients. How you put them together depends upon you, but without all of them, authentic power is not possible any more than bread is possible without the ingredients that are required to make it.

This is how to do it. First, clear the countertop of everything but what you will need to bake authentic power. That means put every intention aside for the moment except the intentions to create harmony, cooperation, sharing, and reverence for Life in your own life.

Second, keep doing it.

Soon you will start to create some harmony, cooperation, sharing, and reverence for Life. The bread is baking. Eventually, you will create these things moment by moment, choice by choice. That is authentic power. Experiences of fulfillment, meaning, and awareness can be created. This is big news.

It is not necessary to be filled with anger, jealousy, sorrow, and fear. All it takes is the desire to create authentic power, and the will to do it — the desire to create harmony, cooperation, sharing, and reverence for Life, and the will to create them when you are angry, jealous, sad, and frightened. Understanding how to create authentic power is easy compared to actually doing it, but the same is true about anything that develops you.

Baseball is easy to understand. Becoming a good player is more difficult. First, you have to get into good condition, and you have to stay that way. Then you have to learn skills, such as pitching, catching, and batting. Then you need to practice, practice, and practice. This requires other people. You need a team to play on, and other teams for your team to play.

Anyone can understand baseball in an afternoon, but no one can become a good player overnight. Everyone needs time to learn, practice, apply, and then learn, practice, and apply again. This takes time and intention. It takes focus and determination.

So does creating authentic power. Knowing how is easy. Just set the intentions to create harmony, cooperation, sharing, and reverence for Life no matter what, and keep them. The rest is learning what these things mean, how to do them, and practice. That takes time. You also need other people to practice with. In this case, you don't have to recruit them. They are always there. They are the ones you get angry at, jealous of, sad about, or frightened of. To improve your ball game, you have to become aware of yourself. For example, you need to become conscious of how your body moves when you swing the bat. Great batters know exactly what they are doing as they do it. They don't close their eyes and swing. They are conscious of every muscle.

Are you aware of your intentions? When you are angry, what are your intentions? When you are jealous, what are your intentions? Trying to change your intentions when you don't know what they are is like trying to go to New York when you don't know where you are starting from. Going to New York from San Francisco is one thing. Getting there from Paris is another.

When you are aware of all of your intentions, you are like a great batter who is conscious of every muscle as he moves his body toward the ball. He can change what needs to be changed. He knows how to get where he wants to go, because he knows exactly where he is.

When you choose your intentions according to what you want to create, that is responsible choice. When you intend to create harmony, cooperation, sharing, and reverence for Life, your intentions and the intentions of your soul are the same. When that happens, you become authentically powerful.

Creating authentic power is a process. Each time you choose harmony, cooperation, sharing, or reverence for Life, you challenge parts of yourself that want other things. They are the parts of you that are angry, sad, jealous, and frightened. The more you challenge them, the less power they have over you, and the more power you have over them. Eventually, their power over you disappears.

That is how authentic power is created — intention by intention, choice by choice. You cannot wish it, pray it, or meditate it into being any more than you can wish, pray, or meditate yourself into being a great baseball player. If you want to bake bread, you have to know how to do it. If you want to create authentic power, you have to know how to do that, too.

Then you have to do it.

The Path of Spirit

NEALE DONALD WALSCH:

What God Wants

Because of the way God made you (that is, because of the way God Is), any feeling can be experienced without a stimulating corollary external event. This is without a doubt one of the greatest secrets of life. This is *how God works*.

Did you know that you can simply *think* of an event and capture the feeling you wish to experience?

Watch a scary movie sometime—or a romantic one. You don't actually have to move through an external experience with your body to have all the feelings that a person who is moving through it is having. You can even know that the person you are watching on the screen is not moving through it, but is simply *acting*. It makes no difference. You can have a feeling anyway. Movie producers call this "suspending disbelief." Their job is to make a movie so realistic that you literally stop the stopping of your believing.

You can use the same technology on the movie screen of your mind, placing yourself in the starring role and calling *action!* You may have any feeling you desire at any moment you wish. And now, here's the real miracle. Often you'll find that creating a feeling inside you can create an event outside you.

Did you hear that? That is not a small statement there! That is an enormous announcement. *Creating a feeling inside you can create an event*

Neale Donald Walsch is author of the wildly successful *Conversations with God* series. In 1992, after four failed marriages, poor health, spotty relationships with his children, and losing his job, he fired off an angry letter to God—and to his surprise, received an answer filled with profound truths. Through his books, those answers have touched the lives of millions of people around the world. Each book in the series has been a *New York Times* best-seller. To deal with the enormous response to his writings, Neale created the Conversations with God Foundation, a nonprofit educational organization dedicated to inspiring the world to move from violence to peace, from confusion to clarity, and from anger to love. www.nealedonaldwalsch.com

outside you. This is because feelings move energy around, and energy is the stuff of life.

This phenomenon is discussed with extraordinary insight in the classic book *The Power of Positive Thinking* written over fifty years ago by the Reverend Dr. Norman Vincent Peale, a Christian minister who understood that feelings are a gift from God, giving us the power of creation. That book has sold millions of copies and is still easy to find today, in libraries, in bookstores, and from any online bookseller.

A more updated and non-Christian-oriented look at this amazing process is offered in the contemporary book *Ask and It Is Given,* by Esther and Jerry Hicks, which speaks about the power of joy—how to get in touch with it, how to create it, and how to use it as a magnificent device with which to produce experiences rich and full.

The fact that you can create something by picturing it in your mind, by *seeing it* as already accomplished, and by allowing yourself to experience *the feeling* associated with that is evidence of the greatest news humanity has ever heard: God wants nothing.

If God wanted something specific from us. God would hardly give us the power to create anything we want! And yet we have this power. Do you believe this? If you do not believe it, then, of course, you do not have the power—because you are *using the power to create the reality that you do not have it.*

("As you believe, so will it be done unto you.")

God says only one thing to humanity: "My will for you is your will for you." This opens up the space for miracles. *Personal* miracles, in your own daily life.

This is how God cares for you. God cares for you by giving you the power to care for yourself. Each human being has the ability to create his or her reality. All human beings are creators, and we are creating our reality in every single moment of now. That is why Now is the most important moment there is—a point made eloquently by Eckhart Tolle in his own extraordinary book *The Power of Now.*

And it is not what you *do* in the moment of Now that is the most important element of the creative process, it is how *you feel.* Your feelings create your inner reality, and your inner reality creates your outer experience.

This puts you squarely in the driver's seat. Unfortunately, many people don't, know how to drive. They are out of control, because feelings can so often "come over them" out of nowhere, and run them. Often, what they have done in such moments has affected their entire lives.

I hear this so often in the Recreating Yourself retreats that I present around the world. In these intensive retreats I tell participants, "You may have any feeling you desire. Feelings can be Things Chosen, they do not have to be Things Endured."

Feelings are created by thoughts, I tell them, and every thought is nothing more than an idea conjured up in your mind *that is not reality, but is merely an idea — your idea — ABOUT reality.*

Part of what we do in the ReCreating Yourself retreats is invite people to give up their "story." A story, in my vocabulary, is a top-to-bottom, start-to-finish scenario that we create in our minds about someone or something based on an Originating Thought that popped into our minds, usually given birth by a judgment.

Once you understand this, you can literally decide to feel any way you wish about any experience you are having — and in that moment experience it in a new way if you choose. You can even decide *ahead of time* how you are going to feel under certain conditions or circumstances.

There is the story of a man who, driving down a country road late one night, had a flat tire. Opening his trunk, he discovered .that he was without a jack. He immediately looked around. "Perhaps I can find someone nearby who will lend me a jack," he thought, and started down the road. But then he began creating his own story about everything as he walked.

"I'm in the middle of the country," he cried. "There won't be a house for miles." But then he saw a farmhouse just ahead. "It's so late," he said to himself. "There's probably no one up." Then he saw a light in the window. "It's probably just a night-light," the man told himself. "The whole family is fast asleep, and the farmer will have worked all day in the fields and be impossible to wake up and I'll have to bang on the door and bang on the door forever until someone comes, and if the farmer does wake up he's going to be furious with me for getting him out of bed, and when I tell him I need a jack he's going to say, 'My God, man, I have to get dressed and go all the way down to the barn to get one!' and he's going to be really angry now and probably slam the door right in my face, and, and…"

By this time the man had arrived at the farmhouse door, agitated beyond all measure. He banged on the door especially hard — and the door swung open almost at once. "Yes?" said the startled farmer inside. "What do you mean, acting like that?" the man blurted. "What kind of a person are you? Can't you see I'm in trouble here? All I want is a simple favor! All I need is a jack! Now don't even *think* about slamming that door on me!"

At which point the farmer slammed the door.

There is scarcely a human being alive who hasn't had at least some version of this happen in his or her life. This is a little-understood experience, even though it is created by one of the most powerful life tools ever used by humans. Most humans use it unwittingly.

This process of deciding our feelings ahead of time can be used in a positive way or in a negative way, and regrettably, it is most often used by people in a negative way—usually because, I'll say again, people do not know they are using it, and would, in fact, *deny* using it. This advance thought about something, given birth by a judgment before the fact, is called a pre-judgment, *or prejudice.*

One can have healthy prejudices, and one can have unhealthy prejudices. Unhealthy prejudices are judgments that you make ahead of time that bring you stress or produce some negativity, such as anger, resentment, or fear. Healthy prejudices are judgments made ahead of time that bring you positive experiences of inner peace, inner joy, or well-being.

You can look at the anticipated events in your life (far more of them are easily predictable than you might at first imagine), and you can decide *before these incidents occur* how you are going to feel about them. This may seem "calculating," and it is! There is nothing "wrong" with being calculating, especially when you are devising the best emotional outcome for you and all concerned. This is what I call Positive Prejudice. You can also create a new perception about what is going on right here, right now.

Byron Katie, the creator of a process that she calls the Work, speaks with marvelous clarity about all this in *Loving What Is,* written with Stephen Mitchell. The Work is very similar to the What's So Process that I use in the ReCreating Yourself retreats. Both processes invite people to look at their thought about something versus their actual experience. That is, their "story" versus their on-the-ground, in-the-moment reality

When people are willing to give up their "story," their perception changes and amazing things happen. And when people are willing to give up their "story" about *What God Wants,* entire lives can be changed.

EDWARD ROACH:
The Twenty-First Century Man

CHAPTER
37

The look on Paul's face said it all. A highly successful real estate investor, Paul was speaking to a small group of men at a personal development seminar, and it was obvious that sharing his inner-most feelings did not come easy. But as he talked, his face seemed to relax, as though the frightening personal realization he was sharing was also somehow liberating.

"I've spent decades working fifty hours a week building a successful business, raising my children, and taking care of my wife, and I don't have a damn clue who I am anymore," Paul said, shaking his head. "I've spent my entire life trying to live up to what I've always been taught about being a man, and I've achieved most of the things that a man is taught to believe a man should achieve, but I feel pretty empty inside."

Paul's deeply felt statements touched us all and sparked a discussion that continued deep into the afternoon. It was clear that Paul was hardly alone in feeling that way. Nearly every man expressed similar feelings. One man noted that outside of being a provider and "enforcer" at home, society hadn't provided him much of a self-definition.

Since that dynamic afternoon, I've talked with hundreds of men individually and in small and large seminars, and it is clear to me that rediscovering our identity is particularly difficult in today's environment in which the bar to manhood has been raised to stratospheric heights.

Edward Roach can be described as a man's man who embodies optimism. At twenty, he purchased and restored a turn-of-the-century cargo ship, then sailed around the world. At twenty-five, he cofounded a manufacturing business, rated in 1984 as one of the fastest growing companies in America. After losing his wife to cancer in 2003, he moved to California to raise his daughter and focus on personal transformation and helping others transform their lives. A life coach for both men and women, he also leads men's groups and workshops. For decades, he has been deeply involved in spiritual practices, including Tibetan Buddhism. www.edwardroach.com

The fact is that many men today do not know what it is to be alive without the feelings of disconnection, sacrifice, and self-doubt. We men have too often accepted the premise that we absorbed subliminally from the time we were small boys: that isolation and unhappiness are not only part of being a man, they are also an essential part; and that lack of these feelings means we are somehow shirking our duties as providers, protectors, and fathers. Without realizing it, we felt that not only was the great American philosopher Ralph Waldo Emerson correct when he said more than a century ago that "most men live lives of quiet desperation," but that it was supposed to be that way!

It is vitally important that men begin to realize that we do not need to sacrifice our happiness and sanity in order for the world to spin correctly on its axis, and that we all deserve—and can achieve—self-fulfillment and complete happiness.

To some, this might seem like an airy-fairy idea. After all, society has measured men for so long in terms of accomplishments and accumulated material wealth that the idea of our importance beyond that is hard to grasp. But it is far more critical than most men think that we build this new paradigm as quickly as we can. *For many men, it is literally a matter of life or death.* It's a little-known, but extremely important fact that older men commit suicide at rates four times higher than any other segment of society. Unfortunately, that's just the tip of the iceberg. Many men suffer deep disillusionment and unhappiness as they get older and realize, often more subconsciously than consciously, that, like Paul, they "don't have a damn clue" who they are anymore. Retired and separated from the only identity they've ever known—their job—men often feel a great sense of loss, disconnection, and isolation. They suffer from great feelings of uselessness and stumble into deep depressions. Many die early of disease, but the real causes are loss of identity and hope.

My Story

For much of my adult life, I struggled with the same destructive definitions of manhood as most other men I knew. Without thinking much about it, I focused nearly all my hours on building a business—on being a good provider. For twenty-five years, I worked almost every day, ending up with more than two hundred employees in my combined businesses. I was fiercely proud of my success. I told my story with some zest: I began my business at the age of twenty-five, building high-end residential homes in Washington, DC; after some success, I ventured into the commercial and industrial construction business.

At first, I was highly pleased with my success, considering that I started with no capital and no previous training in business. After a few years of this, however, the stress and pressure became almost overwhelming and I realized that I was not happy. I had focused on success for years and did not realize I had a deep and beautiful heart to explore.

The more I pursued financial gain, the more happiness seemed to elude me. Because I was focused solely on making a profit, I began to alienate my employees. I created more distance from and less connection with the very people I cared about and sought acknowledgment from. Running a successful business created the illusion that I was important (and therefore happy), but my self-doubt and disillusionment were growing every day.

Then my wife of eighteen years, Jody, died of cancer. Her death brought my life, as I knew it, to a crashing halt. I was devastated and I began to wonder about all the time I had spent on the business that I could have spent with her. I began to question the fundamental meaning of life. After a time of deep soul-searching, I decided to make some serious changes. I stopped working and moved to California with my daughter. I was determined that there was more to life than ten-hour workdays. I shed the old definition of what it is to be a man and came up with one that would help me live a better and happier life. As a result, my life became better every year, far exceeding even my most optimistic expectations. Finally, I had the time to get to know myself and connect with people in a deep and loving way.

The decision to stop living a life that was not working for me was the best thing I ever did. I became aware that my life was getting better and better, and yet I was doing less and less. I observed that I was more healthy and optimistic than I thought possible. I also found that I was "in the present" nearly all the time, not worrying about the past or the future but enjoying the moments of my life. I call this "being in the flow." I have come to believe that when we are moving closer to our destiny of realizing our true nature, grace comes to move us forward. Conversely, grace will not assist us if we are going against our truth or our true nature.

I have begun the practice of surrendering to this unseen and intelligent force, and I feel I have a relationship with it. As long as I am authentic and trusting, I find that the needs of my creative nature and desires are met. The more I am conscious of this process, the more I see this relationship functioning. I have made a conscious choice to slow down and experience my life as a being, not as a doer. I am amazed how full my life has become. My relationship with friends and my beloved has expanded into greater depth as I have taken more time to feel and consciously connect.

I have been living and experiencing life within this expanding and conscious template, which emerged as I dropped the old definitions of manhood that no longer work and rebuilt new ones that do. Living in this way has resulted in an optimism I feel every day, created, I believe, by the fact that I can now stay in the present and no longer feel I have to sacrifice and be unhappy to be a man.

A New and Healthier Definition of Manhood

It's time, gentlemen, for us to do what we do best: build something new—in this case, a new paradigm that embraces the idea that happiness, connectivity, and self-acceptance are essential ingredients in our lives. It's time to blow up the old model and develop a new definition of who we are and why we are important. Optimism should illuminate this new paradigm, lighting the way to the knowledge that we can change, that we no longer need to define ourselves as the sum of what we have accomplished or accumulated. To find the happiness, connectivity, self-acceptance, and love that are all rightful aspects of being a man (or woman), we must come to realize that in the end, it isn't about the corner office, the big house, or the fancy car. It isn't about careers or sending our kids to the most expensive Ivy League school. Those things may be worth striving for, but that isn't who we are. We must come to embrace the fact that is often lost in this society: that every man is vastly important and intrinsically perfect simply because he is a human being.

It's time to build a new definition that discards the old toxic (though seductive) concept of the male as *suffering hero* in favor of an enlightened definition that embraces happiness, self-acceptance, and self-fulfillment. Believe me, the earth will continue to turn after we do this. Many of us were raised with the idea that the happiness of women and children somehow depends on our suffering, sacrifice, and unhappiness. That concept is, in the words of my father, "a dog that don't hunt no more."

The Power of Optimism

I want to take a moment and talk about how important optimism is in this new model. It is the outcome we're aiming for. With it, men can move mountains; without it, we soon lose hope. As a definition, *optimism is the natural and joyful expression of being totally in the present moment.* It emerges when we are no longer burdened by the past (especially in the form of regrets over lack of perceived achievements), the future, or the societal constraints that limit our understanding of who we truly are and what we can become. This requires that we let go of the old destructive definitions of manhood and embrace a state of mind that *chooses* life without suffering.

This new definition says that men do not become irrelevant at the moment they lose their job or retire. Optimism will be our constant companion when we accept that we are important because we exist and because of the character of our souls. It will infuse itself into our heads and hearts when we accept that our happiness is important, that what we feel is important, and that the old ways of being measured by society will go the way of the Edsel, if we take charge and break their dysfunctional hold on us. Being optimistic is a critical part of getting where we need to go and a wonderful outcome of getting there.

Mick Jagger sings, "You can't always get what you want, but you just might find that you get what you need." With all due respect to one of my favorite rock stars, we're going to jettison that whole idea. Our new definition of being a man is that you can and should get what you want, in terms of psychological fulfillment and happiness. We can and will find satisfaction.

It's important to realize, though, that making the change we're talking about here isn't easy. We men are used to being totally unhappy. "I've been down so long, it looks like up to me" are lyrics many men can relate to. To blow past this trap, we have to start asking ourselves questions: How am I truly feeling right now? Am I happy? Do I like who I am? What are my needs? Are they being met? Am I loved and does it feel like love? Am I connected to the world, to nature, to my family, to my lover?

Yes, as men, we get to ask ourselves these questions. Let me ask you, does it feel weird asking yourself these things? It almost makes you feel guilty, doesn't it? Like you're getting self-indulgent, not being "manly" enough. Well, get rid of that garbage — we deserve to spend time finding the answers to those questions. We are worth it and we deserve answers. For many, that will take some getting used to, but the alternative is facing increasing alienation, unhappiness, and depression.

Men Must Adapt

It is my intent to reach out and send support and guidance to everyone who is ready to take the next step in creating the life we deserve. The first step, and it isn't always an easy one, is to make the decision to transform, to help build and buy in psychologically to the new model. After that, it's about identifying and getting rid of our old patterns and outlooks that do not support us, that keep us trapped in sacrifice, unhappiness, and isolation. The bottom line is you are deserving of love.

As we go about creating our new model, it is important to keep in mind that everything has changed and is changing even as you are reading this. You don't need me to tell you how technology is tumultuously tumbling us toward the future. Technology has brought more information into our daily lives, creating a much faster and fuller existence. Everywhere, people are changing careers. Homes, relationships, and everything else in our lives continue to evolve quickly. Those who are aware of this new dynamic through networking and social connections have done well. That which worked well before is now irrelevant. It is mostly woman who have evolved in this new world, as men have stead-fastly held to their worldviews and are now suffering as a result.

This is an important issue because the traditional male qualities of steadfastness and enduring focus on long-term goals, which have served us in the past, are now hurting us and causing us to lag behind. Part of the new model of manhood must contain a new trait of steadfastness through adaptation. In this techno world, those who adapt survive; those who don't are left out in the cold. What does that mean for men who are valued for their ability to remain the same, day after day, year after year? It means we have to change that expectation. It means women must come to understand that men must change, not their core values, but their understanding and interactions with society. Men must be able to change, and change quickly. Those who would sacrifice men in order to maintain their own security must not be pandered to. Adaptability must become part of what is valued in a man.

It is Not Our Job to Save Others

Another outdated element of the male model is the idea that we must be the *heroic rescuer*. The old idea that the life goal of men is the "Gilgamesh journey," which involves constantly rescuing someone or saving something, is fundamentally flawed. It is not our job to save others or to be saved. Our job is to discover who we truly are outside the traditional constraints of manhood and then be that man we were meant to be.

I have found that most of men's heroic efforts are just elaborate ways to get love. Once men become aware of their true innate value, they will be able to receive love for being who they are and will not have to do or prove anything to receive it. Just this realization helps bring us closer to having the love and the life we deserve. Making these moves can save us from the dangerous and forlorn desperation that many men feel. It is critical that we make this transformation.

One of the first steps is to surrender the old ways that are not work-ing for us. We need to look at our present lives to see what is working and what isn't. You may realize that you are not getting the love you really want and that all your efforts so far have not given you what you want. You know on some level that there is more to life. Doing what you were told to do, or taught to do since boyhood, hasn't worked and now it's time to take a stand. It's not always comfortable or easy to make these hard choices, but if you don't act, you will likely fall back into isolation, depression, and defeat. It's not hyperbole to say that many men who don't make this transformation die slow deaths of quiet desperation. It is time to change.

We Choose to Suffer

It is helpful to surrender the illusory notion that we can control everything in our lives. Once we realize that we are not alone, that we don't have to do and control everything, we can begin to perceive the presence of the grace that will bring true harmony and love into our lives. When we begin to trust and surrender to that source, our lives become even richer and filled with more love.

At the same time, we need to realize that we have more control than we think. For example, we have the choice either to be happy or to suffer. We have the choice to live a stressful existence by sinking into regret about what we didn't accomplish yesterday or by worrying about tomorrow, or we can experience the joy of being alive by staying present. Let me ask you: Are you choosing suffering or are you choosing the present moment? You have that kind of control in your life.

Hearing Paul speak about himself reminded me again that men know what a man looks like: strong, successful, confident, and focused on his mission. These are great qualities, but where is the man behind these constructs? As discussed, men are more than providers, steadfast guardians, and stoic minions to the establishment of business. Those who don't realize that will, at some point, reach the empty conclusion that Paul reached and wonder who they really are.

As men, we have accepted far too often that it is our duty to fight and strive to become this twisted ideal of what it means to be a man. We even get used to the struggle and used to being unhappy. Too often we mortgage our present because of our focus on future attainments. Clearly, these are huge impediments to achieving the amazing "Now" of life, all because we are focused on becoming "the perfect man."

Men sometimes react against this tyranny of traditional manhood, but they often do it in ways that do not work. They may become rebellious and angry or continue living life with even more intensity, more effort, more logic and thinking, more sacrifice, more unhappiness. The result is usually less and less.

The Critical Role of Women

I want to address my female readers for a moment. If your man wants to undergo these changes, it is critical that you be a supportive partner. When he reaches the final stage of this transformation and gains a deeper sense of himself and a far happier state, he will have more capacity for love and intimacy with you. With your support and understanding, he is far more likely to reach his goals.

Some of you probably see that your man needs to make this change, but perhaps he is unaware of it. He may not know why he feels so unhappy much of the time. You might start by asking him to read this chapter and then having a casual conversation about it. Let him know you are supportive of the ideas I've presented and that it would be exciting to be part of such a positive transformation. You can help your partner grow healthier, stronger, and happier than he has ever been. It is important that he realize that his past ways of thinking and living may not serve him today and that the two of you should concentrate on directing your focus on the present. With your help, he can make the transformation and you both have an excellent chance of achieving a new level of happiness together. That is a fine reward that you both deserve.

Steps Toward Transformation

There are a number of practical and spiritual steps you can take. The goals are to disconnect from group consciousness that has led us down the wrong path, and then to forge a new path using the new model of what it means to be a man in the twenty-first century. In the end, every man should strive to create a new consciousness that helps him create a fulfilled, loving, and optimistic life. It is important to realize that this new life must reflect your true nature. Discovering your true nature—who you really are beyond your job title—can take time. The first thing you need to do is disconnect from the stubborn, outdated, and dysfunctional matrix of "man as sufferer." Once you have pulled the plug, the process of self-discovery will begin.

There are some practical things you can do to get your transformation started. First, there is an abundance of good material on the Internet about redefining men's roles. I suggest using your search engine to begin to browse through it. Some information will probably resonate with you and some won't. I also highly recommend joining some men's groups, both local and national.

Here's a critical step. Set some meaningful time aside—put it in your daily planner—to think about these things. Go on a walk, or just sit in a peaceful place and let these ideas sink in. Think about what your new definition of being a man is and how you can get there. Think about what you want out of life and how you want to feel about yourself. Give yourself that time; it's one of the most important gifts you'll ever give.

Talk to other men and gently bring up these subjects to see if they have any interest. You'll be surprised to find how many do. I've had long conversations at sports bars and other unlikely places with men I just met. Don't preach, but instead show genuine interest in the subject and you'll find many men eager to talk about it. When you do this, you are on your way to becoming self-directed in your quest. It's critical that you not be judgmental or controlling during these conversations because that is the dynamic we want to change, where men are competitive with each other and the environment is full of distrust and anger. One final, but very important thing is to be aware of and to overcome the old and toxic societal stigma that equates male friendships involving intimate discussions of roles and masculinity with being effeminate. We need to blow that old concept out of the water; it has kept us in the dark ages, and has contributed greatly to men's feelings of isolation and dissatisfaction.

Be aware that you might not get encouragement from those around you as you attempt to change. In fact, you are likely to experience a certain amount of pushback. Your friends and family are comfortable with your conforming and predicable self. They will tell you to come back, sometimes in irritated or even angry ways. They may ignore you. Don't worry; if you persevere and get to the place we're talking about, they will come to accept what you are doing and, ultimately, you will likely receive far more love and blessings than you ever had. Once you have made the decision to change your life radically and begin the process, grace will gather behind you and propel you toward your true destiny, one that is filled with optimism, love, and an excitement for life.

The experience of optimism is created when you fully embrace life in the present and then joyfully witness each moment as you are creating it.

JOEY ADLER:

Faith in Optimism

CHAPTER 38

Most of the time we float through life like a canoe drifting on calm water, but, inevitably, we encounter turbulence. Sometimes the turbulence is so profound that it shakes us to our core and demands of us complete focus and faith—strong faith. These interruptions in the happy narrative of our lives may be short and manageable, but, long or short, ¬each of these harsh awakenings—illness, divorce, financial loss—is a great, though painful, teacher. I believe it is these very struggles that teach us our most valuable life lessons. They test our mettle and build our character. Through adversity, we grow strong. This belief fuels my optimism. And optimism is, after all, what helps us cope and move forward. Call me naïve, but no matter the degree of darkness or the depth of sorrow, I always have faith that I am going to come out the other end with the best outcome possible.

Some of us indulge in a bit of magical thinking. We assume that if we faced tragedy once and survived, we are immune from it the rest of our lives, as if inoculated against a rare virus. Wrong. Lightning can strike twice—can, in fact, strike many times. It has for me. I write this chapter having just learned that my father has multiple myeloma, a dangerous blood cancer. When I lost my husband to cancer eight years ago, I never imagined this painful encore. I actually felt sorry for myself in the first twenty-four hours after my father's diagnosis, but I woke up on day two with a growing clarity, the knowledge that with the help of my family I can do what is necessary and that, in the end, it will turn out right. Here

Joelle (Joey) Berdugo-Adler, president and CEO of Diesel Canada, is the visionary founder of ONEXONE, which has raised millions of dollars for children with the mission that every life is precious and that individuals, one by one, can make profound changes in the lives of others (www.onexone.org). In 2010, she made a dozen trips to Haiti to deliver aid to earthquake victims, and has been recognized for her work by Hope and Cope, Mary J Blige's FFAWN Foundation, and the Urban Zen Foundation. Recipient of an Honorary Doctorate of Laws from Concordia University, she is also the first recipient of the Laurie Normand-Starr Humanitarian Award.

is the wonder of that kind of thinking: the minute I made that choice, I felt empowered and powerfully positive. And what I surely know is that my attitude will directly affect how my dad and those around us, from caregivers to doctors, will react. Expecting good creates good.

Those first few days in the hospital I was shocked at how much my dad had aged. It seemed as if he advanced fifteen years in fifteen days. He was frail and ill, but his smile never wavered. Suddenly, I realized that my positive outlook on life came from him. His incredible joie de vivre never flagged. As I sat in his hospital room, an image of him from my childhood flooded back until it seemed to fill the hospital room. There he was, season after season at our holiday table conducting the prayers with a full glass of ritual wine in his hand. For him, the glass of life has always been full.

His lessons and that outlook have helped me in my career and have fueled my passion to help the children of the world. My day-to-day work is in the fashion industry, a roller-coaster business driven by the vagaries of taste. In the spring of 2008, not only our industry but also the whole economy was beginning to hear whispers of what we would experience so painfully a few months later as we were handed the great financial "correction." What hit us was a crisis as bad as any we had ever experienced. To ride out the storm, we strategized and planned and prayed— and we did it all with a positive attitude, with optimism. We won the round, emerging from the financial debacle stronger. Optimism without strategy is naïve. Strategy without optimism is the fast track to failure.

I bring that same optimism to my philanthropic work. In that, too, I have been tested. I was on the first nonmilitary flight into Haiti soon after the paralyzing earthquake hit the island. In surveying the devastation, any human, no matter how optimistic, would falter. But when the shock subsided, I focused on the millions of dollars of medicine, medical equipment, and water on board the plane. As we transferred our supplies to waiting trucks, I was overwhelmed by joy. From this shipment, these heavy gray boxes now being stacked in dusty trucks, someone's life would be saved—many people's lives would be saved. And a thought even more powerful and positive came to me: helping others is not an obligation but a privilege.

My missions to Haiti marked me in a way I cannot completely explain. Driving through scenes of unimaginable destruction, I searched for signs of hope. In the middle of the devastation, I saw courage in my Canadian police officer escorts. I saw injured and weary expats stoically evacuating a country they had made their home. I saw doctors, nurses, and other health-care workers sleepless and, in total disregard for their own well-being, helping others. Rather than feel hopeless, I felt inspired and blessed to lend a hand to the evacuees on the long air Canada flight to home. I felt elated and honored to go back again and again to Haiti to bring medicine, medical personnel, and equipment. And when my spirits lagged, I thought about the work of people like Duncan Dee, the COO of Air Canada, and the whole Air Canada team who did everything they could to help deal with endless red tape in order to bring orphaned and newly adopted children back to Canada.

How could I bring my optimistic mantra to the worst humanitarian crisis the UN had seen in decades? Here's how. By taking a breath and putting one foot in front of the other. By watching and learning from those braver than I and by knowing absolutely that I would succeed. Though stunned by what I saw on the ground, I realized hopelessness would get us nowhere. Hope and hard work allowed our organization, ONEXONE, to deliver over four million dollars' worth of medicine and medical equipment, over 1,500 tents, and 300,000 bottles of water. On the back end of eight flights in nine weeks, we secured thousands of pounds of food (which had been requested by our partners on the ground) to Partners in Health, the NGO based in Cambridge, Massachusetts. I reminded myself at every juncture, "Optimism without a plan and strategy is naïve; strategy without optimism will not inspire leadership and will often fail."

The work to be done on this planet may seem overwhelming, but the challenges facing us are not insurmountable. The important thing is to shift our focus from the enormity of a problem to whatever contribution, no matter how small, we can make. Collections of individual small acts of kindness are already changing the world. The important thing is to be positive and get started. As the Chinese philosopher Lao-tzu said, "The journey of a thousand miles begins with a single step." And that small step, taken in concert with others, may just lead to saving a life. The Talmud (Jewish text interpreting the Torah) says, "Whoever saves a life, it is considered as if he saved an entire world." ONEXONE was founded on this philosophy, on the belief that each of us has the potential to be an agent of positive change, to save a life, to save the world. All we need is faith in ourselves, a bit of hard work, and optimism.

Why aren't we all more optimistic? Why are so many people pessimistic irrespective of the situation? Is it our education? Our genetic makeup? Our upbringing? It strikes me that when parents talk about their desires for their children, I never hear anyone say, "I want to raise an optimist. I want to teach my children that being an optimist and having a positive outlook will be invaluable in helping get through life's ups and downs." They want their children to be well adjusted, happy, ambitious, and educated, and to have self-esteem. But not to be optimistic. Why not? Shouldn't this be close to the top of our wish list for our children?

And yet the young are naturally optimistic. Even when this quality is not encouraged, it springs to life. I have worked with many young people and am convinced the next generation will be the one to save the world.

This new generation (those from fifteen to twenty-five years old) is the most socially conscious and committed generation in history. They are beautifully linked to one another through social media and are able to voice their thoughts, desires, and personal vision of the world. From this generation will come a core group whose passion and drive will make a profound difference. As that core group achieves, they will disseminate their success and empower and inspire. More important, they understand the gift of collaboration and teamwork, something a bit foreign to us baby boomers.

I recently met a group of four young men in their twenties who retired from their careers and decided to start a movement called the Summit Series. They gather opinion leaders and movers and shakers of their generation and create platforms for speakers and interaction, all based on philanthropy. Their next summit will be on a cruise ship where a thousand young people will debate how best to preserve our environment and rescue our dying oceans. I sat with them over dinner so we could share our visions. I was so impressed by their passion. These young men epitomize optimism.

In the last six years, I have had the privilege of visiting many developing areas—Rwanda, Ethiopia, Kenya, Haiti, and our Canadian native peoples' communities—as well as handing out food in the inner cities of Toronto, San Francisco, and Los Angeles. I've seen the worst conditions in which a human being can live. Friends often say with pity in their voices, "It must be so hard! How you cope with it? How are you able to keep going back?" During my many trips to Haiti—after the beleaguered island's floods in 2008, the earthquake in 2010, and the political unrest in 2011—it never entered my mind that Haiti is not destined for glory. When I see Haiti, I see and experience the most incredible things: billions of dollars pledged for development, a new state of-the-art hospital, brand new schools for the children, and factories being built to put people to work. When I am in Haiti, I see only possibilities. I am positive that in my lifetime things will change. Why are the news reports so negative? The answer is clear to me: sensationalism and conflict sell more than optimism.

One can only wish the stories of conflict were followed by an equal number of stories of peace and healing and rebuilding. And there is much healing to report! In my life, every visit to a troubled place has been a juxtaposition of pain and optimism. Barely two weeks after the earthquake in Haiti, Port-au-Prince was already coming alive with merchants selling their wares on the streets. These street vendors were like rays of sunlight cutting through the devastation, like a rainbow after a violent storm. Seeing them made my heart happy and confirmed my optimism. *When I see Haiti, I see a canvas for true and sustainable change.*

I can remember when I announced my optimism to the world. Like most people from Montréal, I was raised to love hockey and my hockey team. It was at one of those baptismal moments of a Montréal childhood, my first NHL hockey game, that I came out as an optimist. As a child, I believed my thoughts and actions could actually affect the outcome of an event, especially sports. It was my eighth birthday. On that April night, still winter in Montréal, my dad took me to the shrine of our national sport, the Forum (the Yankee Stadium of hockey). I remember the colors and the bright lights and I remember I was breathless. With fifty-six seconds left, Montréal was down by two goals. I turned to my dad and announced to him with certainty that we would come back, tie the score, and then win in overtime. He smiled at me and probably at my child naiveté. As I turned my attention to the ice below, I visualized how the game would unfold because, after all, it was my birthday and if I wished hard enough for my team's victory, I could make it happen. Montréal scored two goals in the fifty-six seconds and then scored in overtime. I will never forget that night. It was transcendent. Maybe it was me or maybe it was the 17,000 fans all wishing hard for a miracle or maybe it was the Montréal team's superior prowess that made it happen. For me, at the time, however, it was simple. I had made it happen. I held the innocent belief that my thoughts and positive actions could effect change.

I am still that hopeful child. When I say to people that Haiti will rise, malaria will be vanquished, there will be no more hungry children, people look at me as if I am a foolish dreamer. Dreamer, yes. Foolish, no. I am as faithful to what I can imagine as I was at eight. I still believe if we marshal our positive energy and marry those energies to action, we will, indeed, win…even if we have to go into overtime.

Mandy Horst: Sacred Joy

T he air was charged with virtuous devotion as the Shaman meticulously arranged raisins, dried figs, llama fat, anise, flowers, and other offerings of tribute on the table to honor the all-powerful source—Mother Earth—Pachamama. As I observed with excited anticipation and heartfelt appreciation, I participated by silently thanking the benevolent matriarch for everything in my life and the opportunity to be a part of this reverent ritual.

When everything was perfectly laid out, the shaman directed my attention to three coca leaves carefully positioned on the table and in a firm yet gentle tone informed me that the leaves symbolized three entities: the etheric cosmos represented by the condor, the earthly plane represented by the puma, and the underworld represented by the snake. Presenting the sacred trio of blades to me, he instructed me to infuse them with my breath, embrace them to my heart, and deeply ponder what I desired.

As I meditated over the question, the shaman began a soul-penetrating chant in his native Andean language of Quechua. Immediately, what came to mind was what I have learned in the past five years to incorporate and specifically desire: my blessed trinity of allowing grace to show me the way, allowing my inner light to shine, and living a life of pure infinite happiness and joy!

When the sacred ceremony was complete, the shaman announced that he would read my coca leaves—my destiny. Placing one leaf in front of him, he explained that the leaf represented my current life—everything

Mandy Horst gracefully transitioned from twenty years of professional hula dancing in Hawai'i into her heartfelt practice of spirituality. She is a yogini, meditator, connoisseur of psychic readings, and a forever seeker of spiritual knowledge and self-expansion. A world traveler from the very beginning, her journeys of enlightenment have spanned the earthly plane to the multiple outer dimensions of the cosmos. She is the creator of *Sacred Journey*, a television show pilot highlighting healers and healing modalities all over the world, and the author of *A Chocoholic's Sacred Journey: A Tale of Spiritual Rags to Riches.* www.sacredjourney.tv

I have learned and accomplished. Placing another in direct line with the first leaf but away from him, positioning it closer to me, he explained this leaf symbolized my future—the manifestation of my goals and achievements. Lastly, he set a leaf on each side of the last leaf, informing me that these leaves depicted change in my life—whether small or vast. He began to flick coca leaves into the air similar to flipping coins. The sixth leaf that was launched landed squarely on top of the coca leaf representing my future. Looking up at me with a huge grin and a sparkle in his eyes, he declared that I was very lucky. The interpreter translated that my luck was equivalent to receiving four aces in a hand of poker! Clasping his hands together, the shaman proclaimed that whatever I wanted to achieve in life would manifest and there was nothing more to say.

I clapped my hands in noisy delight as I heard the prediction, for the shaman's revelations confirmed what I have searched and journeyed to attain for over four and a half decades. My wise, inner guiding light has finally made me aware that, by focusing on any desire, releasing all fears and doubts surrounding that desire, and letting my true light shine through, all my wildest dreams will manifest and many times turn out more amazing than I could ever have envisioned.

The path to this optimistic knowing from a place of fear and doubt has been a journey of finding my true spirit of light and fulfilling my life's purpose—a simple mission of living every day in happiness and joy. Before the shaman took his leave, he gifted me with a huayruru (red legume) used as a lucky charm for protection, a reminder of a cherished and memorable experience in Cusco, Peru—the first stop on a trip around the world.

Yet my life was not always this way. As an unwanted Chinese-Indian baby girl, my start on this planet was a rocky one. My unsteady footing began in the spring of 1964, when the only gift my mother gave me before abandoning me at birth was my name: Mei-Wan (Beautiful Cloud). I don't remember anything about my nearly two years in the Babies Home, a Catholic orphanage in Hong Kong.

I arrived at the San Francisco International Airport on December 22, 1965, kicking and screaming. Distressed, I would not let my new and anxiously awaiting parents hold me and I booted my dad in the stomach when he tried. I was twenty-one months old, and I wore every item of clothing I owned: a red dress, two undershirts, a slip, several layers of diapers, a sweater, and a red satin Chinese-style jacket—you'd think they could have spared a shopping bag! In 1965, it was a big deal for a white couple from America to adopt an Asian baby from Asia. When I and the other children from Asia arrived in San Francisco, there were bright camera lights and television cameras to document the newsworthy event. In the pictures, I looked terrified. The *San Francisco Chronicle* headlined the story as "Flying start to new homes" and "Hong Kong Orphans land here." A newspaper in nearby Stockton, where my new parents lived, headlined it as "Stockton pair gets Chinese orphan for Christmas."

My parents gave me a new name: Amanda. Latin in origin, Amanda means "worthy of love." Worthy is defined as "having worth or possessing merit or value; to be loved or deserving to be loved." My birth and adoptive names seem contradictory to me. As Beautiful Cloud, was I a lovely yet unwanted event that rained on my biological parents' parade? And what about the deeper meaning of "worthy of love" — did it hint that I was once *not* worthy? I know that my adoptive parents had the best intentions when they gave me the name Amanda and I also know that they really wanted me and loved me even before they met me. They chose what, to them, was a precious name that demonstrated their love for me. But to me, the word "worthy" has a negative connotation and vibration. Was I not worthy before my parents adopted me? Is that why my birth parents did not want me? Did I need to do something to become worthy? On a subconscious level, the word "worthy" meant that I needed to *earn* my parents' love and that I somehow needed to establish merit to deserve a place on this planet.

How much significance does a name have anyway? If it is true that your name shapes your destiny or that its meaning empowers your life, then I would have preferred the name Shakti (power) or Shanti (peace). If it were the vibrational sound of Amanda that my parents liked, than Ananda (bliss) would have been a perfect name for me.

My mother wrote in her journal that during my first days in my new home I was afraid of everything, even my polka-dot bed. She also wrote that I ate everything in sight and always seemed to be starving. The one exception to my fears was my new mom. She was the only one who I would let hold me, and I would only sleep on the couch if she was with me. The couch was at the center of the family room and that is where I played most of the day and I felt safe in that room. After a few days, I warmed up to my sister, Lorie, and brother, Doug — Lorie was a year older than I, and Doug, a year older than Lorie.

In those early months in Stockton, California, I had a greater challenge to overcome: I was deathly afraid of my father. Up until then, I had never had contact with any males, and my father's deep, low voice must have been really scary. I would not go near him or let him near me. Every night, my father arrived home from work with M&Ms in his pockets. My sister and brother would run to him and madly search for the hidden treasures. As the days progressed, I would step closer and closer to my dad each evening, longingly wanting the candy. Finally, after two months of the nightly lure of chocolate candy, I quietly slipped up to my father, stuck my hand in his pocket, and retrieved the long-sought reward. Both my parents had to bite their tongues not to shout their delight. They were so relieved but forced themselves to accept this change casually, not wanting me to think my behavior was anything out of the ordinary.

In my first few months with my new family, my biggest issue was food. My mom wrote in her journal that when I was hungry, which was the majority of the time, I would stand by the refrigerator and cry. To add to her distress, I hoarded and hid food under the living room couch. When she vacuumed under the couch, she discovered old and smelly dried-up chicken legs there. As I learned to trust — little by little — that there *would* be another meal and I would never go hungry, I eventually stopped hiding food. Part of me, though, was still unsure and untrusting.

Being an orphan for twenty-one months also set a pattern for challenging emotional issues that I would have to later face, acknowledge, and process in the future as I searched for my higher self on my spiritual journey. In the orphanage, I only received one-on-one attention while I was being fed. As a result, I associated food with love and security. Some people eat when they are happy or sad. I ate for all emotions: happiness, sadness, frustration, and elation. Food fed my buffet of emotions, and learning to distinguish and separate the nourishing of my spirit from the feeding of my emotions was an issue I would parry with for many years to come. Today, I still buy too much food, can never travel without packing snacks, and don't really like to share my food, but I am so much more balanced and at peace with myself. My food issue was like a giant octopus with its four pairs of tentacled arms harboring emotional issues: the first pair harbored insecurity and fear of abandonment; the second, issues of self-confidence and self-worth; the third, inability to love and trust; and the fourth, perfectionism and a negative body image.

Yet being an orphan also created in me a powerful will to survive, a fierce sense of independence, and a burning desire to live in the light — enlightenment. These three traits have served me in both positive and negative ways throughout my life. My journey in search of healing and spirituality — with my clinging emotional octopus in tow — has been a wild and slippery ride. Through my search for spirituality, I have been able to heal my early childhood wounds; my emotional octopus has been boiled, chopped up, arranged on a platter of sushi, and devoured. I have made peace with Mei-Wan (Beautiful Cloud) and Amanda (Worthy of Love), and now both names are beautiful to me. I have come full circle and truly know that I was *always* worthy and I do not have to do anything but be my genuine self to have a beautiful life of love, light, and joy.

*   *   *

My indestructible inner being always knew that I would find my inner light and no matter what challenges life presented to me, I would prevail. Everyone is born with that light, and figuring out how to let it shine ultimately led me to my solution: optimism. Optimism is not just "hopefulness and confidence about the future or the successful outcome of something," it is *knowing* there is a positive result. I have learned to expect and *know* it's going to be positive, abundant, beneficial, and, quite often, surprisingly better than I could have possibly imagined. Optimism is knowing that the outcome will be positive.

To get to that place of knowing, I've looked for my true self, inner spirit, and voice beyond this physical world through adventures or experiences with psychics, healers, spiritual teachers (like the work of Abraham), and in the metaphysical world. All of these offered some insight into the world of spirit and our potential or life purpose. This information gives hope, and reaffirms that we are here for a purpose. How quickly or effectively we fulfill our purpose depends on whether we choose to work through our fears and obstacles.

Happiness is my only goal in life. Not love (I see love as one of the components of happiness). Not money, not material things. Happiness is all-inclusive and everything positive falls under the happiness category. Being happy is the only thing that you can *do* in life and something you can actually control. Truly, no one can make you happy except yourself. You're the only one responsible for your happiness. When you look to someone or something to help you achieve it, that happiness is not ultimately genuine because it's based on external conditions. Only you can generate your own happiness, nurture it, grow it, and expand it. Being happy opens up all the wondrous doors in life, and those portals become material, physical, emotional, and spiritual gifts. When you continually vibrate with such an insightful, positive light, it blocks all darkness—it is deflected away from you. Hang around positive people because their positivity is contagious. Attend laughing workshops¬—do whatever it takes to fill yourself up with happiness.

I feed my spirit and maintain my own happy quotient by surrounding myself with the love of my family and friends—we nurture and support our individual beings by creating a safe space without judgment—whether it's yoga, Zumba, sharing our goals and dreams, eating or shopping, our laughter and love continually nourishes us. I've figured out my "happiness quotient" by learning to discern through my emotions what makes me happy and following that happy track.

How do I consistently live a happy life every single day? I realize that it is unrealistic to be happy 100 percent of the time and know that less-than-ideal circumstances will arise. When they do, I know that the circumstances are arising as an opportunity to fine-tune my personal happy quotient to an even higher level. From a friend's hurtful comment to a death of a loved one, you move through it in grace, knowing that your basic set point is happiness and anything less is not part of the plan because going backward is unacceptable.

I do this on a daily basis—this is my life's work: I work 24/7 at being happy and living in joy. By paying very close attention to my emotions, I vigilantly monitor my psychic, energetic, and physical levels and if I feel uncomfortable or unsure about anything, then I know it's something to be looked at and addressed so that I can transform it, to make sure I'm authentically happy.

Day by day, you can look at the experiences or personal exchanges that are occurring and if any are negative say, "I'm not going to let this affect the tone of my day." When I was asked to be a part of this beautiful anthology, I was so honored and elated. However, I was embarking on an extensive trip around the world the very next day, leaving me no time to think about my contribution, let alone write. The pressure of writing this article could've ruined my trip and, in former days, I would have tortured myself over my unproductiveness. I usually write as insight comes to me in the wee morning hours, but the fast-moving pace of this trip jumbled my sleep patterns and there was no time for my usual lucid mornings of clarity. Every time I began to stress over the self-imposed deadline and doubts of being able to write anything of worth, I just stopped and told myself, "It's okay, Mandy, you are on the most memorable trip of your life—appreciate every moment and know that it will all work out." I reminded myself not to waste any energy on a single negative thought or to beat myself up. I used to be a gold medalist in the game of mental self-flagellation. It took most of my life to realize the search for perfectionism was an illusion and the negative abuse toward myself served no purpose and, in fact, interfered with my achieving my bright inner light.

Knowing is knowing that I'm going to be okay, whether something negative happens or not, knowing that if something happens to me tomorrow, I have a spiritual skill set, which is my foundation for solid grounding. You know when you're vibrating at a positive level—simple things from getting the best parking stall to a huge blessing like being asked to contribute to an anthology with the foremost spiritual writers and world leaders is proof positive.

Of course, I'll be honest—knowing sometimes takes a long time to know. And it's only by putting forth the effort and focusing on working through fears and doubts, working up your emotional scale from insecurities and helplessness to hope, that ultimately brings you to a state of knowing. Everyone will have different tools to assist them in the emotional work, whether spiritual help books, a spiritual teacher, self-improvement workshops, physical work, or energetic healing modalities.

The only way to get to the place of true optimism, spirit, and knowing is by doing your work and toiling at your happy quotient. You're constantly being shown by the universe that your endeavors are effective. Little or big—everything that appears in your life is a direct reflection of your energetic vibration. These signs continually reconfirm your work and efforts. It's a universal law that your energetic vibration is reflected back to you constantly, so pay attention. Wouldn't you want to keep practicing happiness and have the universe keep reflecting it back to you? It's not a big secret—practice happiness every single day and it'll become your second nature; when you're not practicing it, you will know immediately.

I was lovingly reminded of the success of my Happy Formula when it was my turn to hug a baby panda in Chengdu, China, one of the stops during my trip. As soon as the adorable roly-poly bundle of fur was lifted off the prior person's lap and placed onto mine, he began licking and kissing my face all over. His handlers were not happy at all with the physical contact and, scolding him, tried to get him to eat his bamboo lollipop dipped in honey. He still preferred my face and kept licking me. My heart filled with overflowing joy and love for such a beautiful loving mutual exchange from one happy spirit to another.

That baby panda recognized my happiness, which I achieve through my dedicated practice of happiness. Everybody's practice of happiness will look different because we all come from different places, different upbringings, and different point of views, and have accumulated different emotional baggage—different life-forming experiences. My practice involves closely watching my thoughts, emotions, and actions. I try to do this regularly and diligently, but life happens. Then it's a quick reminder to get back to my baseline of happiness and do whatever it takes—possibly a chocolate cupcake.

Try this happiness exercise: think of things that make you happy and, for the next ten days, do these things. Obviously the amount of time you set aside for this depends on your life circumstances, so find as many moments as you can during those ten days, and be aware of, maybe even take notes on, how it makes you feel and the boomerang positive effects that result (Do you notice people going out of their way to be extra nice to you, the shoes you have been admiring all season are now on sale at 75 percent off, or you get a lucrative job offer from out of the blue?) The work of happiness is a muscle and you have to exercise it to make it stronger so you can reap the benefits. Ultimately, don't you want to jump out of bed every morning embracing the day that will unfold with all of its delights? I promise that if you figure out your perfect Happiness Formula and apply it conscientiously and diligently, your life will amaze you.

The daily reinforcement of positive interactions serve as a happy meter for me. Now if something starts going wrong and I get frustrated, I interrupt the negative pattern. I immediately apply the work—my tools—and move on. I strive to never, ever be unhappy. Our visit to Rapa Nui, Easter Island, was a perfect example. Our group was scheduled to stay in a brand-new five-star hotel, but two weeks before our arrival, the hotel was destroyed due to ongoing political strife between the government and the indigenous people. Our group ended up in three very small hotels that, on a good day, could be rated one to two stars. The next day at the beach barbeque it was visibly and audibly obvious how unhappy the majority of the people were. Complaints about the no air-conditioning, restricted hours for hot water, not being allowed to flush the toilet paper, ant armies, and crappy canned food were rampant. Many of my fellow travelers who had been jovial in Cusco the day before were downright grouchy and cantankerous. Refusing to let my external circumstances affect my fabulous trip, I focused on the magnificence of the mo'ai (the huge monolithic stone heads) and the fascinating history of the island and its people. It also reminded me of my wonderful first visit to India thirteen years ago when I stayed in an ashram that would make our hotel on Rapa Nui look like the Ritz.

Something that occurs not quite as you would have liked is a lesson in perception: on how you perceive the situation, how you let it affect you, and how you handle it. What are you doing to make yourself happy? Are you letting external elements dictate your level of happiness for you? How do you process those things in your life that you don't have control over? Do you let them yank you outside of your space of happiness and allow them to spiral out of control, dragging you into an abyss? Or do you acknowledge the challenge and know you are going to get through it, knowing that you have the tools, and that it, too, shall pass?

What happens when the external events are circumstances of sadness, tragedy, or loss? In my bag of happiness tools are my main disciplines of yoga and breathing. I have also trained my mind to look for the next happiest thought. If you think you're happy, your whole body on a cellular level is happy. When I experienced the passing of my father, I kept my daily routine as much as possible, always looking for the things that would keep me happy, even while grieving.

Some people perceive the statement "It's all about me" as selfish, yet it is a mantra for me—yes, it is all about me because my happiness is first and foremost, and it is no one else's responsibility. Only I can take responsibility for the joy in my life, and when I'm happy, I make a better contribution to my friends, my community, and the world.

When negative turns appeared in my journey, I had choices to make. I could've fallen into the victim trap or let my negative emotions control me, but my inner light guided me to positive roads. Intrinsically, by the Light of Grace, I knew which path to take. Through the training of being quiet enough so grace can lead you, you can take the road that is for your highest good.

Every person who is doing what they love to do has figured out their happy quotient. All of the people in this anthology are perfect examples — they're not doing what they're doing because it's their job but because they're inspired by it, and have found that inspiration attracts more inspiration. Light attracts more light. Your awe-inspiring destiny unfolds when you learn how to let your light shine. When you attract the lightness in the world, you will find what inspires you. So be happy and let that light in!

HUSTON SMITH:

The News of Eternity

CHAPTER
40

I taught for a time at Syracuse University. One semester, I invited the author Saul Bellow to appear for three weeks as a guest lecturer. He was a big fish for that area, so the Syracuse press corps mounted a press conference to interview him. When the journalists had assembled, the leader of the press corps asked, "Mr. Bellow, we are all writers here, and you are a writer. What's the difference between us?"

Without batting an eyelid, Bellow replied, "Reporters are interested in the news of the day. Novelists, if they're worthy of their salt, are interested in news of eternity."

We live in a world in flames. There is no issue that calls for more serious thinking than the difference between the news of the day and the news of eternity. When we look at Islam today, the news of the day is dismal, all the way through. But what do the religions have to say about eternity? Here they are in full agreement. The message in Christianity is one of peace, with Jesus as the Prince of Peace. The core of the Koran is similar. It is an absolutely solid message of peace.

What about the jihad that fundamentalist Islamists believe they are waging against the West? The word jihad is usually translated as holy war. But the literal meaning of the word is effort. What's wrong with effort? When people are at war, then effort is directed at furthering their aims in the conflict.

Huston Smith, religious scholar and philosopher, is professor emeritus at Syracuse University and MIT, where he taught philosophy for fifteen years. Most recently, he has served as visiting professor of religious studies at the University of California, Berkeley. He is the holder of twelve honorary degrees and the author of fourteen books, including *Why Religion Matters* and *The World's Religions,* which has sold over two and a half million copies. His film documentaries on Hinduism, Tibetan Buddhism, and Sufism have all won international awards. In 1996, Bill Moyers devoted a five-part PBS special, *The Wisdom of Faith with Huston Smith,* to his life and work. www.hustonsmith.net

Christianity, too, has a doctrine of a holy war, a righteous war. It's spelled out in the Catholic doctrine of the Just War. What the Catholic church teaches about a holy war, and what Islam teaches about a jihad, bear a great deal of resemblance to each other. Yet religion can be hijacked by politics, and used to stir up conflict and violence. In a time of war, each side needs power. The greatest power is to be sanctioned by God. Each side wants to set up a pipeline from God, the greatest power, down to their political maneuvers. This results in both sides claiming to be on God's side.

It's interesting to go back in history and discover the origin of this word jihad in relation to war. It stems from a time when Mohammed and his followers were returning from fighting a war. For ten years, the Meccans were trying to wipe Mohammed and his followers in the city of Medina off the map, because they had stood up for justice. After ten years of battle raging back and forth between Medina and Mecca, Mohammed was victorious. When he got home, Mohammed declared, "We have returned from the lesser jihad to the greater jihad." By the greater jihad, he meant the evil that dwells in the heart of every one of us. He saw the inner struggle, the inner effort, as an infinitely greater battle than the outer one—a historical reality that is missed by all the current press reporting on jihad.

Reinhold Niebuhr, a theologian powerfully affected by World War I, wrote a remarkable book called *Moral Man and Immoral Society*. Hearsay has it that Fidel Castro, John F. Kennedy, and Che Guevara were all reading it at the same time. Niebuhr's thesis is that individuals are moral in and of themselves, and often make selfless choices. But larger groupings like institutions and nations are always selfish and self-interested, and— because they have both power and social momentum on their side—usually coerce individuals to behave in immoral ways.

The faith traditions help us with these behaviors, because they inspire us to do better. They lay down guidelines for societal actions. These traditions are the practices that can transform this selfish behavior, affecting the whole landscape of problems we face.

Rev. William Sloane Coffin, who served as Chaplain of Yale University during the Vietnam War and later founded one of the largest peace organizations in the U.S., was asked what Christianity has to say about war and peace, he quoted the biblical prophet Amos: "Let justice run down like water, and righteousness like a mighty stream."

But when pressed for specifics, he said that Christianity gives us the mighty stream, but it doesn't give us a whole irrigation system; that we have to build for ourselves. The wisdom traditions give us inspiration and comfort, but we have to apply them to our daily lives. Every morning, wherever I am, I read two or three pages from one of the great wisdom traditions. That's my irrigation system. In Robert Frost's phrase, "Everyone must work the ounces of his own strength on the world in his own way." You have to begin with what you have.

A critical turning point for me came in the spring of my junior year in college. It was a day that changed my life forever.

There were only six hundred students in this little college. My major was Activities; I wanted to be a Big Man On Campus, and to do that I thought I needed to be visible, and join as many societies as possible.

The professor who taught philosophy selected the students who showed a genuine interest in philosophy, and set up a monthly class in his home. Each meeting, one of us composed and read a short paper, three to five pages in length, on some philosophical topic. The whole group would then discuss the idea of the day over cherry pie a la mode, made by the professor's wife.

This particular night, my interest in the topic kept mounting, even after we left the professor's house. On the way back to the dormitory we continued the discussion. A little knot of three or four of us talked till midnight, then went to bed.

I turned off the light but I could not sleep. My head would not stop churning. The whole night, I felt as though I were in a tunnel, traveling rapidly through the universe of ideas, with ideas streaking toward me like points of light, some large, some small, then receding into the distance.

When I got up the next morning I was a changed student. I spent the next year-and-a-half getting myself out of all the organizations, so that I could throw myself into the world of ideas. I've been immersed in them ever since.

The list of problems our world faces is endless, from global warming to pollution to economic inequality to hunger to war. One of my books is entitled *Why Religion Matters*. After September 11, my eyes fell on that title, and I reflected that the ideas in the religious traditions surely matter a great deal, because they have endless resources for helping us with our individual spiritual growth, and providing a guideline for society as it confronts its challenges.

One of these challenges is keeping the enormous powers of destruction that technology has given us under our control, and utilizing them for human well-being. Scientist James Lovelock, developer of the Gaia theory, gave our planet only a fifty percent chance of making it through this century. Our consciousness has not caught up with our technology.

Modern society aims for knowledge through science. Science is empirical, meaning that it studies what our sense receptors pick up. The whole panoply of science is an extrapolation from things that our eyes can see. But our sense receptors are not our only receptors. Nobody has ever seen a thought. Nobody has ever seen a feeling, yet that's what our existential lives are awash with. Because modernity makes science the big picture, consciousness — which cannot be seen — has received short shrift. Science believes that matter is the most fundamental stuff of the universe. That's dead wrong.

All the great religions and wisdom traditions turn that belief exactly on its head. They tell us that what's fundamental is consciousness. In the beginning, God. God is consciousness. The heavens and earth — and all the material things that science knows how to deal with — came later. So the truth of the matter is that consciousness is not only all there is, but consciousness is primary, while matter obtrudes into this vast sea of consciousness. This mundane world is just a shadow, like the shadows on the cave walls in Plato's oft-quoted allegory. That's the basic story line of religion, developed in a thousand ways.

I've been involved with science for a long time. I taught at the Massachusetts Institute of Technology for sixteen years. All of my students were scientists. A large number of my colleagues were world class scientists. Science is good.

Scientism, though, is bad. What's the difference? Science is the positive finding, through controlled experiment, of truths about the physical universe — and that's good. Scientism, by way of contrast, says two things. The first is that science is the best if not only probe of truth. The second fallacy of scientism is that it holds that the most fundamental substance in the universe is what scientists deal with, namely matter. There is no scientific basis for those two corollaries. They're a philosophical assumption and a matter of opinion. But this distinction has not been made. I don't want to paint scientists as white-jacketed bad guys. This isn't something that scientists have done to us; we've done it to ourselves. We've wanted all the benefits of science; rapid reproduction of goods, the reduction of drudgery, increases in life expectancy, and so on. But we've wanted these good things about science so much that we've forgotten that these practices deal only with the material aspects of life. We've sold ourselves a bill of goods, and it's pulled our culture askew. It has spawned the most secular culture history has ever witnessed.

I did my doctoral work at the University of Chicago. At that time, academics believed that science had the ability to explain everything. My teachers had persuaded me that science is the big picture; my world view was the scientific world view.

Then, one evening, four months before I was due to complete my dissertation and get my degree, I came upon a book by a mystic. Mysticism is everywhere now, but it wasn't so back then. I started reading. By page two, I realized that this material had nothing to do with my dissertation. I kept on reading that book, and my scientific world view collapsed like a house of cards. I realized that I was a mystic, and that mystics had a depth and accuracy that I'd never heard before.

I've never looked back. I quit philosophy, which has sold out to the scientists and lost touch with the big picture. I went to China and India and Nepal, and found profound ideals there. If you try and understand these great truths on your own, without the guidance of these great traditions, there's no hope. You just wander around and get no place.

At the start of my journey, I apprenticed myself to the most profound thinkers in each of the eight great wisdom traditions. I read their books and contemplated their practices. For instance, while studying Hinduism, I read the Upanishads and studied the Bhagavad Gita. Having done my homework, then I went to study with the teachers of these traditions in person. I focused myself for between two years (the shortest) and fifteen years (the longest) and the wisdom afforded to me through these minds became my guide. At the top of each tradition are the mystics. Whatever the religion, they all speak the same language, with only small differences between them. In this way, I found myself standing at the convergence of the wisdom of all the great traditions.

Truth holds together. You can't fill in all the interstices with just one religion. I haven't found anything in the other religions that are incompatible with my own Christianity. What I learned from Taoism, for instance, is not at all in conflict with the teachings of Jesus. It augments my Christianity by fleshing out different crevices of my experience that I didn't hear Christianity speaking to with the same precision. An example is the Four Yogas of Hinduism. The four ways to God in this tradition are through knowledge (jnana yoga), though love (bhakti yoga), through service (karma yoga), and through meditation (raja yoga).

The same idea appears in the twelfth chapter of Mark's Gospel: "Thou shalt love the lord thy God with all thy heart [bhakti yoga], with all thy soul [raja yoga], with all thy mind, [jnana yoga] and with all thy strength [karma yoga]. Those four ideas are present in both religions. In the Bible, they're dealt with in one verse, whereas in Hinduism, they're explicated in many books of scripture. So the guideline I've discovered is that truth holds together.

There's a fundamental divide in religious people between the mystics, and those that are not of that bent. The minds of mystics work differently. Mystics are comfortable with abstractions. Religious people who are not mystics don't work with abstractions. C. S. Lewis, a great Christian thinker and writer in the mid 1900s, put it very vividly. He said, "When I was a boy, my parents drilled into me, 'Don't attribute a form to God, because God is infinite, beyond all boundaries of form.' I tried

and tried to think of a formless God. But the closest I could come was an infinite sea of gray tapioca." A concrete mind needs something concrete to latch onto. And that's the basic difference between the mystics and orthodox practitioners. The mystics have all the orthodox knowledge too, but they also have the experience of intuitive insight into truths that cannot even be put into words, because words are forms and forms have their boundaries. All the core truths of the wisdom traditions are united in the experience of the mystics.

The big question is this: What is the nature of ultimate reality? How can we best comport our lives in keeping with it? These are the great issues with which the traditional religions and philosophies have never lost touch. Man does not live by bread alone. An upward tilt toward the better is built into us humans. It's a part of our nature. So spirit, and the lord of the spirit will be here no matter what happens. Spirit and its cultivation is the most important pursuit we could possibly undertake. Our work is to tend that life-giving lamp.

World Change

MICHELLE OBAMA:

"To Whom Much Is Given, Much Is Expected"

W e're at a point in time in society where life has gotten increasingly harder for folks. I think because of that, it is difficult to reflect on life and to think through these issues because we're all struggling so very, very much just keeping our heads above water. At least regular people are.

And I do consider myself regular people even though I've gone to Princeton and Harvard, and I'm married to a guy who might be the next president of the United States. In my heart of hearts, deep down inside, I'm still that little girl who grew up on the South Side of Chicago.

I'm a product of that experience, through and through. Everything that I think about and do is shaped by the life that I lived in that little apartment above that bungalow, that my father worked so hard to provide for us.

And I remember every day seeing my father get up and put on that blue uniform and go to that job that I'm sure he didn't love. It was just a blue-collar shift job. No reward. No passion in it.

But the beauty of it was on that little salary, and it must have been small, he was able to care for a family of four: me, my mom, my brother.

Michelle Obama, First Lady of the United States, is an attorney, mother of two daughters, and former executive director of Chicago's Public Allies, a nonprofit organization that encourages youth's work on social issues. Though some media persist in focusing on the First Lady's fashion sense, likening her to Jackie Kennedy (she has been dubbed Michelle O), Michelle has already shown that she will give them much more to report on than what she is wearing. She visits homeless shelters and schools, advocates for military families, and has had an organic garden and bee hives installed on the South Lawn of the White House. With a law degree from Harvard, she is the third First Lady to hold a postgraduate degree. Integrally involved in her husband's presidential campaign, she continues her support of his policies from the White House by publicly endorsing legislation that furthers them, stepping out of the traditional First Lady role. This chapter is excerpted from a speech she gave in New Hampshire in 2008.

CHAPTER FORTY-ONE

We lived in this small apartment, and my father could pay his bills and pay them on time. Because he certainly did tell us about that, "Pay your bills on time."

That was possible back then, just forty-three years ago.

But it wasn't that long ago, that childhood I had, that was very unremarkable in so many ways. People often ask my mother, "What did you do? What did you feed them? There must have been magic going on in the house." No. It was a very ordinary life. Very simple, back then. *Way* back then.

But the fact that you could raise a family of four on a single salary today seems remarkable. Maybe the most remarkable thing that I saw growing up was my father's sacrifice and dedication—that hard work. That work ethic.

And as I've told many people, my father was a man with a disability. And I took that for granted because he never complained. Never. Not once.

And I know that he struggled to get up every day and probably lived in fear that one day he wouldn't be able to get up and care for the family that depended on him.

It was a simple kind of life. Father didn't make excuses but he did what he had to do. We could go to the neighborhood school around the corner. We didn't have magnets, charters, all that stuff. You didn't have to sign up for school when you were two in order to get into the one or two decent schools.

We went to the school around the corner. No questions asked. You get up. You go.

And they were decent schools and I talk about that a lot. Because when people look at me, I want them to see the product of public education. I would not be standing here if it weren't for those simple neighborhood schools. Those solid schools with decent teachers. [I am] what an investment in public education can look like. This is what can happen if we do the right thing. Simple.

What I know now, looking back on my life, what *was* remarkable was that a man like my father, on limited means, could send two kids to Princeton. And the pride he must have felt, being able to accomplish all of that. When all of his dreams must have been shattered, put aside, he still had *that*.

That's where he got his pride. That's what gave him his sense of being. And that's true for all Americans all across this country. The story of my father is the story of America.

Folks don't want much. They just don't want that much. They're not asking for much. People aren't selfish. They aren't naturally greedy. Most folks don't want much. They want to know that if they get up every day and go to work, they'll earn enough to care for their families.

They want to know that their kids can get a decent education at the neighborhood school around the corner. You don't have to drive twelve miles for your kids to get a decent education. And maybe they'll be prepared to go to college if they choose, but if not, they'll be able to get a job and support themselves.

Folks want to know if they get sick, they won't go bankrupt. And that when they're ready to retire after a lifetime of hard work and sacrifice that they'll have a little money in the bank—to be able to live in a little decency. That's all folks want.

But the truth is, that unremarkable life I had all those years ago has become a virtual impossibility today. That life is out of reach for so many people. Everyone is struggling. *Everyone* is struggling.

The jobs that my father had don't exist, or they're dwindling all over the country. If you're lucky enough to have that job, your salaries aren't keeping up with the cost of living, so everybody's got to work.

My mom stayed at home until I went to high school because you could do that. Now, if you make that choice, you do it at your family's financial peril. You do. You make huge sacrifices in order to stay home with your kids.

And the public schools around the corner are all so uneven. You go from block to block, neighborhood to neighborhood, and the quality of the school will change dramatically.

No Child Left Behind is sucking the life out of teaching and education in ways that people are echoing all over the country. It's not working.

I know that kids are being tested to death. I have met so many kids who started out loving learning and by the time they're done, they're so sick of tests, that school no longer speaks to their needs.

They're tired. They're deflated.

So now, parents have to worry if the schools they're sending their kids to are preparing them. Then you've got single moms all over the place. Millions of them. Struggling every single day, and every day feeling like they're failing because when you can't get ahead, all you can do is feel like you're failing. All the while being told, "Your kids aren't where they need to be. You need to be at the parent-teacher conference. Why is your kid overweight? You should be chopping up vegetables and making good meals that you can't afford."

We have made many young mothers feel like they can never get ahead. And college has become out of reach for most families. Kids like me, who've done everything that has been asked of them—studied and prepared, with the hope of going to college—only to get there, look at the cost, and think, "There's no way I'm going to put my family in this kind of jeopardy for a college education."

For those who take the risk and make the investment like I did, like my brother did, like Barack did—we come out in four years with so much debt that many of us forgo the careers of our dreams.

We've become a society where we're pricing our young people out of teaching, and social work, and government, and journalism. Anything that is the backbone of this society, the salary won't cover the cost of the education.

Unless you're a hedge fund manager or a corporate lawyer, it's hard to pay your debt off. Barack and I know this. We talk about it all the time. We're just a few years off of paying down our educational debt because we did what we thought we were supposed to do. We didn't stay in corporate America. We went out and worked in the community.

Every job we took, we made less money. My mother was like, "What is going on with you two?"

We said, "Mom, we're working for the people."

She said, "Yes, but you're broke." And we were.

The only reason we're out of debt now is because Barack wrote these two bestselling books—which I thank you all for. Thank you for buying the books, because I was sitting around waiting for Barack's trust fund to pop up. I kept looking at him: "You sure you don't have a trust fund?"

But we were lucky. We were lucky. There are millions of young couples like us with master's degrees, PhDs, working hard. Barack's other sister is a teacher. She can barely pay off her student loans, and pay for gas, and take care of childcare on her teaching salary.

She is wondering, "How do I create a future for myself? How do I save for my child's college education when I haven't even paid off my own?"

That's the position many young couples are in. Plus, they are struggling to figure out how to care for their kids. These couples, who have two people working, don't have access to affordable and quality childcare. And if you do, you are not *really* secure about it. There are so many of us mothers who are just agonizing over childcare.

I breathe in and out deeply because of my mother who is seventy years old and retired. She is at home with the girls right now—getting them ready to go to school in the morning.

"To Whom Much Is Given, Much Is Expected"   Michelle Obama

There's nothing like Grandma. We have a societal interest in taking care of our seniors. There is nothing like that kind of love. Having someone there helping you, as a young parent, raise those kids—sharing the values that you learned. We need our seniors to be whole, healthy, and in a position financially to contribute.

We're not there. My mom has the pension from my father's job that no longer exists. She is in a financial position to help us, but a lot of our seniors aren't there. This is how we're living today. I'm not exaggerating. I'm not stretching the truth. I know everybody is dealing with some of what I just said. And it's gotten harder and harder over my lifetime.

Through democratic and republican administrations, it's gotten harder for regular people. There are people who have seen some booms and they've profited. But most regular folks are struggling.

Barack says our greatest challenge as a nation, is not that we're suffering from a deficit of resources, because we're a *wealthy* nation. There is money here. And it's not that we're suffering from a deficit of policies and plans.

The truth is this stuff isn't that complicated on a lot of issues. Take public education. We know what we need to do: it costs money; it requires good teaching; it requires resources and investment. You know how we know? Because there are thousands of excellent public schools all over this country. They exist.

The problem is they don't exist for all children. You have to be one of the lucky ones, living in the right neighborhood with the right parent to get you into the one or two good schools in your community. Everybody else is out of luck.

What Barack says we're suffering from right now is a deficit of empathy. We live in a nation where we have a mutual obligation to one another. Those aren't just words. It's true.

I know in my lifetime, as an adult focusing on this stuff, I don't remember us being asked by our leadership to sacrifice or compromise for one another. I don't remember every being asked.

We're a nation at war right now, and the only people who are sacrificing are the soldiers—the men and women and their families who are over there.

We haven't been asked to pay a tax, to collect a can, to darn a sock. Nothing. In fact, we were told, "just keep shopping."

If we're not directly affected by the war, we're not even *thinking* about it on a daily basis.

That's where we are. What we need is a reminder that we are one another's brothers' and sisters' keepers. That's where we start. We have to sacrifice and compromise for one another. If we live in isolation and we don't know one another, it becomes very difficult to want to compromise for people that you don't think share your values.

We need a different leadership because our souls are broken. We have holes in our souls in ways that I don't think we recognize. We need to be inspired first, to want to be a better nation, to want to treat one another better, to make the sacrifices that are necessary to push us to a different place. I know that so fundamentally.

[Barack] learned the values that we're trying to pass on to our daughters. Things like truth and honesty matter in life, all the time. Your word is your bond. When you say you're going to do something, you do it to the best of your ability. And that when you're a working class kid in this society, you don't feel entitled to anything.

You know that you're going to have to work for every single thing. You're going to have to be smarter, faster, better, work harder. You know that. You learn that you treat people with respect and decency, even if you don't know them and even if you don't agree with them. Because that's the right way to treat your neighbor.

We learn that there is nothing more important in this life than commitment to your family and your community. That's why I married Barack Obama. Those values. That is it. He was cute too, that helped.

I knew, with a man like that, I could raise a family with him. I could build a life that would be whole and solid and stable. As I got to know him more, I saw how he struggled to live his values. Not just understand them, but how to make choices with the notion that, "To whom much is given, much is expected."

Barack and I, regardless of not having a lot of stuff when we were growing up, we know we were blessed. When you have love and stability and people sacrificing for you, you know you're blessed. You know not every kid gets that.

To whom much is given, much is expected.

When [Barack] graduated from college, he didn't go to work on Wall Street and make a lot of money—which would have helped him pay down his debt. He became a community organizer, working in some of the toughest neighborhoods on the South Side of Chicago, folks who had reason to be cynical because the government had forgotten a lot of these folks who lived in these neighborhoods.

They had lost their voice and were living in unsafe streets—still are. Barack drove mothers down to City Hall to fight for better schools and safer streets. He worked in those communities for years. Imagine a president of the United States who brings that kind of experience to the Oval Office.

Instead, we give more credit to those who've run corporations or spent years in Washington. I don't know what's wrong with us sometimes. I don't understand it.

To whom much is given, much is expected.

When you have the gift of advocacy, when you are the first African American president of the Harvard Law Review, which Barack was, and you can do anything in the world, you don't give your resources to the most powerful. You don't make money for yourself. You work on issues of justice and fairness.

Bono:

Reimagine the World

The Man of Peace Award…I am really honored to be here to accept this award from all of you. Thank you for taking me seriously because that's not a given when you're a rock star. Even worse, a rock star with a conscience—spare me.

The ONE campaign, the organization that I represent when working on these issues, is very serious, by the way. Deadly serious, thanks to support from people like Bill and Melinda Gates and John Doerr and Susie Buffett who fund our organization and our work. And the world's poor deserve seriousness. They deserve the best representation in the world's capitals. They deserve their own interest group, their own powerful lobby.

The U.S. gun lobby spends nearly $200 million dollars a year making sure you can't get elected if you support gun control. Tobacco companies spend $19 million on lobbying Congress. The world's poor deserve more than that. For them it's quite literally life and death. Four thousand people dying every day of a preventable treatable disease, HIV/AIDS; ten thousand dying every day of a mosquito bite; five thousand children dying every day of diarrhea. I mean, diarrhea can be a problem in our house, but it is not a death sentence.

So that's why we set up the ONE campaign. I think our voices were heard during the presidential campaign in the U.S. Did you notice that

---

Bono, famed singer and songwriter of the Dublin–based rock band U2, is also well known for his social activism, particularly on behalf of Africa and to eliminate AIDS and global poverty. In recognition of this dedication, he was named *Time*'s Person of the Year in 2005 and received an honorary knighthood from Queen Elizabeth II. Among his humanitarian projects is ONE, a nonprofit organization he cofounded to combat extreme poverty and preventable disease (www.one.org). In 2008 in Paris, Bono was awarded the Man of Peace Prize, which was created in 1999 by the annual World Summit of Nobel Peace Prize Laureates to recognize individuals for "outstanding contribution to international social justice and peace." This chapter is his acceptance speech. The Nobel winners present included F. W. de Klerk of South Africa, Lech Walesa of Poland, and Northern Ireland's John Hume, Betty Williams, and Mairead Maguire.

neither Barack Obama nor John McCain ever once criticized aid, never used it as a pawn? Despite the huge economic crisis, Barack Obama has made a bold promise to double aid to Africa. Part of the reason for this, I believe, is the two million members of the ONE campaign that we have in America. They showed up at every town hall meeting during the elections, making sure the candidates knew that this stuff mattered to them. And you know that it's not just Obama himself that's committed; it's his whole team, even his security team, the tough guys.

On the way here yesterday, I got to thinking about this guy Alfred Nobel—what an incredible guy. Then I thought, hang on a second, isn't he the guy that invented dynamite? I know it's a bit of a cliché to talk about Nobel and dynamite. But it is a funny thing, that it's the people who know the real cost of war that fight hardest for peace. I've been working on these issues of extreme poverty for quite a while, maybe ten years now. When I started, I never would have expected a phone call from the head of NATO, General Jim Jones, President Obama's national security advisor.

He's an extraordinary man. A six-foot-three gentle giant. He said to me we have billions of dollars of high tech equipment floating in the Mediterranean Sea and yet we are losing to Hezbollah because they are building schools. And then he said, I'm a marine; the men and women of the marine corps don't mind being shot at for the right reasons but they do not like being shot at for being the wrong reasons. I asked what the wrong reasons were. He said, for being American. That sent a chill down me. I mean, this was America we were talking about: America that liberated Europe after the second world war, America that wiped out smallpox and polio, America that created the Peace Corps. And they are being attacked because they are American?

But America is presenting a new face to the world: Barack Obama, Jim Jones, and the person who said this: "Instability and extremism fester in places where infrastructure, education and opportunity are lacking... The battlespace goes far beyond the battlefield." That's Secretary of State Hillary Clinton. "Security, stability, and development go hand-in-hand." Who said that? That one's Robert Gates, the U.S. Secretary of Defense.

There's new thinking in America—a reimagining of how to deal with some of the greatest challenges of our time, things like extreme climate change, extreme ideologies, and extreme poverty, which is entangled with both. With a new U.S. administration taking the reins, where does Europe stand on all this? Europe that has long led the world on development issues?

Well, let's not be left behind. We do see great leadership from Spain; Zapatero is keeping his promise. We see great leadership from the UK.

Great leadership from Germany, a country that for almost the last 20 years spent 4 percent of GDP on reunification.

Where does France stand, a long-time champion on global health, and you could argue, joined at the hip and the heart to Africa through its history? Truthfully? France isn't quite doing its bit against the promises made. And we're not sure why, because we are pretty sure the French people do care about this stuff. Carla Sarkozy [wife of the French president] certainly does; she's just been named ambassador for the Global AIDS fund—and apparently, rumor has it, she sleeps with the president. He has spoken passionately about these issues, but we might need her to do a bit of pickpocketing. France is not, however slashing, its aid budget, which is what its next-door neighbor Italy is doing. What an embarrassment for the next chair of the G8 to be slashing its aid budget.

And today, not far away from here, President Sarkozy and the rest of the European heads of state are trying to figure out where they stand on the link between extreme climate and extreme poverty. Will a new grand bargain take shape under which the people who created the problem of climate change (us) will make sure the people worst affected (the poorest of the poor) benefit financially from a new carbon deal? Now there's a bold idea.

I think that Europe is a thought that needs to become a feeling. I get the sense that, for many Europeans, Europe is defined by geography and bureaucracy. I think it's through working together on bold projects like this, looking outside of ourselves, that we can start to really feel Europe—what it means, what it's about, the big idea.

I know I am saying all of this at a time when financial markets are melting down and I might sound like I never read a newspaper, but it is in troubled times, when times for ourselves are toughest, that we reveal who we really are. Do we batten down the hatches and protect our own, or do we join forces and make sure the most vulnerable are not forgotten? Do we dwell on the problems, or the solutions? Because in troubled times, I'd argue precisely what we should be doing is looking for new ways to fix old problems.

Just look around this room—the people in this room. That you've all come out of conflict is the truth. You've all seen opportunity in moments of crisis. Just think about Europe at the end of World War II. Germany was in ruins. Britain, penniless. France had been starved and suffocated. Economies, hopes, the future seemed wrecked. And through the wreckage walked giants. De Gaulle, Monnet, Churchill, Keynes. Truman, Marshall, Adenauer. Amid the ruins, they could see a path to a more broadly shared peace and prosperity. And that's what they built—a postwar order of security and opportunity that endured for half a century. Out of that conflict came the Declaration of Human Rights—60 years ago, bbut its basic ideas were older than that. On the ruins, they built a new world. They envisioned it, and then they built it to last. That was their wisdom.

What is ours? Look, we all know it—we're at a moment in time here, just like after the First World War when the League of Nations was set up, just like after the Second World War when the UN and the World Bank and the IMF were formed. The world is up for grabs; a system that has benefited the lucky few and excluded the unlucky many is under the microscope, soon to be on the operating table. New ideas are in play. Creativity is needed—all the creativity in this room.

It raises eyebrows, fists even, when musicians enter these debates. It is unusual but it shouldn't be. I may be biased but I think we need all disciplines (art, commerce, fashion, science) as well as politics to converge on these challenges. Sometimes it takes crisis to reimagine the world and what we are capable of. To shake up the established order. To make old, bad ideas look ridiculous. In fact, history has a way of making ideas that were once acceptable look ridiculous.

Willem de Klerk, you worked side by side with Nelson Mandela to figure out a new future for South Africa. Who would have thought in our lifetime there would be peace in Northern Ireland? You did, John Hume. You did, Betty Williams. You did, Mairead Maguire. Who would have thought that there was to be a peaceful way out of the cold war and the spectre of mutually assured destruction—MAD madness? Mikhail Gorbachev knew that…

As I said, what is our wisdom? Could it be that we decide it is no longer acceptable that an accident of geography—where you are born—can decide whether you live or whether you die? That we decide that human rights, the right to live like a human, belong not just to those who live in the comfort of their freedom. I think so, but we haven't quite got there yet. But with your help, we might get there soon. Since the start of the twenty-first century many millions more African children are in school, millions on life-saving ARVs, millions protected from malaria by bed nets.

Momentum is building. Energies are converging. The wheels of change are turning and the people in this room are living proof that we can alter their direction. This is not a burden; this is an adventure. It's exciting. Together we can make the insanity and injustice and inequality of extreme stupid poverty look ridiculous. A child dying in a world of plenty for lack of food in its belly. Death by mosquito bite or dirty water. These things we can consign to the ash heap of history, and write a new history which makes us all proud. Merci beaucoup.

Cécilia Attias

Walking My Way

CHAPTER
43

Nowadays, optimism is a complicated subject to discuss. Our world is a frightening place for today's youth. Concerns like unemployment, lack of job security, and diseases such as AIDS, do not portend a bright and easy future. How can the next generation be optimistic in such a complicated world?

Anything I say is influenced by my personality, and will go against my true nature, which I cannot change. This is a perfect example of the "genetics versus environment" debate we have been having for so long. How much of us is inherent when we are born? How much of ourselves cannot be fully changed, only softened and tempered or developed and expressed strongly?

Our first task in life should be to know ourselves better so that we can develop and grow in a manner true to our nature. Then comes the impact of our surrounding environment. Our past, our genetics, and our education serve as a foundation for our personality, which is made whole by the knowledge and information we receive from the world around us.

I am deeply convinced that whatever social background, education, religion, and environment we live in, we are inherently optimistic and able to hold on to some hope when we are going through hardships.

Cécilia Attias has dedicated her life to service: as a mother, wife, committed public servant, activist, and ardent supporter of women's rights. After studying law at L'University Assas, she began her political career, serving the people of France in many capacities, including in the office of the Minister of Interior, where she became deeply involved in women's rights and issues relating to domestic violence, immigration, assimilation, and crimes against children. In 2007, she became First Lady of France, where she continued to work with those in need. As First Lady, she successfully negotiated with Colonel Muammar Ghadaffi the release of five Bulgarian nurses and a Palestinian doctor imprisoned on Libya's death row. She is founder and president of the Cécilia Attias Foundation for Women.
www.ceciliaattiasfoundation.org

One cannot learn to look into the future with optimism, wishing that tomorrow will be better than today and that life can and will bring us some moments of peace.

A certain kind of upbringing can teach us to never complain and remain, whatever the circumstances, reserved and confident in the future. However, this is only a small part of our personality we have to learn to live with.

I was born an optimist.

I went through good times and less good times in my life.

Yet I always managed to get a glimpse of "blue sky" in my future.

I can't help it; it even annoys the people around me to be so unconditionally optimistic.

Optimism can be a very powerful driving force. Optimism is key in helping us go through life's hardship.

I was born with a heart defect. I was diagnosed at the age of fifteen. Nowadays, it is a benign condition that can be fixed surgically at birth, but at the time they were just starting to develop these surgical procedures. Father Boulogne was the first French transplant recipient at Broussais Hospital where I was in the room right next to his. I remember quite well the picture of a snowcapped mountain with a beautiful blue sky that he had put on the wall opposite his bed.

He taught me optimism.

He never had doubts about my recovery, or his, for that matter.

Neither of us knew what to expect, where we were headed, if we would experience pain, or what our futures would be like. Despite all this, his face remained confident and calm. I clung to his optimism. He gave me the will to face the pain, uncertainty, and fear of my situation. He inspired me. I am truly convinced that our body is governed by our will even when illness ends up being the strongest.

Even so, we knew we would climb up that mountain someday. Optimism helped us to bear the pain, to view our suffering as temporary, and to endure medical treatments. It acted as a mental anesthetic that kept our daily lives in perspective.

Optimism cannot alter the events in our lives but can change the way we deal with them.

I was very young then and needed this optimism to make me stronger.

It was at this moment in my life that this "quality" came to light as an integral part of my personality. This optimism has never abandoned me since then.

I have led a life strewn with flashes of luck. I was born in France, a country whose geographical location and climate bring us everything we need. There is no lack of water, summers and winters are mild, and this is the country of Montaigne and Rabelais. All the same, life is tough for everyone, wherever they were born. Yet we should learn to look at the magnificence present in this world and value the inner beauty that some people possess so we can live better.

I was very lucky to have been born in a sound family with great parents. I was lucky to bear three wonderful, healthy, and happy children. I was lucky to have crossed the path of exceptional men who helped me grow and I was lucky to live in the countries I lived in. I was also lucky to meet extraordinary people in every field, people who look different, more genuine, and larger than life. This is what makes my life a blessing.

I met people who made me realize that everything was possible provided you had Faith. They showed me the way leading to tolerance and truth. They showed me how to achieve self-esteem and have respect for others whatever the circumstances.

This is the kind of people who provide you with human optimism and show you the beauty in human beings.

I had a lot of luck in my life.

It may be because of or thanks to this driving force that I knew right away when I met the father of my son that I would be at his side to fight with him. Nicolas has always been optimistic and confident. He had just been elected the mayor of Neuilly when we met. His optimism was contagious and we, as one, saw the future confidently.

And yet nothing predisposed him to become, first, a mayor, then a deputy at the French National Assembly, then a secretary of state six times and, finally, the president of France.

That was the result of his relentless work, his incredible resilience, and, especially, his unfailing optimism in making his dreams come true. I immediately fell for it. I never doubted him because he had everything plus his optimism.

He led a daily battle, kept learning every day; he displayed self-confidence and a boundless love for his country.

He had the willingness to dedicate his life to others; that's what being a politician is all about, whether you agree with his ideology or not. Embracing a political career is nothing else than devoting one's life to one's country, to its problems, to its population in the hope of improving the life of everyone with...optimism.

I knew he was the one. In spite of the ordeals he had to go through for twenty years, his trust in the future never failed him. I am not sure he, we, could have endured all the hardships of a life in the spotlight without it.

Then my life took a completely different turn. I changed worlds, changed lives, changed languages, and I lived in the United Arab Emirates for a few months. Life can be sweet there because you can soak up the sun and the temperature averages seventy-five degrees. The sand is everywhere, near the sea or in the desert close by. The flora and fauna are totally different from what I was familiar with.

This was a drastic change of surroundings, with men and women dressed exclusively in black and white. Our routine was disrupted and it was difficult for us to adapt. But we didn't have a choice. It was essential for us to look on the bright side of our new and different life.

Later on, we had the opportunity to go and live in a city, in a country that is everyone's dream. It was our dream to start a new life in New York. Driven by my optimism, and in spite of the recession and the worldwide financial crisis, I managed to convince my husband, Richard, that our future was in New York. We took a huge bet in turning such an important page of our lives. It would never have been possible for us to go live overnight in a country where we were friendless and without any family, and, in addition to that, without really having a good command of English, if we didn't have a good amount of optimism.

But the city of New York and the United States itself were the epitome of optimism. They displayed so much solidarity, patriotism, and mutual assistance after the chaos of 9/11. This country has been able to lick its wounds and start over. I never had any doubts about its resilience and its ability to move on and start anew.

And here we were, full of energy and willpower to succeed. My husband is an optimistic fighter in spite of the tremendous difficulties he had to overcome and those he still has to face. I am filled with admiration and respect for what he does for us today.

Creating a foundation benefiting women or a vast Forum for the Economy seemed to be "hopeless" as one of our friends put it. Nevertheless, my optimism persuaded Richard that anything was possible and that, above all, we had to take risks. I don't think I was mistaken and, now, my foundation donates to a lot of NGOs worldwide. The New York Forum, a call to action gathering the world's top business leaders to discover solutions and reinstill confidence into the global economy, is now a reference in the new economic order.

We needed a lot of determination and confidence in the future to embark on this new challenge and, what's more, in a country regarded by most people as El Dorado. Our own El Dorado was in this city whose clichés—the yellow cabs, the skyscrapers, and the "city that never sleeps" motto—we experienced every day.

So this is the place where we took the decision to start all over, first the three of us, then the four of us, and, finally, the eight of us. Our children had also become optimistic and came to join us here to build their future.

And today, witnessing the events unfolding in front of our eyes in the Middle East and in North Africa, I know optimism will help these peoples to reconstruct their countries. They will be guided by their trust in democracy. They have decided to carry on a terribly hard fight, one country after another, one step at a time taking them closer to a life devoid of totalitarianism. It's optimism that you can see in the demonstrators' eyes, it's optimism that guides the crowd, and it's with optimism that we have to help them.

There's been a lot of optimism lately since the election of Barack Obama, even if you don't agree with his ideas and decisions. Optimism is back. Republicans won the majority in Congress, but it is with optimism that the coalition settled in to try and find the narrow path that will get us out of the crisis. The Middle East is starting a revolution and it is with optimism that the rest of the world must offer its support to maintain freedom and Democracy there.

And, more modestly, optimism settles at home and takes us by the hand to lead us on to a rosy future...

—February 23, 2011

KOFI ANNAN:
The Butterfly Effect

CHAPTER
44

Today, in Afghanistan, a girl will be born. Her mother will hold her and feed her, comfort her and care for her—just as any mother would anywhere in the world. In these most basic acts of human nature, humanity knows no divisions. But to be born a girl in today's Afghanistan is to begin life centuries away from the prosperity that one small part of humanity has achieved. It is to live under conditions that many of us in this hall would consider inhuman. I speak of a girl in Afghanistan, but I might equally well have mentioned a baby boy or girl in Sierra Leone.

No one today is unaware of this divide between the world's rich and poor. No one today can claim ignorance of the cost that this divide imposes on the poor and dispossessed who are no less deserving of human dignity, fundamental freedoms, security, food, and education than any of us. The cost, however, is not borne by them alone. Ultimately, it is borne by all of us—North and South, rich and poor, men and women of all races and religions.

Today's real borders are not between nations, but between powerful and powerless, free and fettered, privileged and humiliated. Today, no walls can separate humanitarian or human rights crises in one part of the world from national security crises in another.

Scientists tell us that the world of nature is so small and interdependent that a butterfly flapping its wings in the Amazon rain forest can generate a violent storm on the other side of the earth. This principle

Kofi Annan, a Ghanaian diplomat, served as secretary-general of the United Nations from 1997 to 2006. He subsequently led the formation of Alliance for a Green Revolution in Africa (AGRA), served as president of the Global Humanitarian Forum in Geneva, and has been instrumental in the global fight against AIDS and poverty. The recipient of the MacArthur Foundation Award for International Justice and myriad other awards for his contributions to human rights and the betterment of society, he and the United Nations were jointly awarded the Nobel Peace Prize in 2001. This chapter is the speech he gave in Oslo in accepting the Nobel Prize.

is known as the "Butterfly Effect." Today, we realize, perhaps more than ever, that the world of human activity also has its own "Butterfly Effect" — for better or for worse.

We have entered the third millennium through a gate of fire. If today, after the horror of 11 September, we see better, and we see further, we will realize that humanity is indivisible. New threats make no distinction between races, nations, or regions. A new insecurity has entered every mind, regardless of wealth or status. A deeper awareness of the bonds that bind us all — in pain as in prosperity — has gripped young and old.

In the early beginnings of the twenty-first century — a century already violently disabused of any hopes that progress towards global peace and prosperity is inevitable — this new reality can no longer be ignored. It must be confronted.

The twentieth century was perhaps the deadliest in human history, devastated by innumerable conflicts, untold suffering, and unimaginable crimes. Time after time, a group or a nation inflicted extreme violence on another, often driven by irrational hatred and suspicion, or unbounded arrogance and thirst for power and resources. In response to these cataclysms, the leaders of the world came together at midcentury to unite the nations as never before.

A forum was created — the United Nations — where all nations could join forces to affirm the dignity and worth of every person, and to secure peace and development for all peoples. Here, states could unite to strengthen the rule of law, recognize and address the needs of the poor, restrain man's brutality and greed, conserve the resources and beauty of nature, sustain the equal rights of men *and* women, and provide for the safety of future generations.

We thus inherit from the twentieth century the political, as well as the scientific and technological power, which — if only we have the will to use them — give us the chance to vanquish poverty, ignorance, and disease.

In the twenty-first century, I believe the mission of the United Nations will be defined by a new, more profound, awareness of the sanctity and dignity of every human life, regardless of race or religion. This will require us to look beyond the framework of states, and beneath the surface of nations or communities. We must focus, as never before, on improving the conditions of the individual men and women who give the state or nation its richness and character. We must begin with the young Afghan girl, recognizing that saving that one life is to save humanity itself.

Over the past five years, I have often recalled that the United Nations' Charter begins with the words: "We the peoples." What is not always recognized is that "we the peoples" are made up of individuals whose claims to the most fundamental rights have too often been sacrificed in the supposed interests of the state or the nation.

A genocide begins with the killing of one man—not for what he has done, but because of who he is. A campaign of "ethnic cleansing" begins with one neighbor turning on another. Poverty begins when even one child is denied his or her fundamental right to education. What begins with the failure to uphold the dignity of one life, all too often ends with a calamity for entire nations.

In this new century, we must start from the understanding that peace belongs not only to states or peoples, but to each and every member of those communities. The sovereignty of states must no longer be used as a shield for gross violations of human rights. Peace must be made real and tangible in the daily existence of every individual in need. Peace must be sought, above all, because it is the condition for every member of the human family to live a life of dignity and security.

The rights of the individual are of no less importance to immigrants and minorities in Europe and the Americas than to women in Afghanistan or children in Africa. They are as fundamental to the poor as to the rich; they are as necessary to the security of the developed world as to that of the developing world.

From this vision of the role of the United Nations in the next century flow three key priorities for the future: eradicating poverty, preventing conflict, and promoting democracy. Only in a world that is rid of poverty can all men and women make the most of their abilities. Only where individual rights are respected can differences be channeled politically and resolved peacefully. Only in a democratic environment, based on respect for diversity and dialogue, can individual self-expression and self-government be secured, and freedom of association be upheld.

Throughout my term as secretary-general, I have sought to place human beings at the center of everything we do—from conflict prevention to development to human rights. Securing real and lasting improvement in the lives of individual men and women is the measure of all we do at the United Nations.

It is in this spirit that I humbly accept the Centennial Nobel Peace Prize. Forty years ago today, the prize for 1961 was awarded for the first time to a secretary-general of the United Nations—posthumously, because Dag Hammarskjöld had already given his life for peace in Central Africa. And on the same day, the prize for 1960 was awarded for the first time to an African—Albert Luthuli, one of the earliest leaders of the struggle against apartheid in South Africa. For me, as a young African beginning his career in the United Nations a few months later, those two men set a standard that I have sought to follow throughout my working life.

This award belongs not just to me. I do not stand here alone. On behalf of all my colleagues in every part of the United Nations, in every corner of the globe, who have devoted their lives — and in many instances risked or given their lives in the cause of peace — I thank the Members of the Nobel Committee for this high honor. My own path to service at the United Nations was made possible by the sacrifice and commitment of my family and many friends from all continents — some of whom have passed away — who taught me and guided me. To them, I offer my most profound gratitude.

In a world filled with weapons of war and all too often words of war, the Nobel Committee has become a vital agent for peace. Sadly, a prize for peace is a rarity in this world. Most nations have monuments or memorials to war, bronze salutations to heroic battles, archways of triumph. But peace has no parade, no pantheon of victory.

What it does have is the Nobel Prize — a statement of hope and courage with unique resonance and authority. Only by understanding and addressing the needs of individuals for peace, for dignity, and for security can we at the United Nations hope to live up to the honor conferred today, and fulfill the vision of our founders. This is the broad mission of peace that United Nations staff members carry out every day in every part of the world.

A few of them, women and men, are with us in this hall today. Among them, for instance, are a military observer from Senegal who is helping to provide basic security in the Democratic Republic of the Congo; a civilian police adviser from the United States who is helping to improve the rule of law in Kosovo; a UNICEF child protection officer from Ecuador who is helping to secure the rights of Colombia's most vulnerable citizens; and a World Food Program officer from China who is helping to feed the people of North Korea.

The idea that there is one people in possession of the truth, one answer to the world's ills, or one solution to humanity's needs, has done untold harm throughout history — especially in the last century. Today, however, even amidst continuing ethnic conflict around the world, there is a growing understanding that human diversity is both the reality that makes dialogue necessary, and the very basis for that dialogue.

We understand, as never before, that each of us is fully worthy of the respect and dignity essential to our common humanity. We recognize that we are the products of many cultures, traditions, and memories; that mutual respect allows us to study and learn from other cultures; and that we gain strength by combining the foreign with the familiar.

In every great faith and tradition, one can find the values of tolerance and mutual understanding. The Qur'an, for example, tells us that: "We created you from a single pair of male and female and made you into nations and tribes, that you may know each other." Confucius urged his followers: "When the good way prevails in the state, speak boldly and act boldly. When the state has lost the way, act boldly and speak softly." In the Jewish tradition, the injunction to "love thy neighbor as thyself" is considered to be the very essence of the Torah. This thought is reflected in the Christian Gospel, which also teaches us to love our enemies and pray for those who wish to persecute us. Hindus are taught that "truth is one, the sages give it various names." And in the Buddhist tradition, individuals are urged to act with compassion in every facet of life.

Each of us has the right to take pride in our particular faith or heritage. But the notion that what is ours is necessarily in conflict with what is theirs is both false and dangerous. It has resulted in endless enmity and conflict, leading men to commit the greatest of crimes in the name of a higher power.

It need not be so. People of different religions and cultures live side by side in almost every part of the world, and most of us have overlapping identities which unite us with very different groups. We *can* love what we are, without hating what—and who—we are *not*. We can thrive in our own tradition, even as we learn from others, and come to respect their teachings.

This will not be possible, however, without freedom of religion, of expression, of assembly, and basic equality under the law. Indeed, the lesson of the past century has been that where the dignity of the individual has been trampled or threatened—where citizens have not enjoyed the basic right to choose their government, or the right to change it regularly—conflict has too often followed, with innocent civilians paying the price, in lives cut short and communities destroyed.

The obstacles to democracy have little to do with culture or religion, and much more to do with the desire of those in power to maintain their position at any cost. This is neither a new phenomenon nor one confined to any particular part of the world. People of all cultures value their freedom of choice, and feel the need to have a say in decisions affecting their lives.

The United Nations, whose membership comprises almost all the states in the world, is founded on the principle of the equal worth of every human being. It is the nearest thing we have to a representative institution that can address the interests of all states, and all peoples. Through this universal, indispensable instrument of human progress, states can serve the interests of their citizens by recognizing common interests and pursuing them in unity. No doubt, that is why the Nobel Committee says that it "wishes, in its centenary year, to proclaim that the only negotiable route to global peace and cooperation goes by way of the United Nations."

I believe the Committee also recognized that this era of global challenges leaves no choice but cooperation at the global level. When states undermine the rule of law and violate the rights of their individual citizens, they become a menace not only to their own people, but also to their neighbors, and indeed the world. What we need today is better governance — legitimate, democratic governance that allows each individual to flourish, and each State to thrive.

You will recall that I began my address with a reference to the girl born in Afghanistan today. Even though her mother will do all in her power to protect and sustain her, there is a one-in-four risk that she will not live to see her fifth birthday. Whether she does is just one test of our common humanity — of our belief in our individual responsibility for our fellow men and women. But it is the only test that matters.

Remember this girl and then our larger aims — to fight poverty, prevent conflict, or cure disease — will not seem distant, or impossible. Indeed, those aims will seem very near, and very achievable — as they should. Because beneath the surface of states and nations, ideas and language, lies the fate of individual human beings in need. Answering their needs will be the mission of the United Nations in the century to come.

Jimmy Carter:

The Exaltation of Service

W hen I left the White House, retired by the results of the 1980 election, I didn't know what I was going to do next. I knew that I had a life expectancy of twenty-five more years, and I wondered how I could capitalize on the experience and knowledge of having been the leader of the greatest nation in the world. Looking to my Christian faith for a way forward, I began teaching Sunday school again at Maranatha Baptist Church—where my wife, Rosalynn, and I attend services in our hometown of Plains, Georgia.

Our religious beliefs are important to us. I have taught Sunday school since I was a teen, and we attend services regularly, but for a time that had been the extent of it. Like many people, Rosalynn and I have searched to find an outlet to put that faith into action. Rarely have we found the opportunity to follow Jesus Christ's example of reaching out to those who are poor and in need and treating them as equals.

The underlying problem is that sometimes it is difficult for people like us—who have homes, good educations, and fruitful careers—to cross the chasm that separates us from people who may have none of these blessings. Often, the needy are scorned by us more affluent people who think to ourselves, *Well, if those poor people would only work as hard as I do or study as hard as I do, then they could provide a good home for their families, just as I do.* That kind of prejudice can be difficult to overcome.

Jimmy Carter, president of the United States from 1977 to 1981, is one of only three U.S. presidents to receive the Nobel Peace Prize. He received the prize in 2002 in recognition of his decades of "untiring effort to find peaceful solutions to international conflicts, to advance democracy and human rights, and to promote economic and social development." Much of this work has been accomplished through the Carter Center, a nongovernmental, not-for-profit organization working on behalf of human rights, which he cofounded with his wife, Rosalynn. The author of more than twenty books, including *Beyond the White House: Waging Peace, Fighting Disease, Building Hope*, he is also a strong advocate of Habitat for Humanity. www.cartercenter.org

---

Fortunately for Rosalynn and me, the international headquarters of Habitat for Humanity was located in Americus, Georgia, just nine miles from Plains. In Habitat's work, building homes for those in need, we saw the opportunity — as so many others have — to put our faith into practice.

The goal of Habitat for Humanity is to rid the world of substandard, or poverty, housing. Habitat works hard to do this by building simple homes in partnership with families in need. These partner families pay the full cost of their new homes over time through no-profit loans that Habitat grants them. The prices of Habitat homes remain affordable because the homes aren't extravagant and because they're built with volunteer labor, including the labor of the partner families.

There's no way to describe exactly why Habitat means so much to me, but I will try. If you are a person of faith, you learn certain basic lessons about truth, justice, love, and sharing that shape your life. It doesn't matter whether you learn these lessons in a church (as I did), in a synagogue, in a mosque, or in a temple. Wherever the lessons are learned, they remain largely the same. One is that people who have been blessed with wealth should share that wealth with others who are in need. Finding a way to do this, however, can be hard because of the divide that separates the rich and the poor.

People tend to feel most comfortable with those just like themselves — people who have the same skin color, who talk like us, who live in equally nice homes — so we often shut out others who are different. It's not easy to break through the barriers that we naturally erect. The great gift of Habitat for Humanity is that it offers us a way to reach out to fellow humans who don't have a decent place in which to live. In fact, it's the best way that I know to live out the highest moral values of my faith, because Habitat sees decent housing as a human right.

Human rights can be defined in many different ways. If you ask Americans on the street to name some human rights, they are likely to say freedom of speech, freedom of religion, the right to assemble, the right to a trial by jury, or the right to elect one's leaders. Those are perfectly good *legal* human rights. But one of the most important — a human right that people often forget — is the right to lead a good life. By this I mean the right to have food to eat, a place to sleep at night, access to doctors and education, and a decent job, as well as self-respect and dignity.

We affluent Americans frequently fail to realize that these things are missing from the lives of many people, not only around the world but also here in our own country. When the new millennium began in 2000, I was asked to make a few speeches in different places around the world about the greatest challenge facing humanity. It didn't take me long to identify what that challenge was: the growing separation between rich and poor.

Did you know that in the year 1900, the people who lived in the world's ten richest countries were, on average, about nine times richer than the people who lived in the world's ten poorest countries? That doesn't seem like a lot, but as time passed, the gap widened. By 1960, the world's richest people were thirty times wealthier than the world's poorest people, and today the world's richest people are more than seventy-five times more wealthy!

Even worse, there are many more poor people than most of us realize. Over half of the world's six billion people live on less than two dollars a day. Over a billion people live on less than one dollar a day. Imagine how you might live on just one dollar a day, and you can get some idea of their plight. That one dollar a day would have to pay for food, shelter, and clothing; and even if it did, which isn't likely, you would have nothing left over for education, health care, or the future. Not surprisingly, most people who earn only a few dollars a day don't eat well and are forced to live in slums. Even in America, the wealthiest nation in the world, nearly one in three people lives in a house that neither you nor I would consider a fit place to live.

Habitat makes it possible for us to work side by side with partner families and help them improve their lives so that they can not just survive but thrive in the world. Helping a family in need move into a home is the primary mission of Habitat for Humanity. Yet, because of the unique way in which Habitat operates, the organization accomplishes much more. It brings together people of different backgrounds and stations in life to create an environment in which everyone is equal.

I've learned that these new homeowners are just as hardworking and ambitious as I am, their family values as just as good as mine, and they want the same things for themselves and their children as I want for me and mine. What Rosalynn and I have seen time and again is that when people become homeowners, their dignity and self-respect increase dramatically. Because they've worked so hard themselves to complete the home, they become filled with a new pride that inspires them to reach for other things that they previously considered out of their grasp, such as an education.

We know this because we often revisit Habitat sites where we have built in the past in order to see what has happened to the homes and the neighborhoods. Never have we seen a Habitat home with graffiti on the walls or a broken windowpane that wasn't repaired or a lawn that wasn't mowed. People who build and pay for their own homes are proud of what they have accomplished, and they don't let their homes deteriorate.

You can see this pride in the faces of the partner families on the day that they receive the keys to their new home. They know that they aren't being given a handout but a hand up, because they have done their share of the work and they will be paying their share of the cost. Participating in this ceremony, especially when you have helped in constructing the house, can be an overwhelming, emotional experience.

There is no question that helping to create a decent home for a partner family is a significant act of giving, but volunteers typically find that they receive something in return that is even more valuable: a feeling of satisfaction and a connection to other people. Knowing that you have worked alongside other volunteers to change a family's life is a powerful feeling that you will want to experience again and again. For this reason, Habitat volunteers keep coming back to work on Habitat projects.

Rosalynn and I began working regularly on Habitat job sites in 1984, when we arranged for a group of forty-two of our friends to travel to New York City for a weeklong project rebuilding an apartment house on the Lower East Side. Since then, we have spent one week every year leading a work project either here in the United States or in a foreign country such as South Africa, Hungary, or the Philippines. We haven't missed a year yet, and we expect to continue as long as we are able.

One reason is the way the work makes us feel. In all of our lives, there are usually a few precious moments when we feel exalted — that is, when we reach above our normal level of existence to a higher plane of excitement and achievement.

I remember feeling that way when Rosalynn agreed to marry me and when our children were born. Taking the oath of office as president of the United States was another moment of exaltation for me, as was seeing the fruition of the time I spent negotiating a peace treaty between Israel and Egypt, not a word of which has been broken to this day. When I went to the army hospital in Germany where the hostages that had been taken in Iran were being treated after their release, I was nervous because I didn't know how they would receive me. But when they all stood up and cheered as I walked into the room and then embraced me one by one with tears in their eyes, I felt exalted.

It may surprise you, but I also experience a feeling of exaltation at the end of each Habitat work project, when I give a Bible as a gift to the new homeowners, along with the keys to their new house. My heart and soul always are exalted, and sometimes tears of joy run down my face.

I predict that every one of you who volunteers to help others in need will feel this same sense of exaltation. I believe that, in making what seems to be a sacrifice, you will find fulfillment in the memorable experience of helping others less fortunate than yourself.

When you pay your own way to a Habitat job site in a distant land and furnish your own tools, and you're working hard and getting up early, you can sometimes think to yourself, *This is a big sacrifice I'm making for the folks who are going to live in this house.* But what you'll find is that the "sacrifice" actually is a blessing. I know this because I've learned the secret that so many other Habitat volunteers have learned: you always get much more out of the work than you put in.

CHARLES, PRINCE OF WALES:

Harmony

It seems to me that we have no choice but to live in harmony. By taking Nature as our tutor it might be easier than we sometimes think to build a more durable and more pleasant society. And what is the alternative? Carrying on as we are now, we know will court disaster. There is no option but to seek change, the question is, what kind, and how?

There is much to be gained from the observance of the natural order and the rhythm in things, whether it be in the lines and shapes of architecture or the processes involved in agriculture, and certainly in the natural world as a whole. Not just because of the aesthetic experience this may bring, but also because it reveals how the same rhythms and patterns underlie all these things. Through the contemplation of the rhythms of life, it is possible to understand the forces that dominate everything we are aware of and to sense and gain from the harmony that exists between all things in their natural state. As all sacred traditions have sought to show, the closer we dance to the rhythms and patterns that lie within us, the closer we get to acting in what is the right way; closer to the good in life, to what is true and what is beautiful — rather than swirling around without an anchor, lost "out there" in the wilderness of a view shaped solely by four hundred years of emphasis on mechanistic thinking and the output of our industrialized processes.

Charles, Prince of Wales, as the eldest son of Queen Elizabeth II, is first in line to the British throne. Dedicated to humanitarian work, he is the founder of the Prince's Charities, a group of twenty not-for-profit organizations, which together raise an estimated £110 million pounds annually and are active in opportunity and enterprise, education, health, preservation of historic buildings, environmental conservation, and numerous other aspects of social well-being. His Foundation for Integrated Health promoted the inclusion of herbal and other alternative treatments in National Health Service options. He is also an advocate of organic farming and sustainability.

Studying the properties of harmony and understanding more clearly how it works at all levels of creation reveals a crucial, timeless principle: that no one part can grow well and true without it relating to—and being in accordance with—the well-being of the whole. We need to remind ourselves of this vital "eternal law" again and again, it seems to me, so as to "re-mind" the world, using it as the gauge we apply to all we do.

Thousands of years ago our ancestors embarked upon a journey to derive comfort and security so that they could expand their knowledge of the world and develop ever more sophisticated tools with which they could use more effectively the natural resources they found in Nature. The progress they made was driven by immense hardships. The long march of investigation and innovation, the application of creativity and technology, the process that we now call "progress," has procured for us immense benefits and opportunities, but it has also, paradoxically, brought us back to the place where we started from: facing a grave threat, surrounded by uncertainty and insecurity. The difference now is that we face those threats not as individuals and families, but as an entire global community, alongside much of the rest of life on Earth.

Unless we temper the side of our nature that has delivered such vast benefits, it could easily be the cause of our ultimate demise, It is already becoming the cause of the decline and looming extinction of countless species which, did we but know it, are part of the intricate web of life on which we all depend. In an age of rights do these species not have some sort of right to inhabit their particular niche? Do we not have some sort of responsibility towards them? It seems to me that we have to find ways to unite within our modern culture the perennial wisdom we have abandoned—the voice of our intuition that we have increasingly ignored as well as the spiritual essence of our being that now lies buried beneath great mountains of materialism. We need to understand that we are born into a universe that has meaning and purpose. All of the sacred traditions tell us that this "purpose" is for life to know itself—this is the meaning of communion, by which we sense and help maintain life's essential balance.

This all ultimately depends upon how we perceive the world and our place within it. And this will mean somehow replacing our obsession with pursuing unlimited growth and competition with a quest for well-being and cooperation. It will mean shaping our culture so that its aims are rooted in relationship and focused on fulfillment rather than on ever more consumption. If we can rebalance our perception and restore a sense of proportion to how we relate to the world—and on what basis we value the miracle of its marvels—it seems possible to me that we could create the conditions that ensure human societies thrive indefinitely.

There will be cynical critics who will scoff at such a utopian suggestion, but if they choose to dismiss such a vision, then it is incumbent upon them to come up with something better. One fact is clear. What seems to be their preferred choice, the one that prevails at the moment, which is to carry on as we have been doing, is not an option. An ever more divided and ecologically bankrupt world will be the consequence of our continuing in that vein and if we have any sense of responsibility for the future we cannot allow that to happen. We must recognize that to continue as we have been doing will only compound the problem.

The better, if not the only, effective course we can take is to see that we are part of the Natural order rather than isolated from it, and to appreciate Nature as a profoundly beautiful world of complexity. This world operates according to an organic grammar of harmony and is informed by the awareness of its own being, making Nature anchored by consciousness. In this way of understanding, life is seen as an interconnected, interdependent function of creation.

We do have within our societies and within our existing technologies the solutions that will enable us to transcend our current predicament. All we lack is the will to establish a more entire and connected perspective that includes giving space in our culture for the sense of the sacred in life; for reverence and even, dare I say it, for a touch of enlightened deference to Nature. After all, she is our ultimate "sustainer." Without such an integrated spiritual outlook, the many indications are that we will continue to deal with each individual crisis in a separate way, never seeing the connections that exist between them and the relationship we have with each element and the whole. And the consequence of that is a collapse of catastrophic proportions. Thus we stand at an historic moment. We face a future where there is a real prospect that if we fail the Earth, we fail humanity.

To avoid such an outcome, which will comprehensively destroy our children's future or even our own, we must make choices now that carry monumental implications. It is beholden upon each and every one of us to help redress the balance that has been so shaken by re-founding our outlook in a firmer set of values that are framed by a clearer, spiritually intact philosophy of life. Only then can we hope to establish a far more sustainable economic system; only then can we live by more rooted values; and only then might we tread more lightly upon this Earth, the miracle of creation that it is our privilege to call "home."